D0916948

THE VIRTUES OF MENDACITY

RICHARD LECTURES FOR 2008

THE VIRTUES OF
MENDACITY

ON LYING IN POLITICS

Martin Jay

UNIVERSITY OF VIRGINIA PRESS
CHARLOTTESVILLE AND LONDON

University of Virginia Press
© 2010 by the Rector and Visitors of the University of Virginia
All rights reserved
Printed in the United States of America on acid-free paper

First published 2010

9 8 7 6 5 4 3 2 1

LIBRARY OF CONGRESS CATALOGING-IN-PUBLICATION DATA

Jay, Martin, 1944–
   The virtues of mendacity : on lying in politics / Martin Jay.
      p.   cm. — (Richard lectures for 2008)
   Includes bibliographical references (p.   ) and index.
   ISBN 978-0-8139-2972-9 (cloth : alk. paper) — ISBN 978-0-8139-2976-7
(e-book)
   1. Truthfulness and falsehood. 2. Political ethics. 3. Political science—
Philosophy.   I. Title.
   BJ1421.J39 2010
   172--dc22

                                      2009039437

For Ruby and Fidel—Let sleeping dogs lie.

CONTENTS

PREFACE

It might easily be assumed that this book was conceived during the ill-starred presidency of George W. Bush when indignation against political mendacity reached new heights in the American public sphere. Matched only in popularity by the widespread charge of "incompetence," which gained special traction after the grievous mishandling of Hurricane Katrina, "duplicity" became the favorite target of the administration's burgeoning legion of critics. Although there were many examples to bolster this image, it was the slew of lies intended to dupe the American people into supporting an immoral and unnecessary war on Iraq that did the most damage. When the war turned sour, even the popular media jumped on the bandwagon, as demonstrated by the cover of the July 21, 2003, issue of *Time,* whose headline read "Untruth and Consequences: How Flawed Was the Case for Going to War against Saddam?"[1] If there had been a quick and easy victory—the confident assurance of which itself turned out to be at best an error and at worst a self-deception—the alleged deceptions about the pretexts for invasion might well have been forgiven. But as the journalist Nicholas von Hoffman cynically noted, "If you are going to tell a Big Lie badly, you have to pull off the crime, you have to make it a success. George Bush didn't."[2]

Although it certainly is the case that the brouhaha over political mendacity during the Bush administration focused my attention, it was in fact first attracted well before it began. In 1999 the *London*

Review of Books invited me to respond to two books on the presidency of Bill Clinton: George Stephanopolous's *All Too Human* and Christopher Hitchens's *No One Left to Lie To.*[3] Hitchens's provocative title was taken from the accusation launched by David Schippers, the majority counsel of the House Judiciary Committee, himself a Democrat: "The President, then, has lied under oath in a civil deposition, lied under oath in a criminal grand jury. He lied to the people, he lied to his Cabinet, he lied to his top aides, and now he's lied under oath to the Congress of the United States. *There's no one left to lie to.*"[4] Taking my cue from this diatribe, which expressed Hitchens's own outrage at the way Clinton's handling of the Monica Lewinsky affair typified his entire tenure in office, I began thinking seriously about the more general role of mendacity in politics.

The review appeared under the title "Mendacious Flowers" in the July 29, 1999, issue of the *LRB,* and tentatively advanced some of the arguments I will be making in this book. The response was vigorous and mostly positive, although there was one critical exception that I will always cherish. Referring to the fact that I had just assumed the chairmanship of my department, the correspondent thundered: "If you believe what you seem to believe, you have no business being the chair of the best history department in the country!" I immediately pondered the implications of this charge, realizing with perverse excitement that any project that might relieve me of the duty of chairing was one worth pursuing. But as luck would have it, I was already deeply involved with another challenging project, which was published in 2004 as *Songs of Experience* after I had completed my term as departmental chair.[5] The evident passion that my initial attempt to think about lying in politics had engendered was not, however, forgotten, and once the opportunity to start a new major project emerged, I returned to the theme.

The result is the book that, as it were, lies before you (or rather tries to tell some truths about lying). It is motivated by one cluster of fundamental questions: Why is there such a frequent and ubiquitous linkage between politics and mendacity? Why is virtually the first accusation hurled at a political opponent when things get ugly the charge of misrepresentation or duplicity? Why is lying in politics both impossible to eradicate and yet never easily condoned? Is there something special about the realm of human behavior we call politics that allows mendacity to prosper, despite all the high-minded attempts to condemn and punish it? Does it perhaps even serve positive functions, despite its all too obvious negative ones? Would different interpretations of the essence of "the political," as it has come to be called, have different implications for answering these questions?

As I began to mull over these perplexing issues and begin my research into the vast literature that has accumulated around the question of lying in general and lying in politics in particular, it was especially instructive to see the transformation of the very same Christopher Hitchens who had so excoriated Bill Clinton as a serial liar into a staunch defender of George Bush's war in Iraq. Turning intellectual somersaults to justify the invasion and applying his considerable rhetorical skills to skewer anyone on the other side, Hitchens lost his righteous indignation about mendacity and focused his attention on the larger strategic and ideological questions served by ridding the world of Saddam Hussein. Was he being hypocritical, applying a double standard, or merely shrewdly selective in directing his wrath? Did he perhaps come to the sober conclusion that there are worse sins in politics than failing to observe the highest standards of veracity? If the latter was the case, he was not the first to come to this conclusion. To explain why it may be more than just a sign of moral weakness, self-serving expediency, or world-weary cynicism is the goal of this exercise.

ACKNOWLEDGMENTS

Truth be told, there is no more perilous enterprise than trying to acknowledge the innumerable acts of kindness—or at times painfully pointed criticisms—that abet the composition and publication of a book. From the initial invitation by the *London Review of Books* in 1998 to review two volumes on the presidency of Bill Clinton, which first aroused my interest in the theme of political mendacity, to the efforts of the University of Virginia Press and its talented staff to turn the manuscript into a book, I have benefited from countless individuals and institutions who have contributed in one way or another to the project. The difficulty, of course, comes in doing justice to all of them, given the vagaries of memory and my failure to record every piece of advice I got along the way. So let me acknowledge at the outset the radical incompleteness of these acknowledgments, and beg the pardon of those who are negligently, but not malevolently, omitted.

I should begin by thanking the institutions that allowed me the time and resources to do the research that underpins my argument, and provided the audiences that helped to hone it with their constructively skeptical responses. I had the great good fortune to spend my 2004–5 sabbatical at the National Humanities Center as the John P. Birkelund Fellow. Geoffrey Galt Harpham, Kent Mullikin, and the extraordinary staff of the Center provided every amenity that a scholar could desire. The forty or so other fellows in residence that year managed to steal enough time away from their own projects to respond with great generosity to my own. I was also supported throughout the years I worked on this book by the Sidney Hellman Ehrman Chair at the University of California, Berkeley, which I have been lucky to share with my distinguished colleague Jan de Vries since 1996. As has always been the case since I went on my first sabbatical in 1974, the Humanities Research Fellowship program at Berkeley has also given generously to top off my sabbatical salary.

Opportunities to air my inchoate ideas on the subject of this book were afforded by a wide range of audiences: the Humanities Institute, University of Buffalo; the Department of History, University of Maryland; the Political Science Department, CUNY; the Philosophy Department, Florida Atlantic University; the Humanities Department, Technological University of Monterrey, Mexico City; the Visiting Scholars Program, James Madison University; the conference "Ethics and Politics," Heraklion, Crete; the Philosophy Department, University of Wroclaw, Poland; the conference "The Politics of the Past," Jyväskylä, Finland; the European University of St. Petersburg, Russia; the Unit for Criticism and Interpretive Theory, University of Illinois; the Department of Performing Arts, Southern Illinois University; a conference on Marx's *Communist Manifesto* in Santiago de Chile; a conference on Derrida at University of California, Davis; the Political Theory and Intellectual History Colloquium, Harvard University; the Lansdowne Visiting Scholar Lecture, University of Victoria, British Columbia; the Pierson Lecture, University of Oregon; the European University, Fiesole, Italy; and the Lionel Trilling Memorial Lecture, Columbia University. Perhaps three such occasions should be singled out for special mention: the conference at the American Academy of Arts and Sciences, organized by David Hollinger, which produced the volume *The Humanities and Dynamics of Inclusion since World War II* (Baltimore, 2006), where an early version of my argument appeared; the 2007 Faculty Research Lecture at the University of California, Berkeley, where I presented the mature version to my colleagues in many different fields; and the three 2007 Richard Lectures at the University of Virginia, which became the nucleus of this book.

I have also benefited in countless ways from the counsel and suggestions of colleagues, students, and friends over the years. At the risk of omitting some, let me single out a few names to thank for especially valuable help: Richard Abrams, Anthony Adamthwaite, Etienne Balibar, David Bates, Seyla Benhabib, Marc Bevir, Warren Breckman, Talbot Brewer, Wendy Brown, Judith Butler, Pheng Cheah, Jean Cohen, John Connelly, Carolyn Dean, John Efron, Jeremy Elkins, Andrew Feenberg, Donald Friedman, Timo Gilmore, Peter Gordon, Ruth Grant, Michael Gubser, Suzanne Guerlac, Agnes Heller, Jeffrey Herf, Carla Hesse, Kinch Hoekstra, David Hollinger, Guo-Juin Hong, Dick Howard, Robert Hullot-Kentor, Andreas Huyssen, the late Norman Jacobson, George Kateb, Robert Kaufmann, Leszek Koczanowicz, Benjamin Krupicka, Dominick LaCapra, Thomas Laqueur, Benjamin Lazier, Jonathan Lear, Lloyd Kramer, Olli-Pekka Moisio, A. Dirk Moses, Samuel Moyn, Elliot Neaman, Andrew Norris, Matthias Obert, Ross Posnock, Mark Poster, Gerhard Richter, Dylan Riley, Paul Robinson, Michael Rosen, Emmanuel Rota, Eduardo Sabrovsky, Jonathan Sheehan, Corey Robin, Hanna Rose Shell, Richard Shusterman, Hans Sluga, David Sorkin, Vincent Sorrentino, Shannon Stimson, Paul Thomas, Michael Ure, Stephen Vincent, Loic Wacquant, Richard Wolin, Benjamin Wurgaft, and Lewis Wurgaft. Superb research assistance came from Knox Peden, Benjamin Wurgaft, Radhika Varadharajan, and Larry Fernández. Thanks also to Eliah Bures for tackling the always daunting task of preparing the index. Kudos as well to Dick Holway and his staff at the University of Virginia Press, as well as the two anonymous readers they selected, whose comments were invaluable. I also very much appreciate the careful copyediting of Ruth Melville.

And as always, I have been sustained in more ways than I can acknowledge by the loving support of my family: Shana, Becca, Beth, Ned, Grayson, Frankie, Sammy, and my most judicious reader, unfailing helpmate, and the constant gardener of my body and soul, Catherine Gallagher.

THE VIRTUES OF MENDACITY

INTRODUCTION
American Democracy and the Dream of Transparent Politics

Nescit vivere qui nescit dissimulare, perire melius.
[He who doesn't know how to dissimulate, doesn't know how to live,
and is better dying.]
    —LATIN MAXIM

Qui nescit dissimulare, nescit regnare.
[He who doesn't know how to dissimulate, doesn't know how to rule.]
    —LOUIS IX OF FRANCE

"We demand that there be a legal campaign against those who propagate deliberate political lies and disseminate them through the press." So began the twenty-third of twenty-five points in a crisp and uncompromising program promulgated by a nascent political party in 1920 with a remarkable future before it. There is no small amount of irony in the fact that the party in question was the National Socialist Party of Germany, whose most lasting contribution to the theory and practice of political mendacity was announced in the autobiography of its leader only three years later. The so-called big lie introduced in *Mein Kampf* quickly became known as the favored technique of totalitarian states. As Adolf Hitler explained in one of the most frequently cited passages from his book,

> The magnitude of a lie always contains a certain factor of credibility, since the great masses of the people in the very bottom

1

of their hearts tend to be corrupted rather than consciously and purposely evil, and that, therefore, in view of the primitive simplicity of their minds, they more easily fall victim to the big lie than to a little one, since they themselves lie in little things, but would be ashamed of lies that were too big. Such a falsehood will never enter their heads, and they will not be able to believe in the possibility of such monstrous effrontery and infamous misrepresentation in others. . . . Therefore, something of even the most insolent lie will always remain and stick—a fact which all the great lie-virtuosi and lying-clubs in the world know only too well and also make the most treacherous use of.[1]

What is often forgotten by those who identify the "big lie" with Nazi propaganda is that Hitler was referring in this passage to its alleged use by Jews and others who had claimed that Germany had lost World War I in the field and not because of a "stab in the back" at home, and was by no means explicitly advocating the technique himself.[2] Indeed, on certain issues, it now seems as if he and his henchmen fully believed the foul ideas they espoused and even made their murderous intentions public.[3] As Theodor W. Adorno bitterly noted in *Minima Moralia,* fascism "openly proclaims the principle of domination that is elsewhere concealed."[4]

But it quickly became apparent to the world—although, alas, not quickly enough to many Germans—that Hitler also knew how to use the big lie to his own advantage (while all the while denouncing his enemies as themselves incapable of telling the truth). Ironically, the awareness that he could fabricate so blatantly allowed him sometimes to employ a strategic use of true statements. According to Alexandre Koyré, "It was just because he knew he would not be believed by the 'others,' that his declarations would not be taken seriously by the uninitiated—it was precisely by telling them the truth, that he made certain of gulling and lulling his foes. Here we have the old Machiavellian technique of the second-degree lie, most perverse of techniques whereby the truth becomes the pure and simple instrument of deception."[5] Because of this sinister manipulation, the German language, some commentators went so far as to warn, was crumbling under the weight of Nazism's deliberate abuse.[6] To be sure, once the full magnitude of Hitler's monstrous deeds became known, the mere accusation of mendacity faded in comparison. As the political theorist Judith Shklar noted, "His sincerity was hardly an issue. When one really knows that someone is evil, one has no time for his possible hypocrisy."[7]

The point, however, is not to focus on the Nazi case, which is too extreme and ineffable to be considered typical. Railing against the "lies" of one's opponents while privately granting to oneself the right to commit one's own in the name of a higher cause than truth-telling was, after all, not an invention of the Nazis, indeed of any twentieth-century political movement. Instead, it has been in play ever since Plato's controversial notion of the "gennaion pseudos" from *The Republic* (414c), which is traditionally—although not without controversy—translated as "noble lie."[8] It was not by chance that Plato—rather than more recent German thinkers like Hegel or Nietzsche—was the favorite philosopher of the Third Reich.[9] Its leaders could also pride themselves on the burden they took on— like the guardians of Plato's Republic—to do great and benevolent deeds while hiding their responsibility from the uncomprehending masses.[10]

Plato, to be sure, was a believer in the authority of reason, singular, in accord with nature, and accessible to the philosopher. In the history of philosophy, he occupies a privileged place as the defender of the universality of logos, expressed in eternal forms which reason can discover and then apply to practical affairs in the life of the city (the polis from which politics was ultimately derived). He had little patience for those rival thinkers like Protagoras or Gorgias who came to be called Sophists, and who developed a reverence for the arts of rhetoric as opposed to those of dialectic. Strictly demarcating knowledge from mere opinion, preferring certainty to probability, and suspicious of arguments that were based on the moral character of those who held them, Plato and his followers favored rigorous demonstration over mere persuasion, which could be based on dubious appeals to emotion and the seductions of language.

One of the most virulent critics of Sophistry was the historian and military leader Xenophon (c. 427–355 BCE). In such works as *Hiero*, a dialogue between the Syracusan despot and the poet Simonides, and the *Education of Cyrus* (*Cyropaedia*), a heavily romanticized history of the Persian king, he made a case for the self-denying tyrant who rules by guile for the benefit of all, a case whose lesson was not lost on later defenders of lying in politics. Leo Strauss, for example, devoted one of his most trenchant analyses, *On Tyranny*, to *Hiero*, extolling the subtlety of the poet's defense of wise tyrannical governance against the hesitant and self-doubting tyrant.[11] As he noted approvingly in an essay on the Greek thinker called "The Spirit of Sparta or the Taste of Xenophon," it was for a wise elite "a matter of duty to hide the truth from the majority of mankind."[12]

This wisdom was revived with enormous panache—if for Strauss, also with a little too much candor—by the Renaissance Florentine politician and would-be adviser to the Medicis Niccolò Machiavelli, whose name has been identified with it ever since. In *The Prince* (1513), his manual for the art of ruling unconstrained by moral scruple or Christian piety, he made a powerful case for the autonomy of the political realm or what became known as the doctrine of *raison d'état*. "Those princes," he cynically observed, "have done great things who have held faith of small account, and who have known, with their cleverness, to trick men's brains, and at the end they have surpassed those who founded themselves on sincerity."[13] In the notorious eighteenth chapter of the book, "In What Way Faith Should Be Kept by Princes," he urged rulers to model themselves on the cunning fox more than the powerful lion, "for the one who has known better how to use the fox has come out better. But it is necessary to know how to color this nature well, and to be a great pretender and dissembler, and men are so very simple, and they so well obey present necessities, that he who deceives will always find someone who allows himself to be deceived."[14]

When it came to his own discourse as an adviser to great men, Machiavelli admitted that "for some time I never say what I believe and I never believe what I say; and if it sometimes occurs to me that I say the truth, I conceal it among so many lies that it is hard to find out."[15] As might be expected, his own intentions in writing the work have been shrouded in controversy, even after the publication of his famous letter of December 10, 1513, to his friend Francesco Vittori, in which he admitted his hopes for a position with the Medicis.[16]

But whatever his motives, most later commentators could agree with Strauss, who called him "the first philosopher who believes that the coincidence of philosophy and political power can be brought about by propaganda which wins over ever larger multitudes to the new modes and orders and thus transforms the thought of one or a few into the opinion of the public and therewith into public power."[17]

Soon after, Machiavelli's name was transformed into a generic term of opprobrium, initially because the Catholic Church identified him with the secularization of politics threatening Christendom in the early modern era.[18] Its Protestant enemies turned the accusation around, and Catholic political tactics were themselves accused of being no less based on deceit and manipulation. Groups like the *Politiques* in France or *Políticos* in Spain, who hoped to end religious strife through compromise, were also slandered for their efforts by being called Machiavellian (and as a result the very word "politics" was given a negative connotation it has labored ever since to escape).[19] If Claude Lefort is right, his name was blackened still further by an association with nascent capitalism, then most evident in Italy, and with the accompanying "disenchantment of the world," which abetted the unmooring of politics from any moral or cosmological ground.[20] Although in time the "realism" he preached found its tacit defenders among the religious parties themselves, his critique of universalism and plea for a politics of responsibility rather than ultimate ends, to borrow Max Weber's famous dichotomy, earned Machiavelli an eponymous immortality of the kind achieved by few others in the history of political thought.[21] Not surprisingly, when a twenty-first-century sociobiologist like David Livingstone Smith looked around for a label to define the hard-wired tendency toward mendacity he saw in the human psyche, he called it "the Machiavellian Mind."[22]

It has, of course, been possible to read Machiavelli in a more forgiving, even favorable way, noting, for example, with Benedetto Croce that he was the first to understand the autonomy of the political in the modern world.[23] His advice to adopt the deceitful tactics of the fox, it is also sometimes argued, was designed to avoid the more violent ones of the lion. Likewise, his stress on the need to dissemble and seem to be moral has been understood as a kind of indirect tribute to the importance of morality in the private sphere rather than a simple cynicism about morality per se. His reluctance to impose abstract moral principles on politics has also been praised for recognizing the ruler's need to act in concrete circumstances where all actions have ambiguous implications and there is no perfect reconciliation of opposing interests. His frank acceptance of the role of illusion and appearance in politics—more broadly speaking, the inevitably symbolic nature of political rule—has been lauded for its acknowledgment of the impossibility of grounding the political in a natural or divine order pretending to absolute truth. And his realization of the ways in which ethical intentions in politics may produce counterethical outcomes has been interpreted to bespeak an ironical attitude toward the consequences of well-intentioned action in a complex world that does not itself often find a way to reward well-meaning actions with positive results.[24]

Nonetheless, the stigma of being a wicked immoralist interested only in power was not one Machiavelli's name easily shed. And when it came to the specific question of political mendacity, one can still see it claimed today that "all subsequent justifications for lying and deceit in politics are in one way or another elaborations, defenses or reinterpretations of Machiavelli's ideas."[25] Not surprisingly, one of the distinguishing marks of the new experiment in politics called The United States of America that emerged in struggle against British tyranny and steadily moved westward to conquer a continent was its steadfast rejection of Machiavellian duplicity. According to Leo Strauss, "The United States of America may be said to be the only country in the world which was founded in explicit opposition to Machiavellian principles."[26] The republican tradition of civic virtue stemming from the Florentine's political philosophy may have had a powerful impact on the nascent American polity, as John Pocock has famously argued, but it did not include a principled embrace of the abandonment of moral principles, such as the censuring of mendacity.[27] "The Machiavellian moment" did not linger for very long in a context in which suspicion of self-aggrandizing central government survived the revolution dedicated to overthrowing it. As the historian Bernard Wishy has argued, "If beyond *The Prince* there was another Machiavelli, the advocate of virtuous republicanism, that influence remained far more limited than his portrait as the vile one, teaching that lies, fear and cruelty were to be judged only for their effectiveness in keeping power and enhancing control by the ruler of the state."[28]

The powerful legacy of ruthless Puritan self-examination and insistence on interpersonal transparency—the antimonastic, uncloistered attitude of "holy watchfulness" designed to root out signs of sinful behavior—left its mark on the political culture of the new nation. Living in John Winthrop's famous "city on a hill" made constant surveillance all the easier. Secrecy and duplicity were stigmatized by being identified with the wiles of Catholic casuists. Self-scrutiny of the conscience of the believer was reinforced by the community's gaze. Ruthless sincerity and plain speaking emerged as antidotes to the feigning and dissembling of courtier life.[29] The long-standing prejudice against the "hypocrisy" of theatrical performance, stretching back to Plato and revived during the Reformation, was directed at the falseness of appearances, rather than visibility itself.[30] (The word "hypocrisy," it should be noted, originally derived from a Greek word for "answer," which included those given by actors on a stage. It then migrated to denote acting itself, both on stage and off).[31] Intensified by its association with aristocratic masques and Catholic ceremony—a linkage reinforced by the Jesuit use of theater for instructional purposes—the suspicion of playacting, transplanted to America by the Puritans, who had closed the theaters in Britain in 1642,[32] became easily displaced into distrust for a politics that was also seen as theatrical in style. The legacy of the secular Enlightenment—at least in its most protoliberal guise[33]— also played a role in the generation of a political culture resistant to the excuse that altruistic motives could justify the noble lies of authoritarian rule.

Popular American culture soon reflected these values. The celebrated fable of six-year-old George Washington's inability to lie about felling a cherry tree—first circulated in the fifth edition of Mason Locke "Parson" Weems's hagiographic rendering of his life in 1806[34]—signaled a higher standard for truthfulness among the politicians on this side of the Atlantic. Although ironically Weems had in fact made up the anecdote, or more accurately, plagiarized it from an earlier story by James Beattie called "The Minstrel," published in London in 1799, it became a staple of American folklore. When the Civil War put paid to a Southern culture that had been more inclined to gallant civility than plain speaking from the heart, the triumph of sincerity seemed secure, at least as a model of public behavior. Soon after his martyrdom, "Honest Abe" Lincoln joined Washington as the apogee of that ideal.[35]

Whereas even seemingly liberal Britain developed a "culture of secrecy" based on the reticence and discretion of "honorable" gentlemen anxious about lower-class unrest, a culture that abetted the hidden augmentation of a political secret service, America prided itself on being transparent, open, and above board.[36] Publicity and accountability rather than opacity were the dominant values of social and political interaction; our Constitution had to be written and explicit, not tacit and invisible. A quest for perfect legibility and transparency informed American culture from well before the founding of the Republic. It drove a readiness to confess that easily moved from the religious to the secular world, as evidenced in the popular reception of psychoanalysis in the twentieth century.[37] In American literature as well, as Michael T. Gilmore notes in *Surface and Depth,* there was a "cult of truth-telling . . . exemplified by Melville's familiar review of *Mosses from an Old Manse,* in which he enthuses over his countryman Hawthorne as Shakespeare's equal—no, the Bard's superior—in the great 'Art of Telling the Truth.'"[38] Ralph Waldo Emerson made a fetish of sincerity, which was not only a human virtue but somehow one of the universe itself. What was not truthfully spoken would be no less forthrightly revealed to the visual scrutiny of the public, which sought signs of deep structures in surface manifestations. From the nineteenth-century craze of phrenology, brought to these shores from Europe, to the twentieth-century love affair with the cinema, Americans sought to expose what had been hidden.

By the end of the nineteenth century, any residues of a gentlemanly code of formal decorum that had survived the defeat of the Confederacy were undermined by a renewed appreciation for plain speech and colloquial language.[39] From 1885 to the end of the century, high diction and ornate verbal performances were gradually replaced by more straightforward anti-rhetorical rhetoric in which the prestige of the literary stylist eroded and that of the scientific or technical expert grew. Urbane "men of letters" with their general education and refined sensibilities were replaced by more sober and professionally narrow scholars. The old "grand style" using Ciceronian techniques to arouse the passions of the crowd was discredited in favor of a simpler, allegedly more "authentic" style in which sincerity was paramount. The "plain style" that supplanted it, according to Kenneth Cmiel, "creates the illusion that language can be like glass, a medium without the infusion of a self. It pretends the facts can speak for themselves in ways that the old rhetoric never did. The very style has helped perpetuate the belief that there are technical, apolitical solutions to political problems."[40]

Some Americans, to be sure, were able to enjoy the so-called arts of deception—from phony fairground freaks and automatons to trompe l'oeil paintings—in the popular culture of what became known as "the age of Barnum."[41] Hoaxes and humbuggery abetted a game of credulous gullibility in which the fun was generated by the willingness to be fooled mixed with satisfaction at seeing through the trick.[42] Theatricality of all kinds survived the Puritan disdain for its practice of hypocrisy; witness the extraordinary popular adulation Americans felt for Shakespeare in the nineteenth century.[43] And with Mark Twain, they could laugh about the costs of "the decay of the art of lying" and bemoan the "growing prevalence of the brutal truth."[44]

But when it came to politics, they remained far less indulgent. A prominent manifestation of that unease was the growing advocacy in the twentieth century of scientific and technological solutions to political problems, which spilled over from the world of experts to actual policy makers. In the academy, ever since Harvard picked its familiar motto, it has been assumed that truth, or at least the quest for it, is an unimpeachable value.[45] Originally that motto was "Veritas pro Christo et ecclesia" ("Truth for Christ and his church"), but was shortened to allow other, more profane purposes to be served by that quest. When the secularization of intellectual life undermined appeals to divinely revealed truth, this often came to mean a surrogate faith in the scientific method, however that might be defined, as a viable alternative. Even when American Pragmatists questioned traditional notions of certainty and referential correspondence in favor of a more consequentialist alternative, they did not abandon the search for truth as the telos of inquiry and action. With the growth of departments of political science, often adopting the approach that came to be called behavioralist, the appeal to honesty in political practice could be reinforced by a comparable attempt to study politics in a disinterested and neutral way.

At times, in fact, some came to believe that technocrats with the tools of political science at their command would be the best leaders of a polity that wanted to avoid the untidiness of ill-informed opinion and untested prejudice. During the Progressive era in particular, advocates of scientific administration like Walter Lippmann and L. L. Bernard advocated organization, efficiency, and enlightened management.[46] Truth in politics, it was argued, would be achieved by transcending the cacophony of competing voices and allowing those with the skills and knowledge to cut through to the core of problems and deal with them effectively. Only they might avoid confusing the news with the truth, as Lippmann contended in *Public Opinion* in 1922.[47] Only they might avoid being duped by deliberate propaganda, a concept that came into its own during World War I but was derived from an earlier religious notion of propagating the true faith (traceable to the Catholic Church's *Sacra Congregatio de Propaganda Fide* of 1622).[48]

One telling example of the search for technological answers to political and social problems, which achieved a certain amount of success in law enforcement circles and widespread public esteem only in America, was the lie detector.[49] Spawned in the laboratory of the distinguished Harvard experimental psychologist Hugo Münsterberg, it was developed on the eve of the First World War by one of his students, the popular psychologist William Moulton Marston (1893–1947). Seeking an objective indicator of the intentions of the subject in his or her physiological response to questions, unavoidably betraying interior states of mind, the polygraph, as it became known, was never, of course, directly administered to politicians to test the veracity of their statements. Indeed, its admissibility in courts of law also was generally denied. But as one commentator has noted, "The lie detector belongs to that particular American strain of the Enlightenment project which seeks to replace personal discretion with objective measures, and politics with science."[50]

That desire was given a powerful displaced expression in an unexpected manner in another of Marston's inventions in a very different field: the comic book superheroine Wonder Woman, who first appeared in the November 1941 issue of *All-Star Comics*. In some respects a feminist statement about empowering women, in others a sadomasochistic fantasy about bondage discipline, Marston's strip also contained a magical version of the lie detector in Wonder Woman's golden "lasso of truth." Fashioned by the Greek blacksmith god Hephaestus, it was unbreakable, infinitely elastic, and able to force anyone caught by it to tell the truth. As one observer remarks, "Like the lie detector upon which it was modeled, Wonder Woman's 'Golden Lasso' produced truth—and by implication justice and freedom too—through coercion."[51]

Accompanying this championing of unvarnished truth-telling was an equally persistent lament about a political culture that had to struggle constantly to avoid the seductions of mendacity. No more rhetorically powerful expression of the distrust of the dangers of unchecked rhetoric can be found than the celebrated essay by the British novelist and critic George Orwell that quickly established itself as a touchstone of political truth-telling on both sides of the Atlantic, "Politics and the English Language," of 1946.[52] Widely anthologized, incessantly taught in schools, and cited with numbing frequency, Orwell's essay claimed that a debased, impure, inflated, euphemistic, pretentious, cliché-ridden language was more than a symptom of political decline; it was one of its main causes. "In our time," he lamented, "political speech and writing are largely the defense of the indefensible. . . . Political language—and with variations this is true of all political parties, from Conservatives to Anarchists—is designed to make lies sound truthful and murder respectable, and to give an appearance of solidity to pure wind."[53] Avoid stale figures of speech, unnecessarily long words, the passive voice, foreign phrases, and abstruse jargon, he urged, and perhaps the wind would die down.

When *Nineteen Eighty-Four* added a brilliant exposition of the ways in which totalitarianism depended on the deliberate lies of Newspeak and Doublethink, Orwell's reputation as the saint of liberal democratic honesty was augmented. By 1955 commentators like Lionel Trilling, representing the New York intellectuals around *Partisan Review*, could describe him in worshipful terms:

> He told the truth, and told it in an exemplary way, quietly, simply, with due warning to the reader that it was only one man's truth. He used no political jargon, and he made no recriminations. He made no effort to show that his heart was in the right place, or the left place. He was not interested in where his heart might be thought to be, since he knew where it was. He was interested only in telling the truth. . . . And what matters most of all is our sense of the man who tells the truth.[54]

Since Trilling's time, to be sure, Orwell has been subjected to considerable scrutiny, revealing some of his own less attractive biases and self-contradictions. As Stefan Collini has pointed out, "Orwell's writing in general made inauthenticity or bad faith the fundamental fault of the intellectuals, but that writing was itself shot through with a systematic inauthenticity of its own, in consistently positioning him outside the group to which, by the very fact of his writing, he so clearly belonged."[55] Nonetheless, his critique of linguistic obfuscation and its political consequences has become itself a standard trope in political rhetoric. For both the right and the left, his legacy has been a ready source of epithets against their allegedly deceitful opponents. In the words of Hanna Fenichel Pitkin, he stood for the "truth of witness"[56] in which it is incumbent on the reporter to tell the facts of the story as they are. It is thus not surprising to find that Orwell still remains a heroic model for contemporary scourges of mendacity in the public realm like Christopher Hitchens and Michael P. Lynch.[57]

As late as the end of the twentieth century, a European observer with considerable experience of America, Jacques Derrida, could claim that

> it is in the United States, to my knowledge, that perjury is named and tracked, by that name, with the greatest frequency, with an

obsessional insistence. Although I have not done an inventory, it seems to me that the occurrence of the word "perjury" is much more frequent than in any other Western country, as threat of legal action against the "perjurer," in official documents, wherever a commitment or declaration is made, and practically everywhere a signature is required.[58]

In the past few decades, however, the self-evident virtue of sincerity, both in personal relations and in the public realm, has begun to shed some of its allure. Indeed, by the time Lionel Trilling delivered the Charles Eliot Norton Lectures at Harvard in 1970, which became the now classic *Sincerity and Authenticity*, he could write that "the hypocrite-villain, the conscious dissembler, has become marginal, even alien, to the modern imagination. The situation in which a person systematically misrepresents himself in order to practice upon the good faith of another does not readily command our interest, scarcely our credence. The deception we best understand and most willingly give our attention to is that which a person works upon himself."[59] Trilling, to be sure, was writing more about literature than politics, and the value that he saw superseding sincerity—authenticity—could also be seen as promoting truthtelling against hypocrisy. But there were signs as well of a loosening of the Puritanical code that had held American culture in its grip, albeit with varying degrees of tightness, for so long.

For example, although propaganda was still overwhelmingly condemned as a tool of totalitarian politics, its inevitable use for the rallying of democratic opinion, even in peacetime, had already been acknowledged by certain social scientists like Harold Lasswell and George Catlin in the interwar era.[60] In theoretical terms, the fetish of sincerity was challenged after the war by the growing reception of many strands of European thought that put into doubt the possibility of language, political or otherwise, being a straightforward vehicle for the conveyance of truth or truthfulness.[61] Orwell's dismissive criticism of the "soggy, half-baked insincerity [that] runs through all 'advanced' opinion"[62] no longer seemed sufficient grounds to dismiss complicated ideas expressed in difficult prose. Whether through the incorporation of ideas brought by German exiles from Nazism,

such as Strauss, Hannah Arendt, or Adorno, or through the later absorption of texts by French poststructuralists like Michel Foucault,
Derrida, and Jean Baudrillard, some Americans—at least those inclined to tackle their notoriously demanding and opaque prose—
came to question Orwell's faith in linguistic purification as an antidote to political chicanery. What became known as "the linguistic
turn" involved a new respect for rhetorical tropes and hermeneutic
suspicion, as well as the deconstruction of univocal meaning and
the liberation of texts from the control of those who had authored
them. A comparable suspicion of what Adorno had damned as "the
jargon of authenticity" cast doubt on pious claims to speak "from
the heart" and communicate directly unmediated truths.[63] "The fet-
ishization of authenticity" and "cultural obsession with sincerity" attracted their share of critics, who denounced them as evidence of
the mass cultural stripping away of the aura of objects and a vain
hope to achieve "semiotic transparency" beyond all representation.[64] We will necessarily return to many of these claims in the discussion to follow.

These unflinchingly esoteric arguments—whose elitist opacity
was explicitly defended by many of their exponents against the typical American demand for plain speaking—of course, filtered down
only imperfectly to the larger population. The general public continued to decry political mendacity. It has, in fact, become ever more
frequently lamented that lying in American politics has increased in
the past few decades, the infamous "credibility gap" introduced during the 1960s growing ever wider.[65] A steady drumbeat of major
examples at the highest levels of government can be adduced to support this judgment: the initial American denial of the Bay of Pigs
invasion, the Tonkin Gulf resolution tricking us into the Vietnam
War, Watergate, the Iran-Contra scandal, the Monica Lewinsky affair, and most recently, George W. Bush's apparently bogus claims
about Iraqi weapons of mass destruction (which by one account tal-
lied a whopping 935 in number!).[66]

"Since the end of the Cold War," a recent commentator remarks,
"American culture has been polarized by this topic, finding it an unlimited source of fascination, amusement and horror."[67] Easy jokes
are made about the most notorious perpetrators, for example: "Wash-

ington couldn't tell a lie, Nixon couldn't tell the truth, and Reagan couldn't tell the difference." Or more generically: "How can you tell when a politician is lying? He moves his lips." Bookshelves fill up with titles accusing one or another opponent of lying: Christopher Hitchens, *No One Left to Lie To: The Triangulations of William Jefferson Clinton;* Ann Coulter, *Slander: Liberal Lies about the American Right;* Al Franken, *Lies and the Lying Liars Who Tell Them: A Fair and Balanced Look at the Right;* Joe Conason, *Big Lies: The Rightwing Propaganda Machine and How It Distorts the Truth;* Sheldon Rampton and John C. Stauber, *Weapons of Mass Deception: The Uses of Propaganda in Bush's War on Iraq;* David Corn, *The Lies of George W. Bush: Mastering the Politics of Deception;* Nicholas von Hoffman, *Hoax: Why Americans Are Suckered by White House Lies;* Paul Waldman, *Fraud: The Strategy behind the Bush Lies and Why the Media Didn't Tell You;* and Eric Alterman, *When Presidents Lie: A History of Official Deception and Its Consequences,*[68] just to name a few.

Benjamin Disraeli's famous cynical witticism, "There are three kinds of lies: lies, damned lies, and statistics," popularized in America by Mark Twain, has spawned a literature of its own, mirroring the public's growing skepticism about the use of polls and surveys by politicians.[69] (One survey that may ironically deserve full trust is cited by Sissela Bok in her widely read book *Lying;* it was conducted in 1976 and found that 69 percent of the public believed that our leaders were consistent liars over the past decade.)[70] The comedian Stephen Colbert's tongue-in-cheek notion of "truthiness," defined as a gut feeling about the truth in the absence of any evidence or logic to support it, was named in two different surveys in 2005 and 2006 as "word of the year" and earned its own Wikipedia entry. A once obscure article by the Princeton philosopher Harry Frankfurt with the provocative title "On Bullshit" became a best seller in 2005 when it was reissued as a slim book, and generated learned responses by philosophers anxious to parse its every meaning.[71] Polls tell us that Americans are increasingly hospitable to the proposition that, as a 2006 headline in the *San Francisco Chronicle* put it, "hedging truth not bad."[72] Search for "lying in politics" on the Internet and you will get a flood of references to articles, blogs, movies (like Robert Greenwald's documentary *Uncovered*), even a gift shop featuring George W. Bush paraphernalia from coffee mugs to dog t-shirts adorned with his face and the motto "Got Mendacity?" We seem to have got it to the point of an obsession, which threatens to crowd out a serious discussion of substantive issues in favor of catching the discussants uttering a falsehood.

But even as the furor over the ubiquity of lying increased, it has been hard to deny that politics and mendacity have been intimate bedfellows for a very long time indeed. It is hard to gainsay the worldly judgment of Hannah Arendt about the perennial nature of the connection: "No one has ever doubted that truth and politics are on rather bad terms with each other, and no one, as far as I know, has ever counted truthfulness among the political virtues. Lies have always been regarded as necessary and justifiable tools not only of the politician's or the demagogue's but also of the statesman's trade."[73] As the contemporary French philosopher Alain Badiou has argued, "We know that the overwhelming majority of empirical instances of politics have nothing to do with truth. They organize a mixture of power and opinions. The subjectivity that animates them is that of demand and *ressentiment*, of the tribe and the lobby, of electoral nihilism and the blind confrontation of communities."[74] In short, to put it in the pithy terms of the great muckraking journalist I. F. Stone, "All governments lie."[75]

But however ubiquitous, however perennial lying in politics may seem to be, it still occasions enormous unease, especially among those who hold out hope for a liberal democratic polity ideally based on transparency, trust, and accountability in what Jürgen Habermas has made famous as the "public sphere."[76] For many of them, a defense of political hypocrisy is seen as inherently conservative and elitist in implication.[77] Broadly speaking, reactions to the entrenched persistence of lying in politics have taken two predictable turns. The first, exemplified by moralists who want to apply the same high standards they insist should be followed in private life, argues that public life must be purged as much as possible of mendacity. Especially those who see democratic politics as inherently more ethical than any alternative insist that an open society must be based on the truth-telling of those entrusted with the power to rule. As Sissela Bok puts it, "It is certainly true that deception can never be completely absent from most human practices. But there are great differences among societies in the kinds of deceit that exist and the extent to which they are practiced, differences also among individuals in the same government and among successive governments within the same society. This strongly suggests that it is worthwhile trying to discover why such differences exist and to seek ways of raising the standards of truthfulness."[78] Although some critics of political mendacity, such as the leftwing American journalist Eric Alterman, claim they are not moralistic but only concerned about the "ultimately and invariably self-destructive"[79] consequences of deception, they draw equally absolutist conclusions: "Do not, under any circumstances, lie."[80]

The second typical response argues instead that a realistic, nonmoralistic politics is a politics that understands that, even in democracies, power and success are still the goals to be sought. Soberly, its defenders claim that at times the struggle to achieve those ends will necessitate and even justify duplicity. What matters most, they will say, are outcomes and effects, rather than abstract moral principles. And truth-telling is only one possible means to bring about a desired and beneficial result, a means with no intrinsic superiority over its rivals. Leadership sometimes involves knowing one thing and saying another, in the service of goals that would otherwise be unattainable. Idealism always seems a nobler stance than cynicism, but sometimes it has counterproductive results. Moreover, as the examples cited above from the 1920 Nazi platform and *Mein Kampf* show, denouncing your enemies as liars is no guarantee of political virtue. We have already seen Machiavelli as the eponymous champion of this realist position.

Framing the question of lying in politics in these conventional terms—moralism vs. realism, principles vs. consequences, absolutism vs. relativism—is hard to avoid, and must serve as an inevitable starting point for any discussion.[81] But what quickly becomes apparent in any serious treatment of the problem is that it has solidified into two predictable positions that have battled each other with no clear victory for either since the issue was first raised. Instead of rehearsing them yet again, it would be more fruitful to approach political mendacity with fresh eyes.[82] Taking into account the perennial nature of the problem, its dogged persistence in every political system yet devised (admittedly with varying frequency), it is necessary to ask if there is something about the realm of human behavior that we call politics that lends itself to a weakening of the normal moral disdain for lying. And if so, to push into more provocative territory, is it part of what makes politics valuable rather than merely an unedifying spectacle of human depravity?

To answer these questions will first necessitate a thorough vetting of the larger debate about lying in general. In the first section of this book, we will examine arguments made over the centuries about the links between deception and nature, lying and socialization, language and duplicity, and morality and mendacity. Our second section will turn to the no less vexed question of what constitutes that realm apart known as politics—or even more portentously, "the political"—to see what aspects of it might be understood to abet and perhaps even justify the practice of lying. We will have to ask how watertight the boundary between politics and its various "others," including society, morality, science, and the law, actually is. Finally, in our third section, we will directly explore the possibility of a more complicated relationship between lying and politics than that presented by the conventional dichotomy between moralism and realism. We will explore the question of power and lying, differentiating the mendacity of the weak and vulnerable from that of the strong and dominating. We will enter the gray area between unvarnished truth-telling and deliberate falsification, the swampy terrain occupied by dissimulation, simulation, hypocrisy, spin, "truthiness," and other stratagems of political life. Whether we will exit with all of our conventional assumptions about lying in politics intact remains to be seen.

1
ON LYING

All men are liars.
—PSALMS 116:11

Mundus vult decipi, ergo decipiatur.
[The world wants to be deceived; therefore it should be deceived.]
—PETRONIUS, *LYING AND NATURE*

LYING AND NATURE

Even benign Nature habitually lies, except when she promises execrable weather.
—MARK TWAIN, "ON THE DECAY OF THE ART OF LYING"

Invoking "nature" as a norm has been a persistent temptation for those unable to provide other, more compelling reasons for value choices. To be called "unnatural" or "against nature" often serves the purpose of stigmatizing behavior or inclinations that are for one reason or another abhorrent to the stigmatizer. To be in tune with nature—both internal and external—seems somehow "healthier" in a moral as well as a physical sense. Natural rights and natural laws are often invoked as a standard against which to measure the limitations of positive law, and not only by conservative Straussians or neo-Thomists.[1]

The virtues of artificiality have, of course, been celebrated by those who recognize the arbitrariness of what counts as "natural"—

Joris-Karl Huysmans's classic "decadent" novel *À Rebours* is sometimes translated as *Against Nature*—and radical constructivists have sometimes promoted a no less one-sided domination of "culture" over "nature." The fallacy of a naturalist ethics has also been subjected to withering criticisms from commentators like G. E. Moore. But no matter how often refuted, the appeal to nature, defined in a myriad of ways,[2] has been a perennial ultima ratio for those repelled by the hubris of humans who claim they can invent out of whole cloth the norms they then feel obliged to follow.

In the case of lying, however, those who are its harshest critics cannot easily resort to the accusation that it is an unnatural act. Although on occasion theologians like Martin Buber have claimed that "the lie is the specific evil which man introduced into nature . . . the lie is our very own invention,"[3] his is very much a minority view. For, as many commentators have pointed out, both the animal and vegetable kingdoms are replete with examples of deception and duplicity, which if not based on speech acts are still designed to produce the effect of a deliberate lie. Even on the molecular level, deceptive strategies have been developed by human pathogens like viruses to defeat our immune systems.[4] In the evolutionary struggle, clear advantage routinely goes to those who can find ways to deceive their enemies or rivals and avoid loosing the battle for survival. Darwin himself approvingly cited the work of Henry Walter Bates, the Victorian entomologist who realized in 1862 that one tasty species of butterfly in the Amazon region, the Pierids, cleverly imitated the coloration of their inedible counterparts, the Heliconids, to fool hungry birds.[5] The never-ending contest between predator and prey involves camouflage, mimicry, and other forms of hiding the truth. Deceptive imitation, in which appearance belies reality, can take place in a variety of ways, including alteration of the animal's own body parts and even a kind of cross-dressing.[6] In the no less critical struggle for sexual selection, similar tactics often decide who gets to pass down his or her genes to the next generation. Although interpreting the adoption of deceptive tactics as evidence of a deliberate intelligence at work—the putative "cunning" of nature—may be dubious, its ubiquity is not.[7]

To the extent that humans are part of nature, it is thus argued by some observers that the ability to lie is an invaluable tool developed to avoid early extinction, either of the individual or of the species.[8] Rather than being against nature, deception—in the broadest sense of unspoken as well as spoken representations and acts—is one of the cleverest instruments the natural world has at its disposal. A soldier's camouflaged uniform and streaked face paint echoes the efforts of the insect to blend in with the leaf on which it sits (and indeed, modern camouflage, historians tell us, was inspired by scientists like Abbot Thayer familiar with animals' mimesis of their environment).[9] The impulse to adorn our bodies and cosmetically improve our appearances in order to increase our desirability to potential sexual partners is on a continuum with the fish who flash a red patch on their sides to show they have robust genes. Recent sociobiologists, such as David Livingstone Smith, who want to make sense of all human behavior by assimilating it to an evolutionary model have been keen to defend the capacity to lie as hardwired in the evolved human unconscious, because of the functional advantage it gives to those who use it skillfully. Not surprisingly, as we will see, political theorists like Machiavelli and Leo Strauss, who recognize the virtues of mendacity in the public sphere, tend to find a norm in nature rather than in a moral law that transcends it (although, to be sure, Strauss didn't share Machiavelli's penchant for comparing us to animals). Livingstone tellingly dubs the area of the unconscious that teaches us to lie "the Machiavellian module." The evolutionary biologist Dario Maestripieri adds that both humans and rhesus macaque monkeys have "macachiavellian intelligence."[10]

Even self-deception may well prove a useful tool, they have conjectured, in certain cases when acknowledging a terrible truth—about for example the odds against defeating a formidable foe—is best ignored if the chances to survive are to be maximized. In addition, the ability to lie to oneself—or more precisely, for one part of a divisible self to lie to another[11]—may also be functional in decreasing the likelihood of competitors discerning deliberate lies through the bodily cues that are given off by even the most accomplished deceiver.[12] As Smith suggests, "The liars' tendencies to betray themselves inadvertently acted as a selection pressure for the evolution of self-deception. Self-deception did not appear in the mental repertoire of our hominid ancestors to protect them from distress *qua* distress, as champions of the mental health industry assume. Instead, it emerged as a tool for social manipulation."[13] Although it would be difficult to maintain that all self-deceivers, or "mythomaniacs," as they are sometimes called, are helping themselves survive, at least some may benefit from their unconscious duplicity. And if Nietzsche is right to argue that the founders of great religions were all believers in their own self-deception, than perhaps others have been as well.[14]

It is also sometimes argued that children come into the world not trailing clouds of glory, innocent and uncorrupted, but rather armed with the potential, even inclination, to deceive. The great developmental psychologist Jean Piaget once said of young children, "The tendency to tell lies is a natural tendency, so spontaneous and universal that we can take it as an essential part of the egocentric thought."[15] The opposite imperative, to tell and honor the truth, may be a learned behavior that comes later. But it is a lesson never fully mastered. As Smith sardonically notes, "Children who are unable to lie, as George Washington reputedly was (in yet another lie often told to children), are not 'good' boys and girls: they may quite possibly be autistic."[16] Indeed, another commentator adds, "a reliable indicator of autism seems to be an incompetence in the arts of hiding, pretending, dissembling and lying."[17] That is, an autistic child is generally unable to tell when someone is simply under a false impression or is deliberately uttering a falsehood.

From a very different perspective, lying was praised as "life-affirming" by Friedrich Nietzsche, who had no use for Darwinian notions of adaptation or the survival of the fittest. As a great hermeneutician of suspicion, to borrow Paul Ricoeur's famous characterization, Nietzsche argued that "healthy" life—and he often fell back on health as a norm—would be promoted, not by trust, but by distrust of all that passed for sincerity in the world of respectable people. The question of truth and lies should be approached from an "extramoral" perspective, with no regard for its ethical implications. For in man this art of simulation reaches its peak: here deception, flattering, lying and cheating, talking behind the back, posing, living in borrowed splendor, being masked, the disguise of convention, acting a role before others and before oneself—in short the constant fluttering around the single flame of vanity is so much the rule and the law that almost nothing is more incomprehensible than how an honest and pure urge for truth could have arisen among men.[18]

Although suspicious of the concept of nature, the later Nietzsche came to believe that something called "life" was abetted by illusions, or rather by the realization that beneath the surface of things there were no essences, no hidden truths, just further illusions. As he put it in the preface to *The Gay Science* in 1886,

> This bad taste, this will to truth, to "truth at any price," this youthful madness in the love of truth, have lost their charm for us; for that we are too experienced, too serious, too merry, too burned, too *profound*. We no longer believe that truth remains truth when the veils are withdrawn. We have lived too much to believe this. Today we consider it a matter of decency not to wish to see everything naked, or to be present at everything, or to understand and "know" everything.[19]

Too much truth is "unhealthy," since we need our illusions, our myths, our lies, to survive the harsh realities of existence. "No living things would have survived if the opposite tendency [to telling the truth]—to err and *make up* things rather than wait, to assent rather than negate, to pass judgment rather than be just—had not been bred to the point where it became extraordinarily strong."[20] Although something explicitly called "nature" could not be a norm for art, the ideal of "life" should determine aesthetic value, not art for its own sake.[21] Whether or not "life" was as open to interpretation as "nature"—just think of the change of meaning in contemporary America when "life-affirming" has become "pro-life"—and thus a cultural construct seemed not to dissuade him from employing it as an absolute value.

Such speculations about the naturalness or "life-affirming" function of deception, however, do not entirely dispel the suspicion that the appeal to nature is no less problematic when it comes to defending stigmatized behavior than criticizing it. For the "natural" propensity to deceive in order to foil a predator or seduce a breeding partner is necessarily based on the no less "natural" propensity—innate or nurtured through experience—to believe in the truthful evidence of one's senses in perceiving the world. No one can be fooled, after all, if there isn't a more fundamental presupposition of experiential veracity; nature, like Descartes' God, would be in trouble if she were a systematic deceiver.[22] Species who can't tell the difference between what is true and what is not are unlikely to prosper for very long. The ability to detect deception is, after all, just as functional in evolutionary terms as the ability to deceive. Animals with improved perceptual systems, capable of differentiating appearance from reality, have an advantage over those with lesser ones. The radical and sustained disjuncture between truthfulness and what is in fact the case—normally called "the truth"—is not inherently in the service of self-preservation or that of the species.

Moreover, just because predator/prey relationships between species often rely on a duel to the death of competing deceptions, it doesn't follow that human behavior can—let alone should—be modeled on this interaction. Just as some animals within and even across species cooperate symbiotically for mutual benefit and may well employ truth-telling as an instrument to that end—the deer alerting the herd to the presence of a wolf rather than prudently running away to save its own hide—humans can also derive evolutionary benefit from assessing their environment as accurately as possible and sharing the results of their investigations with their kind. Altruism, even sociobiologists agree, may be functional in evolutionary terms, and if so, then conveying the truth to a friend may be as useful as deceiving an enemy.

So too might the sharp moral disapproval that is almost universally expressed about lying, even as the practice continues unabated, something totally absent from the nonhuman biosphere. It might, in fact, have emerged at a later evolutionary moment than the initial use of deception, which, to be sure, it could not entirely supplant. As one commentator has noted, "A capacity or propensity that is advantageous at one stage of human evolution need not necessarily remain advantageous indefinitely. . . . Cooperation entailed trust and hence disapproval of deceit, but Machiavellian skill, essential for cooperation, could continue to be used deceptively to further individual interests. Hence deceit persisted despite disapproval."[23] To the extent that humans evolved into beings who are both communal and individual—unlike uniformly social, nonindividuated animals like ants or bees—they needed contrary skills that might allow the flourishing of both the imperative to tell the truth and the ability to subvert it.

Moreover, if it is the case that human culture is a necessary supplement to make up for the inadequacies of human nature, that we are as the anthropologist Arnold Gehlen famously noted a "defective life form" which lacks instinctual self-sufficiency,[24] then there is no reason to posit a parallel between those behaviors that we call natural and explain in evolutionary terms and those that we call cultural and understand as a necessary supplement to what is given to us by our genetic inheritance. As Bernard Williams once remarked, "The insistence on finding explanations of cultural difference in terms of biological evolution exactly misses the point of the great evolutionary innovation represented by *Homo sapiens*, the massive development of non-genetic learning."[25] Culture, itself a word no less polysemic than nature,[26] can, after all, suggest both the cultivation of the potential traits provided us by nature and the contrivance of new modes of being that extend well beyond anything that might be seen as latent in our genes. And to the extent that lying, according to a strict definition, may be best understood as a special case of deception based on language—Wittgenstein saw it as a learned language game not available to other animals—it needs the supplement of culture, nongenetic learning, to make it fully possible.

Deception, in short, may be an inevitable feature of the biosphere and of the human world to the extent that we are part of natural evolution. But it is certainly a more variable practice in cultural—and *a fortiori* individual—terms, with humans generally seeking to avoid it as much as possible and bemoaning their weakness when they are inclined to employ it. For however much evidence we may adduce to show the ubiquity of mendacity in the natural and human worlds, we also have no less abundant evidence to show how widely it is deplored and avoided, at least in the latter.[27] Indeed, insofar as instrumental value is not seen as the sole criterion of worth in most cultures, a purely utilitarian defense of the function of deception in serving evolutionary ends cannot exhaust the debate about its purpose or justification. In short, the argument from nature gives us very little help in understanding the dialectic that results from cultural variation, especially when it comes to politics, an invention of our species that has no real parallel elsewhere in the animal world (*pace* fans of *The Lion King* or visitors to Disney's Animal Kingdom).[28]

LYING AND SOCIETY

The best Composition, and Temperature is, to have *Opennesse*
in Fame and Opinion; *Secrecy* in Habit; *Dissimulation* in seasonable
use; And a Power to faigne, if there be no Remedy.
—FRANCIS BACON, "OF SIMULATION AND DISSIMULATION"

O great and noble lie! But when is truth
so splendid as to be preferred to you?
—TORQUATO TASSO, *JERUSALEM DELIVERED*

Is there, then, any consensus about the place of mendacity in that realm of human behavior we identify with society or culture, that is, with something beyond or in addition to what nature decrees we must do to survive and reproduce? Here too evidence can be easily adduced on both sides of the question. No society, it seems obvious, can operate for very long on the premise that truth-telling is a random, infrequent occurrence or mendacity the default norm. If, as we are often told, trust is a fundamental assumption of sociability in general, it stands to reason that one thing we come very early on to trust is the reliability and integrity of those with whom we interact the most.[29] Infants, the most vulnerable members of any human society, learn to count on the presence and nurturance of their caregivers, and are severely damaged, perhaps even lose their lives, if these gifts are withdrawn or denied. The importance of mutual intersubjective recognition prior to cognitive understanding of the external world of objects—acknowledgment before knowledge—is becoming increasingly appreciated.[30] What might be called affective truth-telling, the consistent affirmation of love we actually feel toward those we nurture, caring for those we care for, is so fundamental a human experience that naïve social optimists often hope it might somehow be generalized to embrace all of human relations.

More sober observers, skeptical of the possibility of universalizing *agape*, let alone eros, have remarked how attenuated it can become the farther away from interpersonal immediacy. Any complex society inevitably builds a network of abstract relations among strangers for whom affective ties are weakened, displaced, and perhaps even nonexistent. We feel far less compulsion to share intimate emotions with those who are distant from us in the social universe (however much the new semianonymous cybersociability of the Internet changes its dynamics). Although it is certainly true that we can feel deeply about public figures we don't actually know firsthand, especially in a culture like ours that promotes the cult of celebrities, for the vast majority of fellow humans we experience little more than imaginary sympathy or vague distaste.

Here too, however, truth-telling is arguably also a crucial dimension of the tacit or explicit contractual relations that make dealing with strangers more than just an affair of naked power or strategic manipulation. Interdependence necessitates faith in the continued realization of our expectations about how the social world replicates itself, carrying out its implicit or explicit promises to do what its members say they will do, fulfilling the role descriptions they have assumed. A century ago, Georg Simmel argued that this faith was of ever-increasing importance in the modern world, whose complexity was dependent on trust more than coercion.[31]

Even before contractual relationships are written down or given the sanction of law, we learn to trust in the word of those who give trust in return for ours. The illocutionary force of speech acts, as theorists like J. L. Austin and John Searle have shown us, is built on expectations about what words do as well as what they mean, expectations that are reinforced by the institutional settings in which the speech acts are performed. A promise, for example, is not a statement about the facts of the world, but an expression of the intentionality of the speaker, which can have social power only if the default expectation is that it truthfully reflects his or her intentions and will be carried out. To the extent that social behavior is inherently rule governed, based on practices that require regularity and replicability, the roles we play are enabled by the assumption that those who inhabit them will faithfully abide by their conventions. We entrust our soles to shoemakers and our souls to clerics, and would be in considerable trouble if there were uncertainty about their sincere intention to carry out their very different assignments.

The real world is, of course, far from ideal, and sometimes that trust is misplaced. There are shoemakers who abscond with our footwear and clerics who are in cahoots with the devil. Rules are, after all, made to be broken and always have exceptions; the laws of men, as we all know, are never as watertight as the laws of nature. Even the commandments supposedly coming from a divine legislator can always be disobeyed, at least by believers who celebrate human free will. Indeed, as we will see when looking at the relationship between lying and morality, the freedom to lie may be a fundamental premise of any moral system, even if there is the fervent hope that it will be the exception, not the rule. And of course, it might be argued—and we will see to what extent it often is—that in politics, rules can be relaxed and procedures circumvented, if there are compelling reasons to do so.

But beyond this experience of lying as a deviant abuse of social trust, a breach of the covenant among humans or between humans and their God, there is a more fundamental way in which it plays a critical role in sociability. The first fig leaf adopted to cover our nudity expressed a fundamental link between culture and hiding the truth, even if the latter could be defended by a rhetoric of wholesome modesty rather than corrupt duplicity. We hide and dissemble not only what we feel guilty about but also what causes us to feel shame. As one commentator, punning on the phrase "habit of lying," has noted, "The traditional moral distinction between lying and concealment, the first generally proscribed and the second frequently prescribed, is suspect."[32] However fashions in clothing may change, they all function to veil the body, even if they may work at the same time to solicit desire for it (thus doubling their mendacious function).

For some commentators, in fact, it is clothing, cosmetics, veils, and masks all the way down, as there is no underlying natural truth to be revealed in an ultimate act of revelation. "Let it not be protested that cosmetics and attractive clothing are distorting lies," writes the psychologist Karl E. Scheibe, "making fictions out of our real selves. For we, in our real selves, are inescapably fictions. Our names are made up, our races, our religions, our political doctrines, our nations, our languages, and certainly every object of clothing since the grape leaf phase has been of human devising—there is no natural way to appear."[33] For other commentators like the German philosophical anthropologists Helmut Plessner and Arnold Gehlen, immediacy is always mediated by an artificial symbolic order that defies reduction to anything authentic beneath or behind the mask. The ideal of naturalness has, to be sure, survived this realization, leading to an unending struggle between its defenders and radical conventionalists like Scheibe, Plessner, and Gehlen. The latter also have to grapple with the fact that although selves may never reach a bedrock of natural identity, it doesn't necessarily follow that more or less integrated subjects are unable to have beliefs or thoughts which they express as sincerely as they can or deliberately hide. Indeed, the very concept of a lie makes sense only if it involves that distinction; it can't be lies all the way down.

It is therefore better to keep the tension between truth-telling and lying alive, and recognize that children are normally socialized in contradictory ways, producing a fragile and unstable balance between two competing codes of behavior. Whatever their allegedly "natural" inclination to lie may be, they are quickly given mixed messages about what is socially expected and morally upright. On the one hand, they are admonished to tell the truth and learn to distinguish between their fantasies and the real world. We signal them that honesty is not only the best policy, that is, prudentially effective, but also a positive value in itself, reflecting on the character of the truth-teller. Stories like George Washington and the cherry tree are exploited to inspire in them a respect—and the word, with all its connotations of obeying a higher authority, is not chosen lightly—for the truth. If you tell too many fibs, they are admonished, you turn into a "confirmed liar," whose essential character has been corrupted by the repetition of bad habits, or at least who is perceived as such by others in the world. You thus risk losing your reputation for trustworthiness and may forfeit the esteem of others.

The same world, however, also honors and instills in a child the virtue of certain kinds of benign mendacity, a sense of when certain lies are merely "white" or as the French say, "pious." If there may be, as we have noted above, a natural propensity for children to dissemble, it is an inclination that can be reinforced as well as blunted. We often make guileful trickster figures heroes of both myth (Odysseus and the Norse god Loki) and popular culture (Till Eulenspiegel, Brer Rabbit, and Bart Simpson). Inevitably, children come to admire their defiance of authority and ability to outwit superior force. Despite what we may preach, we often provide a model of well-intentioned duplicity, regarding, for example, sexuality or Santa Claus, which children ultimately see through. And although we want our children to be able to distinguish between play and reality, fantasy and fact, we also encourage their imaginative ability to create and inhabit worlds they concoct out of thin air or enter through fairy tales, fables, and cartoons. By the age of three, experiments have shown, about 50 percent of American children have learned to lie with enough control of their facial expressions to avoid being caught.[34]

Perhaps even more importantly, we also teach children the virtues of politeness and civility, in which full and unvarnished candor is to be avoided, if possible. Knowing that unrelieved honesty can be brutal, we seek to soften the blow by introducing tact as a virtue of its own.[35] We teach the values of discretion and modesty. Elaborate formality provides prefabricated forms of behavior, shared codes of decorum, to help us navigate the otherwise uncharted waters of interpersonal interaction. It allows us to suspend the demand for absolute and immediate justice in a world more gray than black and white. As one commentator notes, "Civility requires another form of restraint: the willingness to accept small slights or incivilities on the part of others. To be too scrupulous about justice produces unnecessary conflicts, and to treat people with respect implied by good manners is often to treat them as better than they are."[36]

Socialization, in other words, involves learning to be sensitive to context and audience, gaining a *savoir-faire* that relativizes the imperative always to tell the truth, to make private feelings or beliefs fully public. It compels us to judge between competing moral commands, including the command always to be honest, which may not invariably be the best policy in all circumstances. And insofar as such judgments may not be subsumable under a single, uniform moral rule, we learn through practical experience a kind of wisdom—the Greeks called it *phronesis*—which helps us negotiate the difficult passage between competing duties and obligations.

Even the trust that binds personal friendships can mean more than trusting the veracity of what is exchanged between close friends, the referential content of their speech acts. Although, as Bernard Williams emphasized, there is a still potent etymological link in English between truth and trust, the former in fact denoting until perhaps the fourteenth century "fidelity, loyalty or reliability,"[37] trust might also convey the meaning of having confidence that the other person has my best interests at heart, which may involve his or her willingness to fib on my behalf. As the philosopher David Nyberg has pointed out in his spirited defense of varnishing the truth,

> Trust in friendship does not *exclusively* mean trust in the truth of your friend's statement. It also means reliance on some quality or attribute of your friend, a quality such as discretion, which is having the tact with regard to the truth, or wisdom, which is having the good sense to know that not everything that *could* be said *should* be said, or resourcefulness, which is the capacity to make happen what should happen but won't happen unless somebody does something to nudge it along.[38]

Trusting in the person, in other words, is not equivalent to trusting his or her being an unqualified truth-teller, no matter the circumstances.

Many observers have, in fact, recognized that what is construed as the proper balance between sincerity and politeness, truth-telling and tact, in the public realm as well is itself historically variable.[39] They often note that cultures like those found in the Renaissance Italy of Castiglione and the France of Louis XIV were ruled, at least at the aristocratic, courtly level, by elaborate rituals and codes of *politesse* and *courtoisie,* in which sincerity was devalued in favor of sensitivity to appearances and sociability. "Honest dissimulation" could be defended by writers like the seventeenth-century Neapolitan Torquato Accetto, and philosophers like Giordano Bruno could invoke it as a shield against religious persecution of the truth.[40] No less a moralist than Pascal could observe in his *Pensées* that the existence of society is based on mutual deceit.[41] The German word for politeness, *Höflichkeit,* significantly retains the word for court, *Hof.* The ideal of *honnêteté* extended similar values to gentlemen from the rising middle classes, whose manners were always moderate, reasonable, worldly, but not in the most conventional sense of the word "honest." The *honnête homme* knew the rules of good conversation and deportment, of wit and *esprit.* In fact, he was so much a master of the social graces that he is sometimes seen as the prototype for the nineteenth-century dandy, who was resolutely artificial, all surface and no depth, and incapable of ever uttering a sincere word.[42]

For all its later associations with rationality, the French Enlightenment's "republic of letters" was built on an ideal of sociability in *le monde* or *la bonne compagnie* of the salons, normally gendered female in opposition to the older military value system of male honor.[43] More egalitarian and meritocratic than the aristocratic court, the salons lessened the competitiveness of life under the eye of the king, and led to the belief that civilization could be fostered by the fine arts of conversation and wit. In the fictional writings of philosophes like Diderot, the deliberate use of deception, mystification, and persiflage for pedagogical purposes was developed, even if the ultimate goal was demystification or "learning from lying," as a later critic would call it.[44]

What has been called a "culture of politeness" could be found as well in the urbane coffeehouses of eighteenth-century England, where morals and mores, ethics and manners, were understood to be congruent rather than in tension.[45] Tact, which sometimes required suppressing the brutal truth to save the feelings of others, could be praised as itself morally sensitive. Although there were vigorous debates over which groups should be included in that culture— women, servants, and the lower classes were not easily admitted— even hypocrisy could be defended as a social virtue by writers like Shaftesbury, Chesterfield, Swift, and Burke.[46]

From the point of view of those who could not or would not play the conventional social game, however, excessive politeness was a sign of moral weakness, a way to justify self-serving deception and vanity over dispassionate truthfulness and integrity, one step from personal and social corruption. It was also identified with the effeminization of culture, which had undermined male virtue by introducing the weakness for mendacity allegedly typical of women and servants. In fact, at least in seventeenth-century England a connection between mendacity and the lower orders was often assumed, for, as Steven Shapin notes, "Lying was vile, base, mean and ignoble because it arose from circumstances attending the lives of ignoble people. An ignoble life was a *constrained* life, in which one was at the will of another, in which passion or interest compromised the self's spontaneous free action. Gentlemen were truth-tellers because nothing could work upon them that would induce them to be otherwise."[47]

Across the Channel, however, the suspicion that aristocratic manners were less conducive to honesty remained strong, occasioning a powerful response by the end of the eighteenth century. Here the critical figures are often seen as Rousseau, the scourge of courtly manners and superficial appearances, who excoriated lying (or rather, did so if the consequences were harmful and the lies told to people who deserved the truth) in *The Reveries of the Solitary Walker*,[48] and Robespierre, who prided himself on being "incorruptible." For them, hypocrisy was an entirely pejorative term, which could no longer be so easily defended by conflating it with tact and civility. It was the opposite of integrity and authenticity. Not surprisingly, Rousseau increasingly withdrew from society as a whole, at least as it existed in the Europe of his day, and Robespierre ruthlessly employed violence to purge it of its polluted elements.[49]

New single-sex institutions like the fraternal lodges of the Freemasons served to undermine the polite sociability of the female-dominated salons that had been so much a part of the pre-Revolutionary "republic of letters."[50] Although they were bastions of secrecy rather than full transparency, they fostered an ideal of the public sphere that valued rational debate, truthfulness, candor, and plain speaking over ornament, rhetorical style, and wit. The latter were stigmatized as somehow inherently feminine (reinforcing an earlier prejudice since the story of Eve that women were prone to lie). However unreal and based on the model of a perfectly symmetrical speech situation that could never be fully actualized, this ideal helped democratize access to cultural and political power for many who were previously excluded by their low birth or economic dependency. But whether or not this transformation meant the marginalization of women—a claim that has been asserted most vigorously in connection with Jürgen Habermas's celebrated reconstruction of the bourgeois public sphere—has been debated ever since.[51]

A different issue was raised by early feminists who recognized that the protocols of politeness meant different things for men and women. The tangled gender politics underlying codes of male gallantry and female modesty were exposed with withering disdain by the feminist pioneer Mary Wollstonecraft, who directed her ire at conservative defenders of civility like Burke (while being equally critical of aspects of Rousseau's educational program for girls). Coquetry and false modesty, she argued, were marks of women's oppression and had to be combated by sincerity, frankness, and transparency (although tempered by a natural politeness and decency that show women to be fully as civilized as men).[52] Throw out the myriad "conduct books" that taught women how to appear in society, she counseled her readers, and learn to express genuine feelings as directly as possible.[53] Not surprisingly, her most ardent love affair was with the anarchist William Godwin, whose great tract *Political Justice* contained a plea for plain speaking and sincerity (and whose memoirs unflinchingly and without embarrassment exposed the intimate details of their romance).[54]

When the Romantics made a cult of emotional authenticity, which betokened an even more intense mode of personal truth-seeking and candor among lovers than mere sincerity,[55] manners, wit, politeness, and sociability were seen as synonyms for vanity, cynicism, and two-facedness. They suggested a pathological split in the self, whose subjective integrity had to be defended against the pressures of social convention. These were pressures that had successfully survived the fall of the ancien régime and determined the behavior of a new target, the bourgeois philistines, whose moralistic phoniness was hypocritically hidden behind their mask of virtue. Now in addition to the imperative to follow higher moral obligations, in the sense of Kant's categorical imperative, the imperative to be true to one's feelings, to have an integral rather than divided self, provided further reasons to scorn mere politeness as superficial social mendacity. Evangelical righteousness, although easily serving as a cover for hypocritical behavior of its own, nonetheless revived the Puritans' dislike for the allegedly superficial culture of politeness. German disdain for the superficiality of French "civilization," fueled by Pietist earnestness and the cult of individual *Bildung*, could spur Mephistopheles in Goethe's Faust to remark scornfully, "Im Deutschen lügt man, wenn man höflich ist" ("To the Germans, one lies when one is polite").[56] Victorian sages like Thomas Carlyle railed against the "clothes-wearing man," the snobbish dandy enamored of mere display and incapable of revealing the true man beneath. In *Our Mutual Friend* (1864), Charles Dickens created a monster of hypocritical insincerity in the figure of Podsnap, who became a metonym for those who valued propriety while ignoring suffering and suppressing desire. In *David Copperfield* (1845), he had already created the loathsome Uriah Heep, whose "umble" demeanor hid a resentment-filled heart of stone.

Nuda veritas, the naked truth, the Romans had called it, and although Victorians like Carlyle and Dickens were not keen on taking the phrase too literally, it served their metaphoric purposes with admirable force. The journalist and statesmen "honest John" Morley, a disciple of John Stuart Mill, champion of Gladstonian liberalism, and rationalist freethinker, wrote fiery tracts like *On Compromise* (1874), railing against hypocrisy in religion, politics, and elsewhere in the name of pure truth-telling.[57] In America, as noted in the introduction, an excess of manners and elaborate rhetoric, still evident in Victorian Britain, often came to seem a mark of "Old

World" duplicity—or in regional terms, a residue of a mercifully defunct Southern way of life—wisely avoided by plain-speaking common men and women. Rhetorical embellishment and high diction were derided as outmoded by those who valued the straight talk of unpolished truth-tellers.[58]

In response, defenders of politeness would argue that it can be more than a weapon in the struggle for social advantage or a way to maintain aristocratic distinction in an increasingly egalitarian and banal world (as the artificial pose of the dandy was often understood). Instead, it could provide a kind of soothing lubrication for social peace, a way to take into account the feelings of others. It recognizes the uncomfortable fact that utter sincerity can itself be a violent act when directed at humiliating the weak or exposing the vulnerable. In the words of a twentieth-century believer in the moral neutrality of mendacity, "Truth-telling can be as despicable as lying, if its consequences are destructive of confidence, trust, human warmth, and dignity."[59]

Historically aware commentators also pointed out that *politesse* replaced earlier codes of honor, in which martial values were tested through even more explicitly violent means. Instead, the allegedly "feminine" cultivation of elegance, refinement, and grace, which Wollstonecraft had so categorically equated with coquetry and condemned as oppressive to women, could replace literal duels, with their potentially lethal consequences, with more symbolic, and thus less deadly, competitions. There was something genuinely "civil," they argued, in the manners disseminated during the "civilizing process."[60] Not only could this mean tolerating a certain amount of dissembling, but also knowing that it was bogus and yet pretending to accept it as the truth, a kind of double-entry moral bookkeeping. The Russian custom of *vranyo*, in which polite listeners accept fanciful tales or claims as real, even when they know they are not, captures this dynamic.[61] What twentieth-century sociologists like Erving Goffman called "positive" as opposed to "negative politeness" registers its function as a way to help others, whose otherness is respected as such, rather than serve the self-absorbed ego.[62] It could thus be defended as a kind of "minima moralia," a morality of everyday, nonheroic life, which is as moral in its own way as the principled following of rigorous prohibitions against lying under all circumstances, no matter the consequences.

It may also be necessary to practice tactics of ironic detachment and social concealment—"cool conduct," as one student of the Weimar Republic has called it[63]—to hide vulnerability in an essentially hostile or dangerous environment. Tactics of deliberate opacity, keeping profiles low and agendas hidden, may be a necessity in a society in which exposure means ridicule, ostracism, or even a risk to one's life. As shown by the vigorous debate over closeting and outing sexual minorities in a society as intolerant of deviance as ours still is, sincerity may be a trap for those who are forced to adopt it against their deeper interests. As Jean-Paul Sartre pointed out many years ago, an insistence on absolute sincerity may foist a rigid identity on people whose fluid conduct precludes their accepting the labels that society wants to impose on them.[64]

The conflict in child rearing that emerges when we give double messages about sincerity and truthfulness, on the one hand, and politeness and tact, on the other, thus in some sense replays the cultural struggle between two kinds of moral behavior, rather than between deep morality, that of the man of conscience and duty, and superficial, trivial, conventional formality. One may be more abstract, the other more embedded in the mores of the community, but both can lay claim to ethical value. How politics plays into this conflict, whether or not there is a link between politeness and the political, reflecting their common etymology in the polis or ancient city-state, or civility and civic virtue, is a question we will have to address later. But suffice it to say now that training in ambiguity, nuance, duplicity, deception, and even outright lying is part and parcel of the normal socialization of children into the human community, one based to a greater or lesser degree on the beneficent lies of politeness.

Although there are many dubious or self-serving actions intended by lies, not all, of course, should be condemned. One frequent purpose of deception, for example, is to maintain privacy, a sphere of interiority that resists the imperative to be fully transparent to an intrusively curious, probing world. "Speech," the infamously cunning diplomat Talleyrand is reported to have said in 1807, "was given to man to hide his thoughts."[65] Whether through the administering of pharmaceutical means—often dubiously effective "truth serums"— or mechanical devices like lie detectors, coerced honesty can feel like a violation of our most private sphere, our subjective interiority. Lying, in this optic, is an assertion of the right not to confess against our will; it reinforces that sense of autonomy produced, as we noted above, when a child first realizes it can be opaque to the world's prying eyes.

It may also be even more paradoxically related to the fundamental cultural imperative toward hiding what is immodest or shameful, which has been around since Adam and Eve grabbed a leaf from a fig tree to cover their nudity as they were chased out of the Garden. As the critic John Vignaux Smyth has suggested, "The proscription of lying and the prescription of concealment, in short, are fundamentally complicit."[66] At least on a structural level, both attract a certain violence, which Smyth sees in sacrificial terms, directed against those who break the taboo, in the first case against those who tell lies, in the second against those who transgress dress codes. Insofar as those codes are themselves a kind of symbolic language, which may reveal social status or cultural taste at the same time as working to hide the actual naked body, the messages they convey are inherently ambiguous.

In short, it would be mistaken to conclude that the social function of lying is always entirely negative. The same Georg Simmel who stressed the growing importance of trust in modern complex societies also noted that the forces of harmony and cooperation "must nevertheless be interspersed with distance, competition, repulsion, in order to yield the actual configuration of society. The solid, organizational forms which seem to constitute or create society must constantly be disturbed, disbalanced, gnawed-at by individualistic, irregular forces, in order to gain their vital reaction and development through submission and resistance. . . . Relationships what they are, they also presuppose a certain ignorance and a concealment, even though this measure varies immensely," and then he added, "The lie is merely a very crude and, ultimately, often a contradictory form in which this necessity shows itself."[68]

To add one final thought on the issue of truth and trust, there may well also be limits to perfect truthfulness to oneself as well as to others. The idea of self-deception is heatedly contested, depending as it does on an image of a divided self one of whose parts can deceive another, but so too should be the counteridea of self-transparency. Despite all the pressure we often feel to be utterly true to ourselves, becoming fully reflective about our motives, desires, and prejudices, it may be an impossible goal. In *Ethics and the Limits of Philosophy*, Bernard Williams tackles this issue with his customary subtlety, concluding that the goal of "total explicitness" is based on "a misunderstanding of rationality, both personal and political. We must reject any model of personal practical thought according to which all my projects, purposes, and needs should be made, discursively and at once, considerations *for* me. I must deliberate *from* what I am. Truthfulness requires trust in that as well, and not the obsessional and doomed drive to eliminate it."[69]

LYING AND LANGUAGE

Κρῆτες ἀεί ψεῦσται
[All Cretans are liars.]
　　　—EPIMENDES, CA. 600 BCE

Is the famous Cretan Liar's paradox a problem only in logic or in language? Or is it impossible to separate the two? This is not the place to try to resolve this age-old conundrum.[70] But it is clear that training in lying really only gathers momentum with the acquisition of language, which has the capacity to say what is not (as a description either of the world or of the intentions, beliefs, and feelings of the speaker). In the *Philosophical Investigations*, where he saw lying as one language game among many others, Wittgenstein wrote that "a child has much to learn before it can pretend. (A dog cannot be a hypocrite, but neither can he be sincere)."[71] It may well be, in fact, that lying, properly speaking, requires the acquired skill to speak improperly. In Augustine's famous definition, "Mendacium est enuntiatio cum voluntate falsum enuntiandi" (A lie is an utterance accompanied by the desire to utter an untruth).[72] In addition to misrepresenting the beliefs of the liar, a lie also relies on a duplicitous act of what one commentator calls "open sincerity," an attempt to fool the victim into thinking the speaker really means what he says.[73] It thus involves an assertion that intends a dual misrepresentation, which sets it apart from the simple deception found in nature and even from more benign forms of pretending.

According to Jacques Lacan, animal duplicity of the type we have seen invoked by sociobiologists is not really mendacity because it does not involve an explicit and unwarranted truth claim. The latter is possible only after entry into the transcendental, institutional space created by language, a "big Other" (*le grand Autre*) which is beyond the two parties involved. As Lacan put it in *Écrits,*

> For I can lure my adversary by means of a movement contrary to my actual plan of battle, and this movement will have its deceiving effect only in so far as I produce it in reality and for my adversary. But in the propositions with which I open peace negotiations with him, what my negotiations propose to him is situated in a third locus which is neither my speech nor my interlocutor. This locus is none other than the locus of signifying convention, of the sort revealed in the comedy of the sad plaint of the Jew to his crony: "Why do you tell me you are going to Cracow so I believe you are going to Lvov, when you really are going to Cracow?"[74]

Without the existence of the signifying conventions of language, which have a normative truth claim as their premise, lying as a deviant case would be impossible. That is—and here he sounds more like Habermas than Nietzsche—Lacan argues that there is an asymmetrical relationship between truth and falsehood: whereas the former does not make an unjustified claim about falsehood, the latter does make one about the truth. Whether Lacan's rigorous distinction between humans and animals according to the criterion of the former's accession to the Symbolic is fully persuasive—Derrida denounced it as an example of "humanist or anthropocentric dogmatism," which invokes religious notions of the innocence of animals[75]—it draws our attention to the importance of language for the concept of the explicit and deliberate lie.

The priority of truth-telling over lying is seen by some linguists as a function of the most basic purpose of language, whose telos is "the communication of belief."[76] It violates the fundamental language game of assertion, for "to assert is always and inescapably to assert as true, and learning that truth is required from us in assertions is therefore inseparable from learning what it is to assert."[77] It also undermines the implicit promise to tell the truth that is the performative dimension of such speech acts.

Significantly, both the "universal pragmatics" of Habermas and the "deconstruction" of Derrida acknowledge the importance of this promise, even if they acknowledge it has different functions under different circumstances. According to the former, truthfulness

> is a universal implication of speech, as long as the presuppositions of communicative interaction are not altogether suspended. In the cognitive use of language the speaker must, in a trivial sense, truthfully express his thoughts, opinions, assumptions, and so forth; since he asserts a proposition, however, what matters is not the truthfulness of his intentions, but the truth of the proposition. Similarly, in the interactive use of language, the speaker expresses the intention of promising, reprimanding, refusing and so forth; but since he brings about an interpersonal relation with a hearer, the truthfulness of his intention is only a necessary condition, whereas what is important is that the action fit a recognized normative context.[78]

Habermas adds that in the expressive use of language, there is "speech-act-immanent obligation, namely, the *obligation to prove trustworthy.*"[79] Derrida likewise insists on the in-built existence of faith in the trustworthiness of the speaker; indeed there is

> a performative of promising at work even in lying or perjury and without which no address to the other would be possible. Without the performative experience of this elementary act of faith, there would neither be "social bond" nor address of the other, nor any performativity in general: neither convention, nor institution, nor constitution, nor sovereign state, nor law, nor above all,

here, that structural performativity of the productive performance that binds from its very inception the knowledge of the scientific community to doing, and science to technics.[80]

To break the semantic rule of assertion, refusing to fulfill the promise implied in the act of assertion, betraying the trust of the addressee, is thus akin to cheating at a game and has a moral stigma as a result. As the literary critic Christopher Ricks has pointed out, "There is no truth verb that is the counterpart to the verb to lie. . . . You cannot truth, a fact which both makes the telling of the truth a less glib matter than lying ('the truth, the whole truth and nothing but the truth'), and also brings out that speaking has to be posited on a presumption of the speaking of the truth."[81] Liars have as much of a stake in the linguistic priority of truth-telling as everyone else, perhaps even more so because of their dependency on the expectation that their lies will be taken as true assertions. Of course, the normative expectation of truth-telling is itself conventionally variable—we don't expect it, for example, of our enemies in a war or of someone trying to sell us a used car—but in the vast majority of situations, it trumps its opposite.

The special case of truth-telling or lying under sworn oath merits underlining. That is, when engaged in the solemn language game that we call swearing, the tacit linguistic imperative to tell the truth is made explicit, with added penalties for perjury—originally religious, but then secular—carefully spelled out. The different roles played by oaths in the legal and political arenas helps explain why mendacity is not always treated in the same way (and one can, of course, add other special situations, such as bluffing in poker or in business negotiations, as well as writing letters of recommendation).[82] That is, politicians normally don't swear "to tell the truth, the whole truth, and nothing but the truth," as witnesses do in a court of law. Of this issue more in our final chapter.

Children's mastery of the protocols of discourse—their "communicative competence"—is not, however, only expressed in their understanding of the promise to tell the truth. It can also be measured, so other commentators have argued, by the success with which they can deceive and manipulate, both in game situations where they learn to bluff and in real social interactions.[83] When, at about the age of six, they realize that other people have different perspectives on the world, they learn that they can fib not only about what is the case in the external world but also about their own state of mind, their feelings as well as their knowledge. They also come to understand that others may be fibbing in turn and thus gain sensitivity to the clues that give away deception.[84] When they realize that they can hide their inner thoughts, so it has been suggested, children gain a sense of independence. As one commentator puts it, "The first successful true lie would thus mark the flowering of psychic autonomy associated with the realization of opacity."[85] A variant of this skill is learning that one can ignore the intended power of a solemn oath by swearing, not to avoid perjury, but rather to express aggression and anger, thus "taking the Lord's name in vain."

Another related sign of linguistic maturity is the ability to use metaphor, analogy, and other rhetorical tropes, which adherents of linguistic purification and monosemic stability often regard with suspicion as tacit lies. The German linguist and literary critic Harald Weinrich goes so far as to claim, in "The Linguistics of Lying," that "on closer examination, linguistic lies include the majority of rhetorical figures, such as euphemisms, hyperbole, ellipses, amphibole, the forms and formulas of politeness, emphasis, irony, verbal taboos, anthropomorphisms, etc. Only a narrow lane indeed is left for truth."[86] It is at least suggestive that the capacity to pun on the word "lie" (to be prone or at rest, as well as tell a falsehood) has been a rich source of literary play from Shakespeare on.[87] Ever since the Sophists were attacked by Plato, who believed that persuasion in general was a mode of deception, figures of speech have been denounced as impeding the quest for stable truth.[88] In *The Republic*, he also denounced artists for being "three removes from the truth."[89] The imperative to find or concoct a neutral metalanguage purged of semantic play has often implicitly stigmatized ornamental speech as inherently untrustworthy. Bertrand Russell, for example, could baldly declare that all fictions are falsehoods.[90] He thus unwittingly echoed Oscar Wilde's notorious and provocative assertion in "The Decay of Lying," while reversing the valence of the judgment, that "lying, the telling of beautiful untrue things, is the proper aim of Art."[91]

Whether or not rhetoric and fiction amount to lying is no longer much in dispute; Weinrich, for example, points out that "there is no lying attached to metaphors,"[92] which can convey meaning as explicitly as concepts if a shared context exists binding speaker to listener. He cites Herder's dictum that "only a fool would confuse poetry with lying."[93] As a later commentator would put it, "Fictions are not lies, for a fiction is not a set of assertions."[94] The self-evident plausibility of this claim was, however, only slowly conceded by those still suspicious of the bewitching powers of language. In fact, fictionality as a category of discourse understood by readers as neither referring to the real world nor deceptively claiming to do so only emerged as a distinct linguistic category beyond truth and falsehood in the modern era.[95] Readers had to learn that the protagonists of their stories were "nobodies" in the sense that they referred to no living, material bodies in the real world. What Coleridge famously called "the willing suspension of disbelief" in his *Biographia Literaria* necessitated a capacity to detect the literary signals of fictionality that put it in an aesthetic frame. What goes on within that frame is ultimately arbitrary in terms of references to a world outside it; there is no external standard by which fictionality can be judged as true or false. As in the case of prayer, which Aristotle—and much later Derrida[96]— noted was a type of speech that was neither true nor false, fictionality differs from lies, which depend on that very distinction.[97]

For those who doggedly seek a language cleansed of ambiguity and uncertainty, a language solely of concepts and names purged as much as possible of images and figures, rhetoric can still be regarded as a source of confusion at best, and deliberate obfuscation at worst. The difference between mendacity and fictionality, although categorically distinct, they worry, may not always be absolute in the real world. Witness Sissela Bok:

> If an author really means to manipulate through his writing, as in propaganda; if the author mingles fiction and purportedly factual statements without signaling where the "suspension of disbelief" is appropriate; if the conveyor of what the audience takes to be fiction or invention is presenting what to him is straightforward history, as when a schizophrenic recently published his

daily journal; if the author of a play has no intention to deceive anyone but finds that a gullible enthusiast in the audience leaps to the rescue of a victim in distress on the stage, in all these cases, the elements of fiction and deception are interwoven.[98]

Especially when it seems to abet what Walter Benjamin famously called "the aestheticization of politics," the domination of rhetorical or figural over literal and sincere modes of speech has alarmed those who understand politics as essentially based—at least as a desideratum—on rational discourse.[99]

There are several other dimensions of the relationship between mendacity and language that warrant our attention first. Although linguists often argue that all utterances are on some level speech *acts*, lying can lay claim to being even more explicitly involved with action produced by an agent deliberately attempting to make something happen or prevent it from happening. In his essay "The Anacoluthonic Lie," J. Hillis Miller observes that

> contrary to common sense, a lie is a performative, not a constative, form of language. Or rather, it mixes inextricably constative and performative language. A lie is a form of bearing witness. It always explicitly or implicitly contains a speech act: "I swear to you I am telling the truth." This speech-act aspect of a lie is not a matter of truth or falsehood. It is a way of doing something with words. Its functioning depends on faith or lack of faith in the one who hears it, not on referential veracity. If a lie is believed it is as "felicitous" as a truth in making something happen.[100]

Because of its powerful performative dimension, lying is inherently future oriented. In addition to descriptive deception about what is or was the case, children also acquire the capacity to think conditionally, using language to promise or threaten or predict or do something with words that refers to a future state of things. "If . . . then . . ." speech acts allow perhaps even greater latitude for deception than straightforward descriptive ones, because they always involve a set of unarticulated assumptions about the future context in which the conditional is or is not realized. Thus, I may promise to clean my room, but do so with my fingers crossed and silently expressing the mental reservation "when hell freezes over." Insofar as politics is an arena in which promises and threats and predictions are particularly important, it may be the case that there is a greater scope for mendacity than in, say, historical accounts of a past that has already taken place.

The relationship between lying and actively intervening to shape the future has often been stressed. Thus, for example, the literary critic George Steiner argued in his celebrated 1975 book on translation, *After Babel,* "We shall not get much further in understanding the evolution of language and the relations between speech and human performance so long as we see 'falsity' as primarily negative, so long as we consider counter-factuality, contradiction, and the many nuances of conditionality as specialized, often logically bastard modes. *Language is the main instrument of man's refusal to accept the world as it is.*"[101] As Montaigne, who was no friend of lying, noted, "The reverse of truth has a hundred thousand shapes and a limitless field."[102] When it comes to politics, as we will see when looking at some of the arguments of Hannah Arendt in particular, the links between mendacity, imagination, challenging the status quo, and human freedom are mobilized to call sincerity into question as an unequivocal political virtue.

LYING AND MORALITY

> Lying is universal—we *all* do it; we all *must* do it. Therefore, the wise thing is for us diligently to train ourselves to lie thoughtfully, judiciously; to lie with a good object, and not an evil one; to lie for others' advantage, and not our own, to lie healingly, charitably, humanely, not cruelly, hurtfully, maliciously; to lie firmly, frankly, squarely, with head erect, not haltingly, tortuously, with pusillanimous mien, as being ashamed of our high calling.
>
> —MARK TWAIN, "ON THE DECAY OF THE ART OF LYING"

The great Norwegian playwright Henrik Ibsen introduced the notion of a "life-lie" in his drama *The Wild Duck* to indicate a destructive self-delusion that allows, for a while at least, a person to avoid facing an unbearable reality. "You take away the life-lie from the average man, and you take away his happiness with it," observes one of his characters.[103] But what if happiness, collective as well as individual, were not the highest goal set for humankind? What if moral considerations outweighed the value of personal contentment or satisfaction, even the general welfare? Would lying ever be morally justifiable, especially when the lies are not as fundamental as the life-lies that allow us to avoid despair at the meaninglessness of it all?

Lying is, of course, often passionately denounced in moral terms, despite the occasional maverick like Nietzsche who seeks to go beyond conventional notions of good and evil. Why is mendacity so frequently condemned as an ethical offense with no extenuating circumstances? Why do even writers who are in so many ways disciples of Nietzsche, like Jacques Derrida, continue to insist on the "irreducibly ethical dimension of the lie, where the *phenomenon* of the lie as such is intrinsically foreign to the problem of knowledge, truth, the true, and the false."[104] Why are efforts made to defend truthfulness as an unconditional value in itself beyond its instrumental or pragmatic function? Is it by chance that one of the Ur-myths of world religion—the banishment from a life of carefree innocence in the Garden of Eden and the concomitant fall from grace—was caused by a certain snake's intentional deception about the quality of the local produce? Or that the ninth of the Ten Commandments Moses brought back from Mt. Sinai—a pretty select group, considering the 613 total commandments ultimately given by the Law—prohibited bearing false witness against one's neighbors? Why do even atheists like Nietzsche who often scoff at the ideal of truth still hold on tightly to a notion of truthfulness?[105]

There is no simple answer to these questions, but one place to begin is with the inherently intersubjective implications of lying. The lie, Jean-Paul Sartre tells us, is located in the world of what Heidegger called *Mit-sein* (co-being): "It presupposes my existence, the existence of the *Other,* my existence *for* the Other, and the existence of the Other *for* me."[106] Glossing this claim, David Simpson writes,

> When I lie to you I do not just treat you as an object to be deceived, regarding you as an obstacle or a means to an end. When

I lie to you I engage, at the core of the lie, the mutuality of our personhood. I do not just dismiss you as a person; I appeal to you as a person, and then use that against you. Lying has the moral intensity it does because it draws on and abuses the core of interaction and communality.[107]

Deeper than the cognitive recognition of one's own self-interests or the interests of others, ethical theorists from Hegel to Axel Honneth have told us,[108] is the acknowledgment of the other as a subject worthy of our respect (and respecting us in turn). Lying, it seems, impedes the basic trust that underlies that reciprocal acknowledgment.

Not only can mendacity be morally condemned for undermining the dialectic of mutual recognition on which communality is based, it can also be assailed for its affinity to physical harm, the coercive violence that is also traditionally assailed in moral terms. According to Sissela Bok, "Deceit and violence—these are the two forms of deliberate assault on human beings. Both can coerce people into acting against their will. Most harm that can befall victims through violence can come to them also through deceit. But deceit controls more subtly, for it works on the belief as well as action."[109] Although it has been argued against Bok by John Vignaux Smyth that the scapegoating of liars in the name of a general rule of sincerity is itself a form of sacrificial violence committed against those who refuse to conform,[110] it has more often seemed that the initial sacrifice of truthfulness is the greater moral crime.

Whatever the ultimate cause or causes, mendacity has never been free from moral taint, often producing powerful pangs of conscience—"invincible shame," Rousseau called it[111]—in those who indulge in it, as well as external condemnation. In trying to evaluate its moral gravity, two general camps have been perennially opposed: rigorous absolutists or deontologists, who denounce lying in itself as an intrinsic evil to be avoided at all costs, and consequentialists or contextualists, who are concerned with the practical impact of lying, either good or bad.[112] Whereas the first position focuses on the responsibility of moral agents or subjects, the second stresses outcomes that are best interpreted as agent-neutral values, which cannot be judged according to the intentions or principles of any prior actors. Although the Utilitarian tradition—Jeremy Bentham, James Mill, John Stuart Mill, Henry Sidgwick, in particular[113]—is often seen as the most prominent exponent of consequentialist ethics, it appears elsewhere, as in Simmel's claim that "the ethically negative value of the lie must not blind us to its sociologically quite positive significance for the formation of certain concrete relations."[114] Pragmatists like William James voiced similar consequentialist qualms about the universal value of veracity, as in his remark in *The Varieties of Religious Experience:* "There is no worse lie than truth misunderstood by those who hear it, so reasonable arguments, challenges to magnanimity, and appeals to sympathy and justice, are folly when we are dealing with human crocodiles and boaconstrictors. The saint may simply give the universe into the hands of the enemy by his trustfulness."[115]

Often these seemingly opposing positions are difficult to disentangle entirely. For if we take seriously the performative element in telling a lie, as an action with what speech act theorists call perlocutionary effects, then we will be alert to the fact that even the most absolutist deontological critics of mendacity often invoke the ill it allegedly does as a major reason to resist it. Take, for example, one of the classical absolutist positions, that of Michel de Montaigne, who explicitly criticized Machiavelli's *Prince* for its defense of the fox's duplicity. Despite Montaigne's own skepticism about knowing the truth, he was adamantly in favor of truthfulness. In his essay "Of Presumption," which targets the excess of formal ceremony and polite affectation in his day, he sounds like a deontologist, proclaiming his allegiance to a pure doctrine of truth-telling:

> Truth is the first and fundamental part of virtue. We must love it for itself. He who tells the truth because he has some external obligation to do so and because it serves him, and who does not fear to tell a lie when it is not important to anybody, is not sufficiently truthful. My soul by nature shuns lying and hates even to think a lie. I feel an inward shame and a stinging remorse if one escapes me, as sometimes it does, for occasions surprise me and move me unpremeditatively.[116]

But in his essay "Of Liars," Montaigne invoked a more directly consequentialist argument for avoiding mendacity: "In truth lying is an accursed vice. We are men, and hold together, only by our word. If we recognized the horror and gravity of lying, we should persecute it with fire more justly than other crimes."[117] And in another essay on the theme, "Of Giving the Lie," he added, "Since mutual understanding is brought about solely by way of words, he who breaks his word betrays human society. It is the only instrument by means of which our wills and thoughts communicate, it is the interpreter of our soul. If it fails us, we have no more hold on each other, no more knowledge of each other. If it deceives us, it breaks up all our relations and dissolves all the bonds of our society."[118] Here, the relationship between truth-telling and trust is invoked to denounce the damage done to men's reputation and good word by mendacity. Here sociability is understood to rest, not on the polite protection of sensibilities, as we have seen Pascal argue, but on the frank exchange of views.

Montaigne, to be sure, was not a systematic thinker, unwilling to contradict himself. In fact, elsewhere in his *Essays* he even tempered his absolutist condemnation of lying. In "A Trait of Certain Ambassadors," he criticized emissaries who take it upon themselves to sugarcoat information given to their rulers, but then added:

> To alter the truth and hide it from another for fear that he might take it otherwise than he should and that it might push him into some bad course, and meanwhile to leave him ignorant of his affairs—such conduct seems to me proper for him who gives the law, not for him who receives it; for the man in charge and the schoolmaster, not for the man who ought to think himself inferior in prudence and good counsel as well as in authority.[119]

Here Montaigne, ever the wise magistrate, displayed a willingness to defend *mensonges officieux* (altruistic lies that are for someone else's benefit, as opposed to "pernicious" or "jocose" lies)[120] for those in power, echoing Plato's defense of "noble lies" when it comes to inequalities of power and responsibility. The "accursed vice," it turns out, can be justifiably suspended when politics is involved.

Mentioning the Platonic *gennaion pseudos* reminds us that the classical world also wrestled with the question of justifying mendacity and suspending the absolute moral prohibition against it.[121] In Greek plays like Sophocles' *The Women of Trachis* and Euripides' *Helen*, various justifications were advanced for lying to enemies, as well as to friends who needed to be protected from folly or insanity.[122] The use of irony in theatrical performances generated a sophisticated awareness that sometimes the truth was spoken through what seemed liked deception. Although Aristotle generally denounced lies as base and worthy of censure, he made exceptions for cases when lies were self-effacing rather than boastful and when they were meant benevolently, as with physicians or relatives who used them to restore health.[123]

In general, the Greeks held those who told the truth in special esteem when it came to the courage to speak it in the face of power. As Michel Foucault pointed out in the lectures that became *Fearless Speech*, the ideal of *parrhesia* or truth-telling was extolled as early as the fifth century BCE in the plays of Euripides and other texts.[124] He notes that the *parrhesiastes* was known for speaking his mind frankly with as little rhetorical flourish as possible. Although there was a pejorative sense of the term, applied to those who chatter irresponsibly and without regard for the effects of what they say, the more positive sense recognized the courage that it takes to utter unflattering truths to those in power, offering criticism where it is warranted. According to Foucault, explicit risk and danger accompanied the *parrhesiastes*' willingness to anger even tyrants who might have control over life and death. The truth-teller feels a moral obligation to be candid no matter the cost to himself. Foucault summarizes his argument:

> *Parrhesia* is kind of verbal activity where the speaker has a specific relationship to truth through frankness, a certain relationship to his own life through danger, a certain type of relation to himself or other people through criticism (self-criticism or criticism of other people), and a specific relation to moral law through freedom and duty. More precisely, *parrhesia* is a verbal activity in which a speaker expresses his personal relationship to truth, and

risks his life because he recognizes truth-telling as a duty to improve or help other people (as well as himself).[125]

The story that Foucault goes on to tell underscores the initial emphasis on *parrhesia* in the nascent Greek democratic polis, but then follows its decline as the irresponsible abuse of free speech led to accusations of undermining legitimate authority. He pursues it into the more private world of what he calls "care of the self," as all types of political activity are seen as unfitting for a life of virtue. Although acknowledging the various contexts in which it was valued by the Greeks, including communal and public, he focuses on the way in which it became a *techne* for the exemplary philosophical life, a way to abet through self-examination the self-governance and self-sufficiency that was the mark of the Cynics in particular. An obligation to preach the truth was one result of this transformation, which would, of course, have a powerful role in nonpagan religions as well. In the case of figures like Diogenes, who was willing to stand up to the emperor Alexander the Great, *parrhesia* still had a connection with risk taking and danger, "a struggle occurring between two kinds of power: political power and the power of truth."[126]

The crucial point for Foucault is that the latter power was intimately tied up with the ethical character of the truth-teller, whose practices of ascetic/aesthetic self-fashioning were the precondition for knowing and conveying the truth. As Foucault explained elsewhere, "Even if it is true that Greek philosophy founded rationality, it always held that a subject could not have access to the truth if he did not first operate upon himself a certain work which would make him susceptible to knowing the truth—a work of purification, conversion of the soul by contemplation of the soul itself."[127] In the modern era defined by the onset of the Scientific Revolution, truth, in contrast, is established purely by the power of evidence, no matter who the individual subject may be.[128] The subject of science is an anonymous, collective, impersonal knower with no ethical substance of "his" own to fall back on as a ground of verification.

This modern transformation is less important for our purposes than the earlier ethical defense of truthfulness as a virtue in its own right, not because of its social consequences, during the classical era. In a complementary manner in religious traditions, the profound value of telling the truth came to be defended in ways that linked it to the ultimate issue of salvation of the individual soul rather than its beneficial social implications. The logic of faith, after all, is belief in the veracity of God's Word, which is truthfully communicated to those who trust the teller, whether it be a charismatic prophet, a sacred text, or a wondrous sign.[129] As often noted, however, it was not really until St. Augustine in the fourth century that a firm repudiation of lying was given a sustained foundation. Before his two great tracts *On Lying* (*De mendacio*) (395) and *Against Lying* (*Contra mendacium*) (420),[130] both Jewish and early Christian theologians, such as Clement of Alexandria, Origen, Cassian, and St. John Chrysostom, had left an ambiguous legacy with many qualifications and exonerations based on readings of certain passages from the Bible.[131]

Augustine dealt with these apparent contradictions in his earlier tract, written shortly before he became Bishop of Hippo most likely as a response to St. Jerome's reading of Galatians 2:11, by claiming either that they were meant figuratively rather than literally or that they were given as examples less to be followed than to be avoided. Arguing from as broad a definition as possible of the ninth commandment—"Thou shalt not bear false witness against thy neighbor"—and citing the New Testament dictum "The mouth that belieth, killeth the soul,"[132] he claimed that under no circumstances could a lie be defended as useful. Because it would endanger the immortal soul, which can be saved only by just means, it had to be condemned unconditionally. Reviewing eight different kinds of lies, Augustine relentlessly dismissed all of them as unworthy of the true Christian. No distinction between telling the truth "in the heart" and a lie "expressed by the mouth of the body" was valid. Even lying to preserve chastity or to save a life was indefensible: "Since, therefore, eternal life is lost by lying, a lie may never be told for the preservation of the temporal life of another . . . the conclusion is, then, that the good never lie."[133] Purity of the soul was always preferable to purity of the body. The integrity both of the religious message and of the messenger were endangered by deception, which also failed to respect the autonomy of the person to whom the lie was told.

Twenty-five years later, Augustine was forced to revisit the question of lying by the challenge of a heretical Manichaean sect called the Priscillianists, who followed a Spanish ascetic named Priscillian. His disciple Dictinius had written a tract called *The Pound* (*Libra*) in which he claimed that mendacity might be a justifiable means to hide religious belief from hostile strangers. Because the tactic was often successful, orthodox Christians were frustrated in smoking them out, until some came on the ruse of pretending to be Priscillianists themselves. *Against Lying* is Augustine's response to one of their number named Consentius. Decrying the fallacy that heretics should be imitated rather than refuted, Augustine elaborated the arguments he had made twenty-five years earlier against justifying mendacity under any circumstances. Lies told to safeguard faith and avoid martyrdom were never to be condoned; fire should not be used to fight fire.

Now, however, Augustine did grudgingly acknowledge that some lies were less awful than others and, although unjustifiable, might nonetheless be worthy of a subsequent pardon. Although all lies are iniquitous sins and contrary to justice, "let some be called great sins and others small sins, for such is the case, and not as the Stoics would have us think, who maintain they are all alike."[134] For example, perjury calling on God's name to bear false witness was inexcusable, and even more so was blasphemy in which a falsehood is told about God, whereas lies told to help another were less grievous than ones told to help oneself. "That sin is more serious which is committed in the spirit of harm than that which is committed in the spirit of help."[135] But lest it be thought that human sympathy might justify telling a lie to avoid committing an apparently worse transgression—in addition to the oft-repeated case of the murderer who asks the location of his potential victim, he gives the example of the ill father who is denied the truth about his son's demise to avoid a shock—"if we grant that we ought to lie about the son's life for the sake of that patient's health, little by little this evil will grow and by gradual accessions will slowly increase until it becomes such a mass of wicked lies that it will be utterly impossible to find any means of resisting such a plague grown to huge proportions through small additions."[136]

Augustine's grudging willingness to allow certain lies to be pardoned, despite his general condemnation of mendacity, has been compared to the ambivalent idea of the *pharmakon* in Greek medicine, at once poison and cure.[137] Although most medieval theologians, including Thomas Aquinas, sought to uphold Augustine's strict teachings, the ambivalence was hard to avoid.[138] By the time casuistry, reasoning based more on cases than principles, became a developed technique of argumentation in the Church after 1550, absolute prohibitions were considerably relaxed.[139] In such works as the *Handbook for Confessors and Penitents* (*Enchridion, sive Manuale Confessariorum et Paenitentium*) of 1153, written by the Spanish Augustinian canon Navarrus, and *Reasoning about Revealing and Concealing Secrets* (*De Ratione Tegendi et Detegendi Secretum*), published in 1582 by the Spanish Dominican Dominico Soto, a cautious defense of mental reservations or restrictions and deliberate equivocation, the exploitation of verbal ambiguity, was mounted. In cases of questioners who were not owed the truth (the perennial example being the would-be murderer looking for his hidden intended victim), it might be justified not telling it. God hears words said in silence, the casuists argued, and doesn't judge ones spoken aloud to avoid a worse outcome than telling a lie. There were other cases, for example breaking the taboo against revealing secrets told in Confession about heterodox belief, which also suspended the absolute prohibition of lying.

Especially in England, after the Acts of Supremacy and Uniformity in 1559 established a separate Anglican Church, banned the Catholic Mass, and turned the English Prayer Book into the official manual of piety, Catholic theologians were forced to address the practical consequences of the ban on mendacity. Those who refused to join the new church—recusants, as they were called—were often compelled to choose between martyrdom and breaking the ban. Some 183, the majority of them priests, elected the former during the reign of Elizabeth, but many others followed the teachings of Soto, Navarrus, and other casuists, allowing them to profess conformity publicly but with mental reservations or restrictions. Echoing the practice of expressing truth in the privacy of the confessional, this ploy countenanced truthfulness only for the ear of God.

When it came to swearing the truth about inner conviction or perjuring under judicial oath, the latter could be excused by Catholic casuists as the lesser evil because putting the question under coercion was itself "unjust." Ironically, during the period of Puritan power under Cromwell, Anglican Royalists were given the same pass by some of their theologians when it came to strategic equivocation. Because of the intimate entanglement of church and state during the early modern era, many of these battles were as much political as religious in nature. As we will see later, resistance from below to the intrusions of the inquisitive state, the state based on surveillance and forced confessions, was one way in which mendacity might be defended.

Early modern moralists were not, to be sure, equally seduced by the moral reasoning of the casuists. It was famously and effectively denounced by Pascal in his *Provincial Letters* of 1660, an uncompromising attack on the Jesuit order from the perspective of an Augustinian Jansenist.[140] Antoine Arnauld, the leader of the Port-Royal community, had already attacked Jesuit "probabilism" in his 1643 *Moral Theology of the Jesuits,* which decried even the best of ends justifying bad means.[141] In 1679 Pope Innocent XI officially backed away from the overly liberal use of mental reservations and equivocation, attacking laxity in moral matters. Although many Protestants were faced with dangers similar to those threatening recusant Catholics in Elizabethan England, their theologians often followed Calvin in his unqualified denunciation of feigning belief to ensure survival. He condemned the practice as Nicodemism, from Nicodemus the Pharisee, the disciple of Christ who hid his actual faith because of fear of exposure and visited Jesus only at night.[142] Later evangelicals like John Wesley would continue to reject the notion of "officious lies" as "an abomination to the God of Truth."[143]

Puritan New England, it will be recalled from the introduction, carried the Calvinist hostility to lying and secrecy to the new world. As Michael T. Gilmore has demonstrated, strict surveillance in the guise of "holy watchfulness," aimed at rooting out sinful behavior, fostered a cult of sincerity and confessional candor that would long influence American culture.[144] Such seminal texts as John Winthrop's "Model of Christian Charity" radiated hostility to the cloistered monasticism and courtly dissembling of the Old World. Scorning the clandestine confessional of the Catholic tradition meant no tolerance for casuistic distinctions between public profession and interior belief. The word "confession," in fact, could be employed in many Bible translations to mean admitting one's faith publicly, and ultimately became a synonym for religious adherence itself. Public penitential practices were, moreover, soon incorporated into more secular institutions, such as the great Eastern State Penitentiary founded in Philadelphia in 1829 on the panoptical principles of permanent visibility as a means to moral regeneration.

With the Puritans' public righteousness and fetish of moral purity went, of course, a greater risk of denunciation for hypocrisy, which followed if they failed to live up to their high standards.[145] Long identified with theatricality and dramatic irony, it had been associated in the Middle Ages with the trickster figure of the Antichrist in particular.[146] For the seventeenth century, hypocrisy, often involving false protestations of piety, was a particular obsession; one commentator has gone so far as to call it the "vice of the century."[147] The act became the basis for a distinct character type, which had already been identified in the *Characters* of Theophrastus, one of Aristotle's students.[148] From Molière's Tartuffe to the most recent exposure of some congressman's hidden sex life (fill in the blank with the name of the latest sinner), the mendacious moral policeman whose actions betray his principles is a familiar type. Indeed, the endless dialectic of purity and pollution, uprightness and fallenness, sin and redemption, public piety and private transgression, is so much a part of the Puritan legacy that it seems almost impossible to see the latter as an engine of moral rigor alone.

Likewise, the Enlightenment, which might be assumed to favor transparency, accountability, and candor, often developed nuanced attitudes toward the cult of sincerity, partly in response to the coercive religious imperative to confess. The eighteenth-century "republic of letters," as we have noted, was governed by the delicate rules of politeness and sociability cultivated in the female-dominated salons of the ancien régime. Many of the less religiously inclined thinkers of the Scientific Revolution and early Enlightenment, including outright skeptics and libertines, had had to resort to dissimulation to

eir subversive thoughts. Champions of the ostensibly trans-
scientific method like Francis Bacon found it prudent to defend secrecy and the restriction of knowledge to an elite, while
defending cunning and guile for rulers as well.[149] Early advocates of
a rationalist method in politics like Thomas Hobbes were no less
insistent on the necessity of dissimulation, simulation, and secrecy,
if it helped preserve the peace and maintain security.[150] Erasmus
also rejected Augustine's strict repudiation of lying under all circumstances.[151] Leo Strauss may have exaggerated his claim for the
ubiquity of esoteric writing among philosophers.[152] But certainly
during this era, when nonconformity with received doctrine could
have severe penalties, it was a frequent enough practice for Perez
Zagorin to conclude his magisterial *Ways of Lying* by calling the sixteenth and seventeenth centuries "the Age of Dissimulation."[153]

Ambiguities continued to mark the Enlightenment discussion
about the justifications of mendacity throughout the eighteenth century.[154] Worries over the ethical implications of the *mensonge officieux* moved from the religious battles between Jesuits and Jansenists
to more secular ones splitting the philosophes into many different
camps. Some international law realists like Hugh Grotius and Samuel Pufendorf[155] defended lying by noting that not everyone was
owed the truth. "A lie is a vice only when it does harm," Voltaire wrote
his friend Thierot in 1736. "It is a very great virtue when it does
good. So be more virtuous than ever. You must lie like the devil, not
timidly, not for a while, but boldly, and all the time.... Lie, my
friends, lie, I shall repay you when I get the chance."[156] The necessity
to dissemble on the part of persecuted advocates of the Enlightenment against the crushing power of Absolutism—expressed, for example, in the secret mysteries of the Masonic lodges—meant that a
movement that touted publicity and transparency could also coun-
tenance the tactical use of hypocrisy against illegitimate power.
According to Reinhard Koselleck, "What for Voltaire was still tactical camouflage became habitual practice in the hands of his suc-
cessors. They became the victims of their own mystification. Strategy became mendacity. Mendacity was the price exacted for their
humorlessness, for their inability to use lies as tactical weapons.

The essence of that mendacity was the fact that it had no self-insight."[157]

There were, to be sure, many Enlightenment thinkers who refused to go down this path. Frederick the Great of Prussia wrote an *Anti-Machiavel* designed to refute *The Prince* in which he devoted an entire chapter to demonstrating "how princes should keep their faith." Losing the confidence of other princes as well as their subjects is the inevitable result of deception, he argued. "Men are not judged by their words— these are always misleading—but by their actions, so that falseness and dissimulation can never prevail . . . people would prefer an irreligious but honest prince who is their benefactor to an orthodox scoundrel and malefactor. It is not the thoughts of princes, but their actions that render men happy."[158] Protoliberal utilitarian theorists like Helvétius and Mercier added that happiness was served only by unqualified honesty.[159] They spurred defenders of the ancien régime like Antoine de Rivarol to respond that illusion, even superstition, was necessary to maintain social stability and ultimately the happiness of those to whom lies were told for their own benefit.[160] The majority of philosophes were utilitarian consequentialists, albeit with a penchant for long-range rather than short-range usefulness. But the deontological argument was not entirely abandoned, as the work of the Encyclopedist François Vincent Toussaint and, more importantly, Kant, to whom we will return shortly, demonstrated.[161] Samuel Johnson put the anticonsequentialist case in a nutshell when he explained to Boswell:

> But I deny the lawfulness of telling a lie to a sick man for fear of alarming him. You have no business with consequences; you are to tell the truth. Besides, you are not sure what effect your telling him that he is in danger may have. It may bring his distemper to a crisis, and that may cure him. Of all lying, I have the greatest abhorrence of this, because I believe it has been frequently practiced on myself.[162]

Virtually all the conflicting impulses of the moral responses to mendacity during this period, and not it alone, were played out in the writings of the most tortured of all the philosophes, Jean-Jacques

Rousseau. He is, of course, remembered as the scourge of salon culture with its superficial and hypocritical protocols of *politesse,* and as such one of the harbingers of the Romantic fetish of sincerity and authenticity.[163] His personal motto was a line from Juvenal, "Vitam impendere vero" (To consecrate one's life to truth).[164] Hostile to the pretense of theatricality, which he directly identified with lies, he denounced the deceptive lures of the distanced spectacle for direct immersion in the ecstatic participation of the open-air festival where audience and players are one. His autobiographical *Confessions* were often taken as a model of the new candor that secularized and psychologized the religious imperative to bare one's soul. Rousseau bragged of his own sincerity as incomparable and belittled that of his great predecessor Montaigne. Not for nothing was he a son of Calvin's Geneva, dedicated to making himself fully open to the eyes of others.

But as Jean Starobinski famously demonstrated, Rousseau's struggle for full transparency and visibility was thwarted time and again by obstacles of his own making.[165] Not only did he remember the many embarrassing times in his past when he had told lies, but he also had difficulty coming to an end on his voyage of self-discovery and self-revelation. The ideal of authenticity was hard to attain when the self to be shown was so elusive, so fragmented, in the modern world. He may have valued the integrity of the personality as an antidote to hypocrisy and corruption,[166] but was not sure how to secure it. Sometimes Rousseau counseled a return to natural unity; at others, he advocated moving ahead to the new unity of the citizen.

Not surprisingly, Rousseau's direct ruminations on the morality of lying were filled with ambiguities and qualifications. As Ruth Grant notes, "Throughout Rousseau's works there are examples of compromises he considers tolerable, lies he considers acceptable, and political manipulations he considers beneficial."[167] The most concentrated of his ruminations on mendacity appears in the fourth walk of his *Reveries of a Solitary Walker,* composed in the years shortly before his death in 1778. One of the most subtle analyses of the theme, it earned Derrida's praise as "another great 'pseudology,' another abyssal treatise on lying and fiction that we should consider with infinite patience."[168] It begins with an expression of his determination to examine his own past and to reveal all he can about his own mendacity. Much to his surprise and chagrin, he is immediately struck by the memory of a terrible lie he had told in his youth, which inspired a feeling of guilt that should have broken him of the habit of lying for life. But then he acknowledges that he had continued to tell many lies and what was worse, felt no real remorse or regret.

To make sense of this baffling and embarrassing outcome, Rousseau recalls the definition of lying he had read somewhere in a "Philosophy Book," "that to lie is to conceal a truth we ought to make manifest."[169] What he immediately takes from this definition, with its added condition of a worthy addressee, is a qualification of the absolute prohibition against mendacity: "It indeed follows that to withhold a truth we have no obligation to declare is not to lie." We do not always owe the truth, Rousseau continues, and there may well be other reasons to lie depending on the consequences. "General truth," he admits, "is the most precious of goods. Without it, man is blind. It is the eye of reason." But "particular and individual truth is not always a good; it is sometimes an evil, very often an indifferent thing" (30). Invoking a utilitarian argument, Rousseau notes that truths that have no use are not ones that are owed to anyone, for "the truth owed is that which concerns justice, and this sacred truth is debased if applied to vain things whose existence is indifferent to all and knowledge of which is useless for anything."

But then backtracking a bit, Rousseau acknowledges that "if the obligation to tell the truth is founded only on its usefulness, how will I make myself the judge of this usefulness? Very often, what is to one person's advantage is to another's prejudice; private interest is almost always opposed to public interest" (31). This qualm is, of course, always one that bedevils utilitarian or consequentialist arguments: Whose usefulness is the criterion? Can we ever find a universal norm of usefulness? Does even the greatest-happiness principle really work when it is impossible to measure and compare happiness? Can we fall back on vaguer notions like satisfaction or welfare without risking tautological formulas?

Moreover, Rousseau ruminates, what about the damage we do ourselves by not telling the truth? "If I do no harm to another in deceiving him, does it follow that I do none to myself, and is it sufficient to be never unjust in order to be always innocent?" With all these considerations to take into account, Rousseau wonders, can we ever find a sure rule for distinguishing cases in which lying is justified from those in which it is not? Perhaps, in fact, there is no universal principle. "In all difficult questions of morality like this, I have always found myself better off answering them according to the *dictamen* of my conscience than according to the insights of my reason. Moral instinct had never deceived me." What that instinct tells him is that it is rare to lie with utter innocence. "To lie for our own advantage is deceit; to lie for the advantage of another is fraud; to lie in order to harm is slander and is the worst kind of lie. To lie without profit or prejudice to ourselves or another is not to lie: it is not a lie; it is a fiction" (32). Fictions may not be true, but they are not an insult to justice, which even white lies are. As Victor Gourevitch notes, "The distinction fiction/lie is thus assigned the central position traditionally occupied by the distinction fact/fiction. Lies and fictions do not differ in that lies deceive. Fictions may do so as well. They differ in their moral import."[170]

Rousseau then goes on to consider the question of who is a truthful man, tacitly alluding to the ancient Greek ideal of the *parrhesiastes*, although he doesn't draw the precise parallel. His answer is the man who may often fib about petty, insubstantial facts to amuse his friends with fanciful stories, "but every speech which leads to profit or hurt, esteem or scorn, praise or blame for someone, contrary to justice and truth, is a lie which will never approach his heart, his mouth or his pen" (34). Such was the answer provided by his moral instinct rather than any general principle. Had he himself lived up to this ideal? No, Rousseau immediately admits; he had told a grievous lie as a youth to extricate himself from an embarrassing situation, and had been haunted by guilt ever since. But, much to his chagrin, he confesses that he continues to fib when finding himself in awkward social circumstances, although never from self-interest or self-love (*amour-propre*). Even in his *Confessions,* when he consciously sought to tell the entire truth, he nonetheless could not avoid lying, although ironically not self-indulgently to defend his actions or inflate his exploits but rather to chastise himself more severely than was warranted.

What was the general lesson Rousseau derived from these puzzling and embarrassing recollections? "It follows that the commitment I made to truthfulness," he writes, "is founded more on feelings of uprightness and equity than on the reality of things, and that in practice I have more readily followed the moral dictates of my conscience than abstract notions of the true and the false. . . . I have wronged no one at all, and I have never given myself any more of an advantage than was due to me. It is solely in that, it seems to me, that truth is a virtue" (39). But nonetheless, he would not let himself off the hook so easily, concluding by reproaching himself for the dishonor he has done to his own dignity by lying and his hypocrisy in choosing a motto to which he could not adhere. "I should have had the courage and the strength to be truthful always, on every occasion, and never to let fictions or fables come out of my mouth and a pen which had been specifically consecrated to the truth" (40). In the future, he hopes, he will strive to exercise the iron will that will allow him to live up to the motto he had taken from Juvenal, "Vitam impendere vero."

Rousseau's tortured and complicated musings on mendacity have several salient features. First, he is clearly more interested in the ideal of the truthful man, the integrated character who reveals his interior virtue by the consistency of his behavior, than he is in the single act of lying. If the intentions of that man are not self-serving or dishonorable and he seeks to serve justice, then individual acts of bending the truth can be excused more readily than if his character is ignoble and his motives base. In political terms, this means that Rousseau accepts the necessity of the legislator legitimating the state by falsely claiming the sanction of nature or the gods, a ploy that Plato had also adopted. Second, he rejects abstract moral principles for a more ineffable moral intuition, which allows one to judge whether or not an individual act of lying can be justified. But third, he worries that such judgment may not be universally binding, because it is hard to know what the usefulness of an act will be to everyone concerned. The implication of this final worry is that another political system than the one under which Rousseau lived would be necessary to assure the coordination of interior intention and public good, a new order in which higher moral selves would not be in tension with a corrupt society and unjust polity. It was precisely to promote such a new order that he wrote *The Social Contract*, envisaging a polity in which the disparate wills of all would be fused into a coherent and unified general will and the conflict between intentions and consequences would be ultimately reconciled. For Rousseau, as Gourevitch puts it, "only in a society of equals might men lead lives free of deceit. Rousseau is the first thinker to have so consistently judged political conditions in terms of whether they do or do not make for false men and false lives."[171] The efficacy of his version of the social contract as a means to achieve a collective moral rectitude and the banishment of lying is, however, highly uncertain.[172]

What was perhaps more of a challenge was coming up with a way to treat the morality of lying in the imperfect society of the present, before voluntary adherence to the general will lifted men beyond their selfish interests. This issue was joined in what has come down to us as one of most celebrated debates on the morality of lying, a debate with explicit political overtones, between the French proto-liberal philosopher Benjamin Constant and the German protoliberal philosopher Immanuel Kant.[173] Kant had been concerned with lying as a moral issue from at least the lectures on ethics he gave from 1775 to 1781, which were preserved in the form of student notes.[174] Here he grappled with the ambiguities left by earlier theorists such as Aristotle, Grotius, Pufendorf, and Wolff, often acknowledging the force of consequentialist arguments. But it wasn't until his mature writings on practical reason, in particular his *Metaphysics of Morals* of 1785, that he first published his better known and more rigorously deontological thoughts on the question. They were developed, albeit by implication, in such subsequent works as "Theory and Practice: On the Common Saying: That May be True in Theory But Does Not Apply to Practice" of 1793, where, among other things, he denied the right to rebel against unjust laws for reasons similar to his prohibition on lying.

Kant's defense of the deontological position against the consequentialists reflected his debts to his early religious training in

Pietism, a particularly rigorous brand of Lutheran Protestantism. Not by chance did he come to call the duty to tell the truth a "sacred [*heiliges*] and unconditional commanding law of reason."[175] It also expressed his hostility to that aristocratic, salon culture of *politesse,* with all its indulgence of superficial sociability, conduct books, and courtly decorum which had already so irritated Rousseau. "Culture," not "civilization," was his idol.[176] "We are highly civilized by art and science," he scoffed, "we are civilized in all kinds of social graces and decency to the point where it becomes exasperating, but much (must be discarded) before we can consider ourselves truly ethicized."[177] Among the foibles that would have to be rejected was tolerance for mendacity.

During the mid-1790s, under the rule of the Directory, Kant's work in translation began to play a major role in the political debates across the Rhine, as France grappled with the uncertain legacy of the Revolution.[178] During the post-Terror moment that has come to be called Thermidor, some French theorists found in Kant an anti-dote to the Rousseauian attempt to create a fully transparent un-mediated polity, which had led to the stifling of representational government under Robespierre. Reasserting government patronage of culture also involved curbing the excesses of the marketplace, which had led to the unleashing of desires that threatened disorder. According to the historian Carla Hesse, "The government found in Kant's political writings a powerful idiom for legitimating and inter-nationalizing its faith in a secular republicanism rooted in the fra-ternal discourse of universal reason. . . . The academic, the univer-sity man who stood apart from the men of the world and advocated conformity to philosophical principles rooted in abstract reason rather than religious faith or historical materialism, he could offer the moral stability critical to the success of the universalizing repub-licanism of the Directory."[179]

The Kant who rejected the right of rebellion and stressed obedi-ence to the state could help legitimate the new political order (while continuing the masculinist bias of Rousseauian republicanism). His stress on the need to follow the moral law no matter the context or consequences struck a chord with officials anxious to head off yet another moment of transgression from below. But there were those who chafed at its abstract, formalist, and legalistic implications, considering Kant himself a moral absolutist uncomfortably close to the attitude that justified the Terror. Among them was a group of intellectuals—the novelist Isabelle de Charrière, the translator and journalist Louis-Ferdinand Huber, and the liberal political theorist and novelist Benjamin Constant—who took seriously consequentialist objections and, especially in the case of Charrière in her novel *Three Women,* challenged Kant's gender assumptions.

On the specific issue of mendacity, it was Constant who struck the most direct blow against Kant in his "On Political Reaction" of 1797, a pamphlet that then evoked the speedy reply "On a Supposed Right to Lie because of Philanthropic Concerns" later that year.[180] Constant's pamphlet, it has been argued, was also a politically charged document aimed at influencing Directory policy—he was a constitutional monarchist, not a republican—and ultimately winning him influence in the new government. According to Robert J. Benton, it was in fact closer to their actual ideas than Kant's were: "Since Constant's pamphlet was written to provide a justification of the policies of the Directory, it reflects their views: it professes a firm commitment to principles, but at the same time its primary aim is to guard against 'excess' by fixing strict limits in the application of principles."[181]

Whichever philosopher best expressed the views of the Directory is less important for us to establish than the debate that ensued between Constant and Kant, which quickly became a classic episode in the endless quarrel between moralism and expediency. Because Constant had been exposed to the world of Jacobin surveillance and the vulnerability of political fugitives, he was impatient with the purism of Kant, who had had the luxury of formulating it from the safe haven of Königsberg. As his biographer Stephen Holmes notes, "In a situation of intense mutual distrust, selective lying can assume a modest community-building function. In 1797, France was still rent by reciprocal hatreds and the desire for revenge. How much men revealed depended upon with whom, and about what, they were speaking. No one could assume that police informers chose their maxims on Kantian grounds."[182]

Constant's first volley was aimed at an unnamed "German philosopher"[183] who had failed to understand the need for "intermediate or midrange principles" to temper the absoluteness of the prohibition against lying under all circumstances. Such principles were required to help move from the level of general rule to that of application to specific cases. The requirement to be truthful, Constant argued, is a duty, but there are no duties without concomitant rights. There is, in other words, a reciprocity of duties and rights in which one never automatically trumps the other. No one has a right to a truth, Constant then added, that might, if known, cause harm. Not everyone deserves the truth (as we've noted Grotius and Rousseau also argued), for example the proverbial murderer who demands to know where his victim is.[184] This is not to say there are no abstract principles or that they are empty—indeed, to proclaim such a belief is itself no less abstract—just that they are always in a context with other, possibly opposing principles.[185] Without principles, there would be only passion and anarchy, Constant conceded, but they have to be tempered by others, which are no less exigent. Moral principles are conditional, not categorical.

Constant, in other words, was not simply arguing against rational principles in the name of romantic feelings, or universal rules in favor of qualitative particularity, as might have his lover Mme de Staël.[186] He was saying instead that no society can function which raises one of its principles to an absolute above all others. For insofar as there is no perfect unity of man and citizen or of duties and rights, there is no foolproof way to overcome the inevitable conflict between moral principles.[187] What Constant would later make famous as the distinction between modern and ancient forms of liberty—one based on negative freedom from coercion, the other on positive participation in the polity—cannot be happily reconciled. Nor should one alternative always trump the other.

Constant went further to defend the inevitability, even value, of hypocrisy in the modern world, where the quest for a true and authentic self beneath appearances was bound to fail. Always to strive to be sincere, he argued against Rousseau, was designed to appeal to an audience that would applaud such virtuous behavior, and as such could paradoxically be a sign of a deeper insincerity. The state might also benefit from hypocritical behavior if ultimately what it feigns to be doing or believing becomes its actual policy. Holmes notes that, for Constant, "lies can be 'noble' precisely because they set in motion a process whereby they become truths,"[188] an argument that goes as far back as Aristotle. Accordingly, it may be wrong, as F. R. Ankersmit has argued, to dismiss his arguments as cynical: "Because of his insistence on the educational value of hypocrisy, Constant's defense of state deceit should decidedly not be put on a par with Plato's 'noble lie' or with Machiavelli's eulogies of pretext and lying."[189]

But despite the nuance and moderation of Constant's position, Kant was not convinced. This is not to say that Kant himself was always above using clever stratagems to avoid having to tell the truth. A famous example of his manipulative use of language came in his promise under coercion in 1794 to the reactionary Prussian king Friedrich Wilhelm II to refrain from writing about religion from a purely rational point of view: "As your Majesty's faithful subject, I shall in the future completely desist from all public lectures or papers concerning religion." When the king died in 1797, Kant revealed that he had slyly meant "as your Majesty's faithful subject" to apply only as long as the king lived, thus applying the doctrine of mental reservation without explicitly telling an untruth.[190] Perhaps this was an example of *aequivocatio,* which Kant in his lectures on ethics had said was "permitted, in order to reduce the other to silence and get rid of him, so that he shall no longer try to extract the truth from us, once he sees that we cannot give it to him, and do not wish to tell him a lie."[191]

But when it came to outright lies, deliberate statements intended to deceive by someone who knows the truth, Kant was unyielding in his hostility, rehearsing in rationalist guise the position Augustine had defended in the idiom of Christianity.[192] In his 1797 reply to "the French philosopher" who had argued otherwise—there may have some indirect nationalist jousting at work here—Kant brooked no exceptions to the general principle of rejecting mendacity, which was entailed by the more fundamental categorical imperative prohibiting acts that were not universalizable. Principles are only genuinely principles if they are categorically valid under all circumstances, not like mere conditional maxims of prudential behavior.

The prohibition against lying was a perfect one, never allowing exceptions. In so arguing, Kant invited the reproach ever since that he was unrealistic, formalistic, rigorist, even "frankly lunatic"[193] in his inflexibility, always advocating "clean hands" no matter how dirty the game that was being played. Even those who generally admire him, like Hans Saner, could speak of his essay as a "strange retort venturing to carry the consequences to the point of absurdity."[194]

That absurdity is perhaps most evident if Kant's rigorous rejection of lying is compared with his more flexible attitude toward violence, which many might see as more morally reprehensible than mendacity. Although he may have held out hope for the ultimate achievement of "perpetual peace," in such writings as "Idea for a Universal History with Cosmopolitan Intent" (1784) Kant defended war as a variant of the "asocial sociability" that moves the species closer and closer to the realization of reason in history. "Thanks are due to nature for [man's] quarrelsomeness, his enviously competitive vanity, and for his insatiable desire to possess or to rule," Kant wrote, "for without them all the excellent natural faculties of mankind would forever remain undeveloped."[195]

Kant's radically anticonsequentialist argument rested on two basic premises. The first was that Constant's attempt to make duties and rights codependent was misguided. Whereas a duty (*Pflicht*) was felt as an internal moral "ought," an immanent imperative, a right (*Recht*) was only an external law, a juridical rather than ethical command. The obligation to tell the truth had nothing to do with the right of the hearer to be told it. In fact, the so-called right to truth was itself meaningless in an objective sense, even if it might have some subjective warrant. This distinction between objective and subjective rights, which many commentators have found confusing and unconvincing, was itself based on a deeper premise of Kant's argument, which he had developed in his first two *Critiques:* that humans are divided into phenomenal selves, beholden to the laws of nature, and noumenal selves, in which the primacy of practical (i.e., moral) reason holds sway. Insofar as men are noumenal beings with the free will to make moral choices, they have an absolute, unconditional duty not to lie. For there is no way, Kant claims, to will that lying become a universal rule, as the categorical imperative enjoins us to do. The empirical consequences in the phenomenal world that might follow from their decision to lie, such as the happiness of those to whom they lied or the welfare of those about whom they lied, is of no moment. Even if the murderer's intended victim is one of our friends, we have no right to lie to save his life. Moral obligation is binding on humans qua moral subjects; personal happiness, which might follow from the right to be told the truth, is merely a state of empirical man, man qua sentient being determined by natural laws. The subjective right to be told the truth is part of the phenomenal world, the world of man as creaturely being, whereas there is no comparable objective right in the noumenal world of men understood as absolute ends in themselves.

Thus, the man questioned by the murderer about his victim was morally obliged to tell the truth, allowing the chips to fall where they may. Moreover, Kant reasoned, there was no guarantee that telling a lie would have the intended good consequence, which might be unexpectedly abetted by veracity instead (the murderer might outsmart himself and distrust the word of the honest man). And even if the murderer did find his intended victim and carry out the crime, the truth-teller would not be morally responsible for an offense he did not commit, which is not the case if he had lied and unintentionally brought about the same result.

The second main premise of Kant's argument is that telling a lie is an injury to the moral character of the liar (a point we have seen Augustine and Rousseau also make). We have a duty to ourselves as rational beings that transcends any material interest or even intersubjective good. That duty is to uphold the moral law that assures our dignity as ends in ourselves. Otherwise we risk becoming "a mere deceptive appearance of a human being, not a human being himself."[196] Or as Kant put it in his lectures on ethics, "A liar is a cowardly fellow, for since he has no other way of obtaining something, or getting out of trouble, he starts to tell lies."[197] Even considering exceptions to the universal principle is a slippery slope toward breaking the taboo. A lie is also an affront to the universal humanity embodied in each of our noumenal selves. As Augustine had noted, it tacitly calls into question the autonomy of the victim by denying him or her information that will allow a rational response; even the white lie of the well-intentioned doctor robs the patient of his dignity as an entirely autonomous adult.[198]

Moreover, and here Kant moves in a subtly consequentialist direction, trust is the basis of all contracts, which are the foundation of all society, so lying is inherently antisocial in long-term effect, whatever its short-term benefit. For lying would undermine belief in the general veracity of statements, which would harm humankind in general. It is thus an offense against both truth, on the one hand, and credibility and trust, on the other.[199] There can be no particular social contract allowing for some lying in certain circumstances, if the general validity of contracts depends on the premise of trustworthiness.[200] As he noted in his lectures on ethics, even if a lie does no specific injury to the party to whom the lie is told, if I lie, "I violate the right of mankind; for I have acted contrary to the condition, and the means, under which a society of men can come about, and thus contrary to the right of humanity."[201]

Another way to present this claim involves the latent linguistic dimension of Kant's position on lying, which Derrida has noted. The absolutist critique of lying, he writes, "can also be described as a modest and tenacious description, a simple, constative analysis of the essence of language. 'Of course you can always lie and lie while promising, who hasn't done that,' Kant himself might say, 'but in that case, you cease speaking, you no longer address another, another as a human being; you have renounced language because all language is structured by this promise of veracity.'"[202] So even if the "possible lie" always haunts veracity, the default position has to be telling the truth.

Kant's argument has always generated considerable resistance, some even claiming that it was an example of his waning powers at the advanced age of seventy-three. "Surely," one particularly vehement critic scoffs, "his prohibition of mendacity in any circumstances was intended as a joke—or, better, as a 'noble lie' constructed out of fear of mendacity's mimetic contagiousness!"[203] In particular, Kant's infamous example of the would-be murderer has persuaded few commentators. Herbert J. Paton voices the typical rejoinder:

We are not entitled to tell lies in order to save either ourselves or our friend from some temporary embarrassment. But surely we must recognize the difference between a desire to please and the duty of helping the innocent in peril of their life. The life of a man is not a mere matter of convenience; and even in the very strong case of contract, if I had contracted to build a dam and discovered later that this would cause the death of many innocent people, I should be acting rightly if I refused to carry out the contract. The case of lying to a would-be murderer is no less plain.[204]

Even Sissela Bok, who in many respects is in the deontological camp, observes that force has been traditionally justified to prevent a murder and "if to use force in self-defense or in defending those at risk of murder is right, why then should a lie in such cases be ruled out? Surely if force is allowed, a lie should be equally, perhaps at times, more justified."[205] As for Kant's claim that only the murderer is really morally responsible for the crime, she adds, "It is a very narrow view of responsibility which does not also take some blame for a disaster one could easily have averted, no matter how much others are also to blame."[206]

Is it also possible that the defense of potentially innocent victims by lying about their whereabouts to a would-be murderer can pass the test of universalizability posed by the categorical imperative? If we conceptualize the act, not as an example of the larger category of mendacity, but as a more specific moral action to be judged in its own terms, why not follow Mme. de Staël and tax Kant for forgetting "that sacrificing truth only to another virtue might be made a general law, for as soon as private interest is set aside in a question sophisms are no more to be feared and consciousness adjudicates everything in agreement with equity."[207] Moreover, as Jules Vuillemin points out, "To tell the truth, or to assist someone in danger, are not maxims of the will, but simply actions. Truth may be spoken out of malice and the required maxim is the rule according to which I only act for the sake of duty."[208]

Another frequent objection follows from the always vexed relationship in Kant's philosophy between the noumenal and phenom-

enal worlds, the worlds of rigorously moral practical reason and instrumental, pragmatic behavior. How can we go from one to the
other? How can absolute moral principles be applied in the world of
imperfect human actions? Why should we prefer the benefit of a
universal "mankind in general" to the specific interests of particular
men and women? Should sacrificing the latter become a means for
the good of the former, an ironic conclusion in the face of that variant of Kant's categorical imperative commanding us always to treat
individual men as ends, never as means? Is the Kantian moral purist
a kind of free rider who indirectly benefits from the "dirty hands" of
those who compromise their absolute integrity to get things done?
How can we judge when a principle should be applied to a specific
case and when it is inappropriate? Is it true that rights are merely
external and juridical rather than moral and internal?[209] Is there
never a conflict between equally powerful moral imperatives, so that
rebellion against an unjust tyrant can sometimes be justified (and
thus under certain circumstances lying as well)? Why assume there
is a coherent and hierarchically organized system of moral imperatives, a consistent set with an unequivocal order, that allow us always
to choose among them with absolute certainty?[210] Even if we identify one that satisfies us, will it be the same for all cultures and all
times?[211] Can we, in other words, find in Kant's purity of principle a
way back to the messiness of the historical world?

Many commentators have shared Derrida's concern that for all
his use of a juridical vocabulary, "Kant seems all the same to exclude
in his definition of the lie all the historicity that, by contrast, Hannah Arendt introduces into the very essence, in the event and the
performance of the lie."[212] Similarly, Hans Saner notes, "Kant thus
aims at a different principle of reflection. It is not to reflect toward
the historical circumstances of a particular case, but from that case
toward the suprahistoric principle. Kant sees this in the categorical
imperative, which has the pure intent of any act in mind and at the
same time its extreme consequence for the principle. In this sense
alone is Kant an ethicist of responsibility."[213]

Saner's final reference in this passage is, of course, to Max Weber's
famous distinction between an "ethics of absolute ends" (*Gesinnungsethik*) and an "ethics of responsibility" (*Verantwortungsethik*)

in his 1920 essay "Politics as a Vocation." Significantly, Weber introduces the issue of lying in politics to illustrate the distinction. Referring to the recent controversial decision to reveal secret documents about the war aims of the defeated Germans, he notes:

> Finally, let us consider the duty of truthfulness. For the absolute ethic it holds unconditionally. Hence the conclusion was reached to publish all documents, especially those placing blame on one's own country. On the basis of these one-sided publications the confessions of guilt followed—and they were one-sided, unconditional, and without regard to consequences. The politician will find that as a result truth will not be furthered but certainly obscured through abuse and unleashing of passion; only an all-around methodical investigation by non-partisans could bear fruit; any other procedure may have consequences for a nation that cannot be remedied for decades. But the absolute ethic just does not *ask* for "consequences." That is the decisive point.[214]

Although in many respects, Weber was indebted to Kant, at least as mediated by the late nineteenth-century neo-Kantians, here he sides with "the politician" who is not beholden to Kant's "ethic of absolute ends." In his account of the debate with Constant, Hans Saner comes to a similar conclusion about the opposition between Kantian morality and the values of politics. "Kant," he writes, "does not name the hostile power that is at work in Constant, but it can be felt in the polemic. It is the politician's way of thinking—the thought of one who, starting from whatever is historically given and seeking to limit his own responsibility, will prudently tackle the problems of each particular situation and make a principle of adjusting his principles to the situation."[215]

Although there have been many efforts to derive a plausible politics from Kant, and there continue to be new ones all the time,[216] when it came to the question of mendacity, a radical disjuncture separated moral rigor from prudential expediency in a way that made moral politics almost an oxymoron. Or to be more precise, consequentialist ethics, by virtually all accounts, has been a more comfortable bedfellow of the political than Kantian deontology, even if it too is beset by a fundamental problem, which plagues all utilitarianism: generating and defending a plausible principle of usefulness that will have universal implications rather than partial ones.

But even before we worry about the tension between the Kantian prohibition on lying and politics, we have to address an even more fundamental question: what exactly is "the political"? Can we simply assume that we know its essential nature and then draw straightforward conclusions about the role of lying in politics? Or is it as contested a conceptual terrain as lying itself? Can it be utterly isolated from other practices and discourses, including the moral, which allows whatever mendacity it abets to be spared the stigma that accompanies lying in other contexts? It would be prudent to pause and ponder some of the multiple meanings and implications of politics and "the political" before reaching any judgments. In the next chapter, I will attempt just such a survey of that territory, which has some well-known landmarks but also some uncharted corners with surprising implications.

2

ON THE POLITICAL

CONCEPTUALIZING THE POLITICAL

In 1927 the right-wing German political theorist Carl Schmitt published a short but enormously influential essay entitled *The Concept of the Political.*[1] Revised twice, in 1932 and 1933, as its author moved closer to his notorious role as "crown jurist" for the Nazis, and reissued in 1963 with added material, the book became a controversial classic of twentieth-century political theory, whose resonance ironically only increased after the collapse of the Third Reich.[2] Although earlier in the decade, Max Weber had famously called politics a separate "vocation" or "calling" (*Beruf*), thus giving it the dignity of more than a mere self-interested career, and set it apart from science (*Wissenschaft*) and moral absolutism, he had not raised "the political" to a conceptual status apart from mere politics.[3] That step was taken by Schmitt, writing in the midst of the ongoing legitimacy crisis of the Weimar Republic.

We will return later to the content of Schmitt's argument, but for now what is important to register is the abiding power of his stronger claim that something called "the political" deserves an entirely distinct treatment under an inherently self-contained "concept" of its own. Although he was careful to say that this did not mean positing a rigid, universally binding definition—as his later disciple and father of *Begriffsgeschichte* (conceptual history) Reinhard Koselleck explained, concepts always contain the sedimented history of their different meanings[4]—Schmitt nonetheless allowed a cryptotrans-

cendentalism to color his argument. For despite his urging a historical analysis of the concept, he never provided more than one basic
criterion. Moreover, with the claim that "the political" had "a concept" went the implication that it was a categorical mistake, and perhaps even a dangerous one at that, to conflate "the political" with
anything else, say, the social, the economic, the aesthetic, the legal,
and perhaps most important of all, the moral.[5] So that those political theories that did so were somehow not living up to the pure conceptual meaning of the term.

In the decades since Schmitt's book appeared, the substantive
idea of "the political," the elevation of an adjective into a singular
noun, distinct from mere politics and irreducible to other spheres of
human endeavor, attracted a great following, and not only in Germany.[6] French political theorists, for example, would come to distinguish between *le politique* and *la politique* to signal the same
distinction. Appearing as early as the 1950s in the work of Paul Ricoeur, the dichotomy became widely adopted during the 1980s.[7] In
English-speaking countries, it would take slightly longer to become
an opposition almost as eagerly embraced.

The new elevation and segregation of "the political" might be
understood in part as a delayed expression of the overcoming of
the massive disaffection of intellectuals from political activity that
followed the failures of the 1848 revolutions and was perhaps not
reversed until the Dreyfus affair near the end of the nineteenth century in France, and in Germany not until the Weimar Republic.[8]
When intellectuals felt less politically alienated, they could theorize
the specificity of the political with greater enthusiasm. But even more
likely, its conceptual emergence also registered a powerful, indeed
often brutal reality of political life in the new twentieth century. Politics, in particular in fascist and Leninist contexts (but also in capitalist welfare states), grew increasingly active and intrusive as cen-
tralized governments seized and exercised more and more power.
Ironically, Schmitt's book was written to challenge the hegemony of
an allegedly apolitical liberalism, that of the legally normative *Rechtstaat,* precisely at the moment when it was most in peril.

As the twentieth century wore on and the beleaguered center lost
ground to the totalitarian extremes, any vision of politics as merely

derivative of something more fundamental seemed increasingly inadequate. Both liberal and orthodox, pre-Leninist Marxist versions of the primacy of the economic no longer persuaded many observers, who acknowledged the growing power of the activist state or the vanguard party over civil society and the market. The "steering power" of the state—or parties and movements that claimed to speak for it—increasingly dominated the self-regulating mechanisms of society or the economy. Whether or not such an activist state was seen as fostering or impeding "genuine" or "emancipatory" politics, it became much more difficult to see it as merely epiphenomenal. Even Marxists began to speak of "state capitalism" and acknowledge the latter-day relevance of the Bonapartist liberation from rigid class determination that Marx had discussed so trenchantly in "The 18th Brumaire of Louis Bonaparte."[10] The Bolshevik Revolution of 1917 came itself to be understood, to borrow the phrase of Antonio Gramsci, as a "revolution against *Das Kapital*,"[11] because it had rejected economic determinism and refused to wait for the automatic explosion of the contradictions of capitalism.

Throughout the history of theorizing about politics, from Protagoras to the American philosopher Stanley Cavell, there have been thinkers who have insisted that everything is always already political.[12] For them, attempts to confine the political to the great matters of state or even the petty ones of normal government are in vain. Even everyday life at its most seemingly banal can be understood as inherently political. Others, claiming that the autonomy of the political was an unfortunate historical development, have held out hope for the reintegration of "alien politics" into a less fractured social totality, beyond the differentiations of modernity.[13] But still others came to celebrate or at least urge the "the return of the political" to what they saw as its rightful status as an irreducible realm of its own.[14]

In fact, as the philosopher Agnes Heller has pointed out, the term can imply both meanings: "a certain 'thing' (a quality, a factor) that may be shared (or not) by other 'things'" or "a domain, for example a sphere or system, which endows whatever enters it, with political nature; whatever leaves this domain ceases to be political, whenever it makes its exit."[15] Whichever meaning predominates, what has to be acknowledged is that the concept—when it was clearly promoted as such—became a way to rejuvenate political theory, which had so long labored to free itself from its reduction to political science or subsumption under a more general science of society as a whole. By the twenty-first century, a publishing series entitled Thinking the Political could commission volumes on a wide range of philosophers—Foucault, Derrida, Nietzsche, Heidegger, Lacan, Lyotard, Deleuze, Levinas, Kristeva, Adorno—whether or not they would have recognized the concept as meaningful in their own work.[16]

Theorizing "the political" rested on two controversial premises. One follows from the "thing" definition noted by Heller, and the other from the "domain" alternative. The first entails the claim that a transcendental notion of "the political" can be discerned beneath all the various institutional forms and cultural practices that have been called political throughout history. Like the phenomenological reduction advocated by Edmund Husserl, it assumes that the *eidos* or essential idea can be revealed by bracketing all the specific manifestations of political activity.[17]

Although the enduring characteristics of its transcendental nature have been much contested, the idea that such an inherent essence of "the political" might be found was assumed by Schmitt and those who shared his belief in having located not "a" but "the" concept. As one of their contemporary number, the Belgian-born theorist Chantal Mouffe, puts it, "If we wanted to express such a distinction in a philosophical way, we could, borrowing the vocabulary of Heidegger, say that politics refers to the 'ontic' level while 'the political' has to do with the 'ontological' one. This means that the ontic has to do with the manifold practices of conventional politics, while the ontological concerns the very way in which society is instituted."[18] A somewhat less philosophically exalted—and less exclusively singular—definition is offered by the contemporary French political theorist Pierre Rosenvallon: "To refer to 'the political' rather than to 'politics' is to speak of power and law, state and nation, equality and justice, identity and difference, citizenship and civility—

in sum, of everything that constitutes political life beyond the immediate field of partisan competition for political power, everyday governmental action, and the ordinary functioning of institutions."[19]

The distinction of "the political" from mere politics allows it to be transferable to other arenas of human endeavor as a quality or "thing." But it also paradoxically enables a search for the distinguishing characteristics that set it apart from other dimensions of human existence, which are often still intertwined with "ontic" politics. Although Schmitt had argued that contemporary political concepts had roots in medieval theology,[20] he claimed that once they became secularized in the "disenchanted world" of modernity, "the political" operated according to its own internal logic and followed its own rules. In the 1927 edition of his book, he argued that it constituted an independent "value sphere"—the term was originally Weber's—separate from those designated moral (where good and bad reigned), aesthetic (ruled by the beautiful and the ugly), or economic (dominated by profitability and unprofitability). It was, to use a term from political theory itself, "sovereign" in its own house, unbeholden to norms or moral constraints from elsewhere.

Schmitt vigorously argued against "the political" being subordinated to what he saw as external standards, such as those derived from Christian morality. But cryptonormative implications nonetheless followed, as the descriptive hunt for the essence of "the political" became a prescriptive warning against polluting it with what it had abjected (as we will see, liberalism in Schmitt's understanding was deemed particularly guilty of defiling the purity of "the political" and needed to be cast aside). Only if some positive valence was given to "the political" could such a worry be meaningful, and as will become apparent when examining Schmitt's own theory, it was not hard to find. It also could serve as a standard against which mere "ontic" politics could be measured, also with normative implications. With reference to the question of lying, if "the political" could be construed as somehow abetting mendacity, perhaps even justifying it, then the widespread condemnation of the latter in daily politics might be understood as inadequate to the deeper affinities that lay beneath the surface.

A generation later, Hannah Arendt likewise sought to protect the integrity of "the political" as a special form of the *vita activa* from its absorption into "the social" with its bloblike capacity to swallow up what it touched,[21] and resisted the reduction of "the political" to philosophical or technical rationality, as well as the alleged laws of historical development. The progressive atrophy of "the political," whose highest moment had come in the Athenian polis or city-state, ultimately led, she argued, to the modern phenomenon of totalitarianism, which did not involve the primacy of politics in the normative sense of the word in her vocabulary. Once "the political" was subordinated to the imperatives of labor, reproducing the species, or fabrication, the making of a world of human objects, it lost its raison d'être, which was a valuable activity in itself, the very mark of human freedom, and not a means to produce something outside it, such as the material welfare of citizens or subjects. *Le politique*, we might say, *pour le politique*, not for justice or welfare or peace or any other extraneous goal.

The second controversial premise underlying the discourse of "the political" is thus the assumption that a boundary can be drawn between its domain and what lies outside it, a boundary that could more or less preserve its purity from external pollution.[22] As the French political theorist Jacques Rancière has noted,

> To speak of the boundaries of the political realm would seem to evoke no precise or current reality. Yet legend invariably has the political begin at one boundary, be it the Tiber or the Neva, and end up at another, be it Syracuse or the Kolyma: riverbanks of foundation, island shores of refoundation, abysses of horror or ruin. There must surely be something of the essence in this landscape for politics to be so stubbornly represented within it.[23]

Here the literal and metaphorical spatial qualities of political life are mingled. All politics in this sense is geopolitics. Whether identified with a special location such as the *agora* (the marketplace or public arena) within the ancient Greek polis (itself a metonymic term derived from the Athenian Acropolis),[24] the city limits of medieval urban republics, or the general territorial boundaries of a modern nation-state, "the political" is often understood to happen—to "take place"[25]—in a defined and limited area. Whether metaphorically identified with a clearing, an arena, a container, a stage, or an elevated site, that place is a privileged locus of political activity. Within the agora it was identified even more closely with the circle or semicircle formed by those who came together to create an assembly gathered to discuss matters of common interest.[26] Fittingly, later place names like "the White House" or "Westminster" or "the Kremlin" came to stand metonymically for the locus of political power (in the case of the American presidency, it was even more precisely located in the "Oval Office").

For Plato, as Rancière notes, it was dry, solid land, the space of caves and mountains, rather than the uncertain waters of the sea, which he identified with the vagaries of democracy rather than the grounded reason of philosophy.[27] For Aristotle, it was categorically distinguished from the different space identified with the household—the *oikos* in classical Greek—which was occupied with other, more domestic tasks and populated by other kinds of people, specifically women and unfree noncitizens or slaves. For Hannah Arendt, it was "where the citizens assemble, it is the realm in which all things can first be recognized in their many-sidedness,"[28] a place of visibility where all can view and be viewed. Unlike the solitary mediation of the philosopher's *vita contemplativa*, politics can only take place in the "world" of humanly constructed spaces that bind together people who nonetheless remain distinct and unique. But it is inherently fragile and ungrounded: "Its peculiarity is that, unlike the spaces which are the work of our hands, it does not survive the actuality of the movement which brought it into being, but disappears not only with the dispersal of men—as in the case of great catastrophes when the body politic of a people is destroyed—but with the disappearance or arrest of the activities themselves. Whenever people gather together, it is potentially there, not necessarily and not forever."[29] The antithesis of politics, she argued, was also a place: the infinite "desert" swept by the blinding "sandstorms" of totalitarian rule in which the internal boundaries between men provided by laws and institutions was absent.[30]

Even when the three-dimensional metaphor of a "public sphere" emerged in the modern world, with its faint echo of the sublunar and celestial spheres of ancient astronomy, the symbolic power of locating it spatially did not wane. In addition to the spatial locations of the hegemonic bourgeois public sphere, such as the coffeehouse, the Masonic lodge, or the debating society, there have also been alternate spaces, what one commentator has called "heterotopia[s] of resistance."[31] Sometimes these emerge in refunctioned nonpolitical locations, like the shop floor of a factory; at others, in places that are designed to abet association and solidarity on the part of people excluded from the dominant culture, like the "houses of the people" established by French and Italian socialists in Europe. Whenever they arise, they serve as the arena in which politics can happen.

It is perhaps not by design but nonetheless telling that the word for an ideal order that left behind the messy conflicts of partisan politics, "utopia," meant a no-place, an unlocatable space, a permanent elsewhere. Although within the perimeter of a polity, politics might be restricted to certain actors, who came to be called citizens, all who dwelled beyond its limits were excluded from participation, strangers not brothers (or later in the development of political participation, sisters as well). For with the idea of location often went the more or less strict demarcation of an inside and outside, undergirding such dichotomies as citizen and alien, city and country, and public and private. Even international relations carried on in the interstices of states were circumscribed in a negative way by the borders of those states, which could not—at least since the modern order of sovereignty largely initiated by the Peace of Westphalia ending the Thirty Years' War in 1648[32]—be breached or violated with impunity. In fact, in the world of capitalist globalization, which might be understood as kind of neoliberal utopia based on the erosion of state sovereignty, meaningful political action becomes increasingly difficult. Without a discrete location for its performance, it is hard to generate the coherent will-formation that is necessary for collective action. In this sense, all politics is not only geopolitics but also local politics, situated in a specific, circumscribed locus, not abstractly universal.

Another way to understand the boundaried, spatial quality of the political with its inevitably local quality is to compare it with another space, which was occupied by something the ancient Greeks called *theoria*. The distinction between theory and practice, among its many other meanings, involved a contrast between the universal and the particular. As the classicist Andrea Wilson Nightingale has noted, *theoria* began as a journey away from home for the goal of watching a spectacle or finding out something about the larger world, seeing for oneself rather than merely obtaining hearsay. When the theorist went to a religious festival, for example, he entered "a panhellenic 'space' which (at least in principle) transcended political differences and encouraged a sense of identity that was much broader and more universal than that defined by the individual polis. . . . The fourth-century philosophers took this model to its extreme: philosophic *theoria* operates in a sphere that completely transcends social and political life."[33] The space of the political life, unlike that of the *vita contemplativa,* was thus always circumscribed, partial, never extending to the totality of the human.

ESSENCES: VARIETIES OF THE POLITICAL

Let us look more carefully at each of these premises in turn to prepare our discussion of the more specific matter at hand, the role of lying in politics. First, if there is an ontological nature of "the political," as opposed to its various ontic manifestations, can we identify its essence, the distinct quality or characteristic that either can be transferred or that defines the limited domain in which it operates? Is it to domestic affairs, as the Greeks thought, or to foreign ones, as the Romans believed, that we must go to find "the political" in its purest form?[34] Without pretending to be exhaustive, we can identify several salient candidates for "the political" that go beyond traditional regime categories (e.g., monarchy, oligarchy, democracy). Each of these will have implications for the question of lying in politics that may well differ, as I hope to demonstrate in the final section of this book. But if we discover that there is an affinity between a significant number of versions of "the political," on the one hand, and hypocrisy and mendacity, on the other, then it may be possible to conclude that lying in politics is not a degeneration or aberration, but is somehow inherent in that realm of human endeavor we have come to call politics.

Before examining the range of candidates, one obvious question has to be addressed. All arguments for the essence of "the political" seek to provide a plausible common denominator for everything justifiably called politics, often banishing certain inferior versions by definition from their (sometimes crypto-) normative model. But in so doing, can they avoid the reproach of ethnocentrism or cultural myopia, privileging one tradition and assuming it reveals universal standards? Can the Greek polis or the Roman Republic, for example, easily serve as a model for, say, political life in Africa or pre-Columbian America? Might it not be wiser to adopt a more frankly nominalist strategy and abandon any search for the essence of "the political"? Can we even comfortably fall back on the method of Weberian "ideal types" and at the same time take into account the full variety of the empirical evidence about differences in the behavior and institutions that have come to be called political? Is it perhaps better to rest content with Wittgenstein's even fuzzier formula of "family resemblances," which gives us some warrant for using a collective noun, but not pretending that we can employ it as an umbrella concept under which all of its examples must fall?

There is, I think, no fully satisfactory response to the doubts that prevent us from confidently adopting one of the candidates and identifying it with a universal notion of "the political." For this reason, I will not myself defend one as superior to the rest or adopt the dubious practice of dismissing the others as impudent imposters. But it may nonetheless be useful for our purposes to canvass the answers that various commentators have given over the years to the question of what is the essence of "the political." For before we can talk about lying in politics, we have to try to sort out the various meanings that have clustered around the latter term.

Several salient alternatives warrant our special attention, two identifying the essence of "the political" with the primacy of foreign affairs, four with the primacy of internal affairs (what the great German historians Leopold von Ranke and Eckhart Kehr called respectively *Primat der Aussenpolitik* and *Primat der Innenpolitik*).[35] The first in the initial group stresses the antagonistic struggle for supremacy or survival, which at its most virulent leads to war. The second emphasizes the agonistic conflict between or among competing states, which involves diplomacy and manipulation rather than outright hostility. Both tend to see the state as an end in itself, sometimes a self-sufficient ethical telos unconstrained by other moral constraints. Although there are domestic versions of both the antagonistic and the agonistic models, the third variant of "the political" I want to examine stresses contractual collaboration among individuals rather than competition; it can be roughly identified with the tradition that has come to be called liberal. The next two are also domestic traditions, more communitarian than individualist, known as Platonic and republican. The first is derived from a Platonic belief in a single model of the Good knowable to reason, which may justify rule by an elite of wise men. The second, often associated with Florentine civic humanism and Machiavellian realism, accepts the pluralism of irreconcilable values, eschewing the possibility of ruling on the basis of access to universal reason. Rather than wise rulership, it stresses inclusive participation and active citizenship. Finally, and somewhat athwart the others rather than parallel with them, is a concept of "the political" as inherently aesthetic. Depending on the version of aesthetic practice which is deemed relevant, this model can analogize between politics and a work of art or politics and performance.

THE POLITICAL AS ANTAGONISM

The most extensive defense of "the concept of the political" in terms of antagonistic foreign relations can be found in the work of Carl Schmitt. Schmitt argued that only at the extremes do essences become apparent, only in seeming moments of exception or emergency do underlying principles reveal themselves. As in the case of what Thomas Kuhn famously called paradigm shifts in science, what is most at stake became apparent only when a given system, previously taken for granted, is in danger of collapsing. At those moments, Schmitt reasoned, the normal authority of existing laws is put into question and more basic questions of ultimate political legitimacy are raised.[36] The rule of law becomes revealed as the power—or perhaps better put, the authority—to make and enforce (or dissolve and suspend) the laws that rule.[37] He who decides in a state of emergency is the indivisible sovereign, unconstrained by any principles, rules, or rational limits. Like the voluntarist God of the medieval nominalists, his absolute will is unconstrained by any laws or norms or rational principles.

What such exceptional states of emergency reveal, Schmitt claimed, is an unending conflict between friends and foes lurking beneath the surface of even the most seemingly irenic political activity. If war is politics conducted by other means, as the Prussian general Carl von Clausewitz famously argued, "the political" may well be at its heart the continuation of war by other means (although Schmitt always denied he was advocating it as a good in itself). Indeed, it can be understood as inherently adversarial even to the point of death.[38] Of the utmost seriousness, politics is, in fact, one of the few human pursuits worth putting one's own life at risk. Contrary to those who see it as a collaborative venture, a way to solve common problems peacefully, it is always at bottom an "existential"[39] struggle for domination, indeed perhaps even survival, in which there are always both allies and enemies, winners and losers. The fundamental fact about human nature, Schmitt argued, is that humans are dangerous to each other and that fear is more powerful than love, leading to group solidarity based on "the eternal relation of protection and obedience."[40]

Does this mean that international politics, where war is always a possible threat, is more "political" than domestic? In the eighteenth century, Schmitt argued, a distinction arose between two words derived from the Greek *polis,* "police" (in German *Polizei*) and "politics" (*Politik*).[41] The former referred to internal governance, based on benevolent administration, the latter to foreign affairs. As one of Schmitt's interpreters, Ernst-Wolfgang Böckenförde, has argued, within the state, which is a "pacified unity," homogeneity rather than adversarial relations or even pluralist ones are assumed to exist, so that it is only in a "derivative sense" that the friend/foe distinction defines internal politics, which may intensify into a state of civil war, but rarely does so.[42] In his 1926 study *The Crisis of Parliamentary Democracy,* Schmitt had made the implications of this position clear. Democracy requires not only homogeneity but also, "if the need arises—elimination or eradication of heterogeneity."[43] He then cited approvingly the Turkish expulsion of their Greek citizens after

World War I, and the restricted immigration policy of Australia, which allowed only "the right kind of settler" into the country. That is, within normal states, unless they are in crisis during an *Ausnahmezustand* (variously translated as "state of emergency" or "state of exception"), "the political" is displaced outward to foreign states who are classified as friends or foes. Sovereign states are never subordinate to an overarching humanity-wide high authority, moral or institutional.

In this version of "the political," the unregulated competitive state system is closer to its conceptual essence than the competition of factions or parties within a state. For it is only at the highest level of collective actors that the requisite intensity of identification is achieved:

> The enemy is not merely any competitor or just any partner of a conflict in general. He is also not the private adversary whom one hates. An enemy exists only when, at least potentially, one fighting collectivity of people confronts a similar collectivity. The enemy is solely the public enemy, because everything that has a relationship to such a collectivity of men, particularly to a whole nation, becomes public by virtue of such a relationship. The enemy is *hostis,* not *inimicus* in the broader sense.[44]

The latter, the *inimicus,* means a personal, psychologically driven enemy not a public one; it is typical of an individualism which for Schmitt is the source of antipolitical thinking, that of liberal bourgeois society with its fetish of self-preservation and the security of the isolated subject. Both ethics and economics, moral imperatives and self-interest, are allied against the autonomy of the political, which is in danger of being lost amid the growing power of bourgeois ideology and the cult of technology.[45] Only through a politics in which life is worth being sacrificed can the triviality of a culture of mere entertainment and distraction be avoided. Against the vain search for compromise typical of the Weimar Republic, Schmitt could go so far as to write approvingly in 1936 that "Adolf Hitler's book *Mein Kampf* [My Struggle] juxtaposes with its title another concept of the political."[46]

These characteristics have also at times been identified with a version of "the political" that is more domestic than international, for example in the early work of Ernesto Laclau and Chantal Mouffe.[47] In cases of radical instability—and remember Schmitt's argument was forged in the volatile conditions of the Weimar Republic, whose very legitimacy was almost always in doubt—internal politics may appear no less existentially at risk than their external counterpart. But by and large this version of "the political" is more plausibly situated in the often hostile or suspicious relations among state actors, who monopolize (more or less) the means of domestic violence, but are unable to do so internationally.

THE POLITICAL AS AGONISM

Must the violence of war—or its constant threat—be seen as the essence of "the political" even in relations among states, where no universal morality, no ethnic or ideological homogeneity, no overarching community, can be assumed? Must extreme situations, states of crisis producing a collapse of normative order, be taken as the key to revealing that essence, rather than "normal" political practices? Even Schmitt tried to distinguish between pure war for its own sake, whose defense he attributed to Heraclitus and in his own day Ernst Jünger, and "the political" properly understood.[48] Perhaps the fluid and delicate diplomatic relations among those entities that have come to be called "states"[49] in the modern world will serve instead? For those who prefer this alternative, nonviolent international relations, the realm of diplomatic compromise, negotiation, and maneuvering becomes the model for a different version of "the political." It implies the never-ending process of building fragile alliances and forging friendships of reciprocal convenience among mutually suspicious metaindividuals, who resist being subordinated to binding international law and observe the imperatives of *raison d'état*.[50] In the European state system established after the Peace of Westphalia, interference in the sovereign affairs of other states was more or less banished to avoid endless religious strife. Ideological justifications for intervening were outlawed in principle, if, to be sure, not always in practice (as during the Napoleonic era and the Cold War).[51]

Although war remains an ultimate resort, this version of the political prefers to solve or at least postpone the inflammation of problems by more irenic means (or a tense balance of power between unfriendly rivals). It resists the black and white bifurcation of the political field into friends and foes, preferring instead to forge temporary and shifting alliances and arrangements of power sharing. These tactics draw on the lessons in *politesse* nurtured in more intimate settings of sociability; indeed, the adjective "diplomatic" means observing the protocols of tact and decorum (as well as practicing a benign kind of hypocrisy). But their champions never fool themselves into thinking that a permanent consensus can be built that will resolve conflicts of interest or value forever. "The political" in this acceptation is thus agonistic and pluralistic rather than antagonistic to the death and polarized, but it is not at the deepest level collaborative or cooperative.

In both of these instances, the operative unit of the political is a collective entity, usually but not exclusively a state (whether a city-state, a dynastic state, or a nation-state), which can neither be subordinated to larger sovereign institutions, such as a universal world state, nor dissolved into its constituent elements understood in social or economic terms. Whether explicitly organicist or not, this version of "the political" privileges those metaindividuals of history that find their justification in themselves, their self-preservation, or in some cases their "natural" expansion of power.[52] Following a postcosmopolitan version of the state, classically articulated in the German historicist critique of Enlightenment natural law theory,[53] its champions argued that such entities were valuable expressions of the infinite creative genius of the species, which manifested itself in particular rather than universal forms. Because each was unique and irreducible, there was no way to overcome their agonistic and perhaps antagonistic rivalries. Politics in this sense might be understood at its most brutal as a variant of the notorious war of all against all that Thomas Hobbes had seen as the state of nature prior to culture.

In some cases, at least for those who developed the *raison d'état* tradition in a more idealist direction, the actors in that struggle gained an aura of ethical value in themselves, which meant they were not constrained in the exercise of the brutality they needed to survive and prosper. In the early nineteenth century in Germany, according to the historian Friedrich Meinecke, "something quite new and extraordinary occurred: Machiavellism came to form an integral part in the complex of an idealist view of the universe, a view which at the same time embraced and confirmed all moral values—whereas in former times Machiavellism had only been able to exist alongside the moral cosmos that had been built up. What happened now was almost like the legitimization of a bastard."[54] Rather than there being a tension between power and morality, *kratos* and *ethos* in the classical Greek formulation, the two were wedded in the individual actor in history that became known as the "ethical state." The moral right to self-realization, individuality (which was so much a part of the Humboldtian idea of developmental as opposed to empirical individual*ism*), was now bestowed on the state itself, which was understood as more than just the holder of legitimate power over a territorial entity. That striving for realization of an inherent telos—in German *Bildung* or self-formation—was understood to be a moral good in itself, which could not be subordinated to abstract, universal principles hovering above the concrete particularities of history.

It was perhaps in Hegel's *Philosophy of Right and Law* that the most elaborate defense of the ethical state was mounted.[55] It was an ideal state, only approximated by its existing exemplars (including the Restoration Prussia in which he invested his hopes in the 1820s). It was a modern, articulated state, based on representation, and thus going beyond the direct, unmediated democracy of the classical polis.[56] Transcending as well the instrumental, self-interested rationality of civil society (*Verstand*), but not abolishing it either, it was the embodiment or hieroglyph of a universal, substantive reason (*Vernunft*). "The state," Hegel argued, "is the actual reality of the ethical *idea; it is ethical spirit as the *manifest* substantial will that is fully self-cognizant, and that thinks and knows itself and realizes what it knows and insofar as it knows."[57] Complementing the "particular altruism" of the family and the "universal egoism" of civil society, it instantiated "universal altruism." The free will of the people, their "sound common sense," was ultimately one with the autonomous will of the state. They did not play a role in constituting the state, however, for constitutions are not "made" by anyone, but are rather "divine and lasting and above the sphere of that which is made."[58]

In historical terms, the ethical state was a hybrid amalgam, a "complex institutional structure synthesizing hereditary monarchy, rationalistic bureaucracy, corporatist-estatist social representation, and an established church."[59] As such, it did not rigorously distinguish between administration and politics, as would later theorists like Max Weber. But whatever its mongrel character, it served for Hegel as the highest embodiment of ethical life (*Sittlichkeit*), mediating contradictions, actively overcoming alienation, uniting subjective with objective freedom. Although defending the life-risking sacrifices of war as a test of ethical virtue and scoffing at Kant's Enlightenment hope for a "perpetual peace" among nations,[60] he did not make of friend-foe antagonism the essence of "the political." That would have been too undialectical a binary opposition. But he did locate the political in a collective rather than individual subject, a higher community whose ethical life was the locus of rationality and freedom.

The ideal of the "ethical state" also had repercussions elsewhere, for example nineteenth-century Britain, where German ideas has been transmitted by figures like Samuel Taylor Coleridge and Thomas Carlyle.[61] By the time of Matthew Arnold, it had become a powerful weapon in the development of loyal citizens who left their class or ethnic status behind and found solidarity on the level of participation in an uplifting moral project through which the state could represent collective interests and express common cultural values. Fostered by a national education system and identification with colonial conquests abroad, the good citizen put aside his narrow class or regional identities and willingly accepted the "higher" status provided by belonging to the United Kingdom.

More domestic adaptations of the agonistic model of "the political" have also emerged in which the groups involved are not identified with states, ethical or otherwise. Thus, for example, in her more recent work Chantal Mouffe replaces Schmittian antagonism to the death between mortal enemies understood in terms of good and evil with a more benign adversarial competition, which she calls democratic agonism. "While antagonism is a we/they relation in which the two sides are enemies who do not share any common ground, agonism is a we/they relation where the conflicting parties, although acknowledging that there is no rational solution to their conflict, nevertheless recognize the legitimacy of their opponents. They are 'adversaries' not enemies."[62] Arguing against both the homogeneity by ethnic unity argument of Schmitt and the homogeneity by rational consensus building argument of Jürgen Habermas, which we will encounter shortly, she identifies "the political" with a permanent, if shifting pluralistic competition of groups for hegemony within a polity. Building on Derrida's ideas about the fragile and unstable nature of group identity and Arendt's belief in pluralistic heterogeneity, Mouffe understands the groups that struggle for supremacy as inherently ephemeral and shifting in composition. Relationally constituted and always in danger of being dissolved, they are not eternal solidarities that have ontological solidity. But such politically adversarial groups do exist and can never be fully reconciled by rational persuasion: "Contrary to the dialogic approach, the democratic debate is conceived as a real confrontation," Mouffe writes. "Adversaries do fight—even fiercely—but according to a shared set of rules, and their positions, despite being ultimately irreconcilable, are accepted as legitimate perspectives. . . . It is not the revolutionary politics of the jacobin type, but neither is it the liberal one of competing interests within a neutral terrain or the discursive formation of a democratic consensus."[63]

THE POLITICAL AS CONTRACTUALISM AMONG INDIVIDUALS

Liberalism was not merely hopeful of reconciling interests through rational deliberation, albeit more often procedural than substantive, but also inclined to understand the players in the game of politics in more particularist terms.[64] Hobbes, one of its founding fathers, had been a nominalist who understood the state of nature to be made up of single individuals rather than collective entities like tribes, nations, or states. For this reason, he cannot be seen as anticipating Schmitt's collectivist version of "the political," as Leo Strauss correctly pointed out in his early response to *The Concept of the Political*.[65] Hobbes hoped to escape the dangers of the bellicose state of nature, with all its insecurities, and to do so contrived a contract among individuals, whose self-preservation was a higher goal than that of the state understood as an organic end in itself. As a result, for all the authoritarian potential in his version of the absolute sovereign, the state as Leviathan into whose benevolent care vulnerable individuals gave themselves, he can be accounted a father, along with John Locke, of what became known as the liberal tradition (or more precisely, classical liberalism, to distinguish it from the New Deal welfare state variant that displaced it in twentieth-century America).

For many exponents of this tradition, politics begins, whether logically or historically is unclear, with a contractual arrangement— or in some cases a broad "compact," to use a word with less legal force—among equals in a prepolitical state of nature. Their rational decision to alienate their full autonomy to a benign sovereign is premised on the assumption that if the latter fails to live up to its contractual obligations to safeguard their liberties, citizens have a right to resist its power and seek another sovereign (Locke, of course, more than Hobbes, stressed that right of resistance, which, as we noted earlier, was not always defended by other liberals, such as Kant). Although rights, understood in natural or religious terms, might be said to antedate the creation of political entities, it was one of the duties of those entities to honor and preserve those rights. Likewise, there is no inherent clash between unconstrained political will or sovereignty and the binding rule of law, between legitimacy and legality, as theorists like Schmitt came to argue.

Not surprisingly, the latter saw liberalism as inherently and irremediably antipolitical because of its naïve yearning to replace permanent antagonism between enemies with rational deliberation or at least mutually beneficial calculation among friends. Whether hoping for a consensus based on the persuasion of the better argument or settling for an agreement to split the difference between positions that remained at odds, liberalism thought that foes could become friends or at least noncombatant acquaintances in a framework of legal constraints. From the restrictive perspective of Schmitt and his followers, it thus elevated the values of the marketplace (negotiated compromise) and the university classroom (persuasion through rational argument) above the passionate antagonism of genuinely existential political struggle. Later liberals like John Rawls insisted instead that liberalism was "a doctrine that falls under the category of the political. It works entirely within that domain and does not rely on anything outside it.... Political philosophy, as understood in political liberalism, consists largely of different political conceptions of right and justice viewed as *freestanding*."[66] Nancy Fraser has made a similar point, albeit from the perspective of a socialist critic of liberalism's indifference to real substantive inequalities: "Liberalism assumes the autonomy of the political in a very strong form. Liberal political theory assumes that it is possible to organize a democratic form of political life on the basis of socioeconomic and sociosexual structures that generate systematic inequalities."[67]

What was the essence of "the political" for liberalism? Believing, *pace* Schmitt, that it can be found in domestic rather than international relations, liberals generally favor negotiated contracts or compacts resting on mutual trust rather than countervailing fear. Locke talked of governments as "fiduciary trusts," which earned the obedience of their citizens only so long as they carried out the mandate on which they were founded.[68] As in the case of contractual arrange ments in other areas of human interaction—say, economic agreements or marriage alliances—the element of trustworthiness, the keeping of one's word, was paramount. In a commercial society, credit and credibility were seen as closely related, even if some commentators like Daniel Defoe did acknowledge that even honest tradesmen were not obliged to tell the whole truth all the time.[69]

After a while, trustworthiness becomes valued as intrinsically good, as more than just a useful tactic in a game of mutual convenience. Perhaps even more significantly, trust for liberals ultimately became an explicit political policy with certain safeguards to reinforce personal declarations of intention. As Peter Johnson has noted, liberals generally believe that "modern political societies are better constituted by trust conceived as a strategically defined reliance on well-designed procedures and institutions agreed to by agents who are notionally rational and free."[70] In other words, fallible human beings need to trust in more than just the word of their no less fallible fellows. The rule of impersonal law backed by sanctions and penalties compensated for failures to keep that word. In fact, the need to establish the rule of law with checks and balances against the abusive concentration of power was a powerful dimension of the liberal version of "the political." Trust, moreover, was often placed by liberals more in the extrapolitical workings of the market than in government per se, which meant that for all their stress on the autonomy of the political, *pace* Rawls and Fraser, the role it was supposed to play was limited.

As a result, from certain perspectives—and not only those endorsing Schmitt's bellicose antagonism or Mouffe's less lethal agonism—liberalism has been accused of having too wan and underdeveloped a notion of "the political." The British political philosopher Bernard Crick, for example, complained in *In Defense of Politics* that the liberal "likes to honor the fruit but not see the tree; he wishes to pluck each fruit—representative government, economic prosperity, and free or general education, etc.—and then preserve them from further contact with politics. He may treat certain things as natural rights—thus by definition outside of politics—or he may think that politics is simply the acts of political parties and politicians—thus narrowing the scope of politics drastically and unrealistically."[71] Excessively nervous about state intervention in the economy or religious practice, zealous about guarding private rights against the common good, anxious about restricting public power in the name of personal freedom, the liberal often understands only limits to politics and not the positive effects of politics themselves. Rather than positing a substantive notion of the good life to be realized through politics, he assigns the pursuit of happiness to individuals in their capacities as private persons (as "men" rather than "citizens"). Politics is often reduced to procedural safeguards for rights that are construed as prepolitical rather than understood as a good in itself. Meaning cannot be found in or generated by a common political project but rather in the motley variety of different projects pursued in civil society. Like the technocrat—and here the utilitarian strand in the liberal tradition identified most clearly with Jeremy

Bentham is exemplary—the liberal sometimes wishes to substitute enlightened administration for the messiness of political life. Or more frequently he falls back on the power of market mechanisms or social conformism to provide the stability that political action failed to create.[72]

THE POLITICAL AS GOVERNANCE BY THE WISE

These reproaches have accompanied other defenses of "the political" that still privilege domestic over international relations but understand them in a different way from contractualist, individualist, rights-protecting liberalism. These alternatives are skeptical of the fiction of a prepolitical state of nature in which individuals, tacitly understood along the lines of *Homo economicus,* band together to create the polity through a contractual alienation of their individual autonomy in order to safeguard their security or guarantee their rights. Instead, they draw on the classical tradition that sees humans more as *zoon politikon,* inherently communal and thus political animals. We may, however, usefully distinguish between two fundamentally different versions of the classical political tradition, that descending from Plato's political treatise *The Republic* (and his other dialogues *The Laws, The Statesman,* and *Gorgias*)[73] and that based on the actual Roman Republic, whose supposed founding by refugees from the Trojan War is told in Virgil's *Aeneid*. It is the latter, more friendly to Ciceronian rhetoric than dialectical reason, that has more often been accorded pride of place in the republican tradition, but both left a powerful legacy.

Although Plato has sometimes been called "the father of Western political thought," in certain respects his legacy can paradoxically be seen as antipolitical, at least if one understands it in the terms of the other republican tradition. But insofar as it generated an influential understanding of "the political" as the art of wise governance, it cannot be ignored. Writing when the Athenian polis was on the decline and seeking to establish the superiority of the philosopher with his rational dialectic over the rhetorical evasiveness of the Sophists, Plato developed a singular model of the good political order ruled by men of distinction.[74] They would be able to do what the divine creator had done in fashioning the world, following an ideal model, harmonious, balanced, and ordered.

The essence of "the political" for Plato, we might say, was enlightened, disinterested rulership, which would be able to tame the passions and reconcile the warring interests of the unruly mass of people. Their disparate and uninformed opinions—the mere *doxa* of the marketplace—would be straightened out, made orthodox, by benevolent guardians who knew how to steer the ship of state on a steady course, in his telling metaphor.[75] The exemplary guardian was a *sophos,* a wise man, who ruled over an "ideocracy," in which human laws were fashioned by dialectical science from the eternal ideal forms. Or he might be a member of a nobility of like-minded rulers, who identified themselves with the state rather than its populace. Although a "republic" in the English translation of the original Greek, πολιτεία (*politeia*), Plato's state could just as easily be ruled by a king or aristocracy as by leading common citizens. According to Sheldon Wolin, "Plato understood *political* philosophy to mean knowledge pertaining to the good life at the public level and *political* ruling to be the right management of the public affairs of the community," but the actual messy and undisciplined politics of the actual world was "evil, and hence the task of philosophy and of ruling was to rid the community of politics."[76]

If there is any privileged political space in the Platonic worldview, it is not the agora but the academy, in which a small number of philosophers can gather and decide on what is best for the rest of the citizenry. The model of politics for Plato, as Arendt argued, is thus making rather than acting, man as *Homo faber* rather than as agent or participant in a public sphere of words and deeds. For all his hostility to the illusions of art and the deceptions of mere appearance, Plato's version of the lawgiver is thus not all that far from the artist who fashions his work out of the unformed, raw materials in front of him.

Not surprisingly, Plato's utopian version of "the political" has often been taxed with spawning authoritarian or even totalitarian politics, with his popularity during the Third Reich taken as evidence for this claim.[77] It has been seen as a betrayal of the more complex legacy of Socrates, whose death at the hands of an ungrateful city has been seen as the beginning of the split between philosophy and politics.[78] Rather than a dialogic exchange of opinions in which the better argument won out over the weaker through persuasion, a victory that was always provisional and open to further revision, Platonic rationality was based on deductive demonstration producing a single right answer that rendered future discussion otiose. Theory thus guided practice rather than learning from it.

Read somewhat more generously, Plato could be understood as the inspiration for a benign elitism, the rule of philosopher-kings, who really do try to rule wisely and moderately and are a check against the irrationalism of the masses and the demagogues who exploit it. Translated into the modern vocabulary of technocracy, which to be sure Plato did not embrace, they were benevolent administrators, who governed according to the principles of scientific management. As we will see, the claim that some falsehoods are permissible as well-intentioned "noble lies" derives from this more positive version of the Platonic legacy, which believed that truth and certainty are obtainable, the Good is universal for all men, unchanging nature rather than variable history provides a standard for the Good, and passive obedience is preferable to active participation for most citizens.

Leo Strauss and his followers are often credited with—or blamed for—reviving this tradition in the twentieth century, although debate still swirls around their reading of its implications.[79] Scorning hedonistic modernity and historicist relativism, they seek in the Platonic legacy a fixed norm for all political life. Strauss did not shy away from repudiating the democratic model of the Athenian polis in favor of one that would better foster the contemplative philosophical life, which he claimed was man's highest goal, at least for the chosen few. "The severest indictment of democracy that ever was written," he noted approvingly in his seminal essay "What Is Political Philosophy?" "occurs in the eighth book of Plato's *Republic*. . . . The classics rejected democracy because they thought the aim of human life, and hence of social life, is not freedom but virtue. Freedom as a goal is ambiguous, because it is freedom for evil as well as for good."[80] Because virtue had to be taught through the education of character, and such an education could only be enabled by the leisure brought by wealth, an aristocracy—"the rule of the best"[81]—was preferable to popular rule.

THE POLITICAL AS REPUBLICAN VIRTUE

In contrast, the so-called republican tradition, which we have already encountered in connection with Machiavelli and which includes later figures like James Harrington, Algernon Sydney, and Rousseau, is usually understood to celebrate the role of the active citizen able to leave behind his or her petty interests and selflessly serve the whole. Understood in terms of the celebrated contrast between ancient and modern liberty posited by the nineteenth-century French liberal Benjamin Constant, it resurrects the classical ideal of "active participation in collective power rather than in the peaceful enjoyment of individual independence. . . . The exercise of the rights of citizenship represented the occupation and, so to speak, the amusement of all."[82] Although lacking an appreciation of what the moderns had called civil liberties as guarantees against the tyranny of the state, it had flourished in small states where everyone might rule. The primary value of republicanism, according to Philip Pettit's influential recent reading, is freedom as "non-domination" by the will of others, which goes beyond the liberal notion of noninterference in one's affairs because it implies a positive acceptance of the rule of self-imposed laws.[83] In line with its descent from the Latin *res publica,* the "public thing" that was distinguished from private, familial life in ancient Rome, it rejects the model of vertical rulership, typical of the patriarchal family, in favor of a more egalitarian ideal of common citizenship in a free state or perhaps even a smaller entity like the polis. Whereas the former is more unitarian in inclination, based on the single family unity, the latter acknowledges the pluralism of different viewpoints within a community. It eschews what Arendt called the coercive potential in the Platonic "tyranny of reason."[84]

As Claude Lefort noted with reference to Machiavelli's contribution to this anti-Platonic republicanism: "There is a fundamental opposition between two forms of government: the government of a *single one*—a prince whose power is limited, a tyrant, or a despot—

and the Republic. . . . Machiavelli is abandoning the idea of a harmonious society, one governed by the best, whose constitution would be conceived as a way of warding off the dangers of innovations and would proceed from the knowledge of the ultimate ends of man and of the city."[85] Not surprisingly, defenders of the Platonic tradition like Strauss could claim that although Machiavelli may have sought the revival of classical *virtù*, it was precisely his rejection of the ideal of the one good political order based on philosophical wisdom that led him to undermine the moderation of the ancient authors. Others found that rejection to be the beginning of a genuinely modern politics that understood the impossibility of resurrecting the discredited ideal of a universally valid natural telos waiting to be discovered by the wise philosopher.

Often honoring the code of civic humanism generated in Florence and other Renaissance city-states, republicanism supports a view of patriotic virtue that transcends narrow personal advantage.[86] As Montesquieu contended in his celebrated discussion of the spirit of the laws, virtue, the ruling principle of republics, is derived from a love of equality, whereas honor, which rules monarchies, comes from a love of distinction (fear, the dominant principle of despotisms, implicitly derives from the desire for security). The republican image of man is not of an isolated, anxious, self-regarding *Homo economicus*, maximizing profit and minimizing loss, but Aristotle's other-regarding *zoon politikon*, belonging to a larger community and willing to sacrifice personal gain for the public good. Republicanism thus often—but not always, as shown by the cases of Harrington and Sydney—culminates in democratic (or at least populist) calls for the sovereignty of "the people" rather than exalting the state, and stresses the value of universal participation and equality of all citizens before the law.

At times the ideology of republican equality could, of course, translate into the more limited participation of only those with sufficient personal means and leisure to engage in the public business of the polity, a privilege that slaveholding had afforded to the (male) citizens of the classical polis. Machiavelli had no hesitation, for example, about defending state secrets, the *arcana imperii*, against the prying eyes of still immature multitudes. But the republican ideal was generally increased inclusiveness. For republicans, rulers and ruled did not constitute separate groups in a natural hierarchy, as in Plato. Here the implied notion of "the political" entails seeking as wide a consensus as possible about what the public good actually might be, combined with a belief that "acting in concert," to use Arendt's definition of power (derived from Burke), is preferable to an antagonistic, or even agonistic, struggle without end.[87] Pluralism does not mean eternal adversarial incommensurability; what Arendt called an "enlarged mentality" suggested incorporating as many viewpoints as possible, even if total consensus may always be impossible. Permanent factions are nonetheless to be avoided in the name of the general good (and the no less general will that can discern and seek to implement it).

The republican exaltation of public service may at times be coupled with a diminution of probity in the private realm. As David Hume noted in his essay "That Politics May be Reduced to a Science," citing the Roman Republic during the Punic Wars, "The ages of greatest public spirit are not always most eminent for private virtue. Good laws may beget order and moderation in the government, where the manners and customs have instilled little humanity or justice into the tempers of men."[88] Conversely, private rectitude may not always inform the actions of the wise or at least effective political leader. For what constitutes political virtue in a statesman may be very different from the moral virtue of the good man or woman. Underlying the republican tradition, it is sometimes conjectured, can be found a secularized version of the religious practice of sacrifice for the solidarity of the community, an inference that is strengthened when one considers its frequent advocacy of a concocted "civic religion" (as Rousseau called it) to cement feelings of group fusion and inspire the willingness to serve a higher good. What might have to be sacrificed is the moral rectitude of the private man, who chooses to get his hands dirty for the good of the whole.

The republican tradition's belief in popular sovereignty may also have the potential to posit a single general good embodied in a single institution, sometimes understood as a vanguard party or even an individual leader. Disappointed by the indirect rule of representative government, it may call for more direct democracy in the form of councils of active citizens, which at the extreme seeks a full isonomy, in which rulers and ruled are identical. Impatient with the intermittent participation of voters at elections, who then leave the real decisions to their elected representatives, it may demand constant involvement with the business of self-government through such institutions as town meetings or, in larger communities, plebiscites affirming the popular will. Even in a more liberal democratic society, it may thus abet the tyranny of the majority, who disdain the rights of recalcitrant minorities. That is, the ghost of Plato's ideal of monologic rulership by the wise guardians may still haunt the more pluralist and egalitarian version identified with Machiavelli and the Renaissance tradition of civic humanism, even if it is collective will rather than singular reason that is the justification for the tyranny. The "soft" coercion of what Foucault famously called "governmentality," in which direct state control through legal constraints and punishments was replaced by a more subtle use of incentives and pressures to induce correct conduct, could be understood as coercive nonetheless.[89]

This threat has led other nonliberal interpreters of "the political," who also remain convinced of the primacy of domestic over foreign affairs, to seek safeguards against its abuse. A salient example is the defense of pluralist, deliberative democracy based on communicative power emerging out of civil society rather than located entirely in the state, a defense most effectively mounted by the second generation Frankfurt School theorist Jürgen Habermas.[90] "The political" may be too Schmittian, too essentializing, a locution for Habermas's more analytic inclinations, which lead him to spurn any attempt to posit the inherent "nature" of politics.[91] But he has nonetheless provided a powerful analysis of the ways in which politics—at least as a counterfactual norm—depends in the modern world on a combination of organized and unorganized deliberations about the laws and institutions of a society. The former takes place in governmental bodies like parliaments and legislatures, the latter in a more diffuse public sphere of opinion and argumentation (or as he ultimately conceded, in a variety of different and distinct public spheres). In both cases, the operative source of political power—or to be more precise, justified political authority—is the discursive

force of the better argument in an uncoerced intersubjective interaction (Weber's rational-legal, as opposed to traditional or charismatic authority, with rational understood in terms of communicative rather than instrumental reason).

Although acknowledging with regret that in the modern world
the rational-critical public sphere has been overwhelmed by manipulative mass communication, Habermas held on to the belief that
only a collective will formed by the persuasiveness of the better
argument could be called genuinely legitimate. While Habermas
clearly took much from the republican tradition—liberals like Rawls
worried that he was, in fact, too indebted to the idealization of the
political by civic humanists[92]—he insisted that the Greek polis could
no longer be a model for modern societies and claimed that Rousseau's ideal of a uniform general will could lead to plebiscitarian
coercion. As Seyla Benhabib notes, for Habermas,

> public space is not understood *agonistically* as a space of com-
> petition for acclaim and immortality among a political elite; it is
> viewed democratically as the creation of procedures whereby
> those affected by general social norms and by collective political
> decisions can have a say in their formulation, stipulation and
> adoption. This conception of the public is also different than the
> liberal one; for although Habermas and liberal thinkers believe
> that legitimation in a democratic society can only result from a
> public dialogue, in the Habermasian model this dialogue does
> not stand under the constraint of neutrality, but is judged ac-
> cording to the criteria represented by the idea of a "practical
> discourse."[93]

Although Habermas also recognized the importance of administrative, bureaucratic rationality—more instrumental and strategic
than communicative—in the political realm, as well as the inevitable
role of compromise when differences can't be bridged, he advocated
an increase in mutual understanding and consensus building without the stifling of pluralist difference.[94] The importance of language
in his argument is paramount. The awkward term "linguistification"
implies that what was previously an unreflected practice or belief,
followed out of tradition or unquestioned prejudice, can become

available for discursive adjudication, which can then lead to self-conscious political change. Not surprisingly, truthfulness is among the general premises of a successful mutual understanding, in politics as everywhere else. "Agreement," Habermas writes in his seminal essay "What Is Universal Pragmatics?" "is based on recognition of the corresponding validity claims of comprehensibility, truth, truthfulness, and rightness."[95]

THE POLITICAL AS THE AESTHETIC

All these versions of "the political"—existential antagonism between friend and foe; agonism in a nonlethal, diplomatic dance of shifting alliances and rivalries; compacts or contracts based on trust and mutual benefit; the benign rule of rational philosopher-kings, self-sacrificing virtue for the good of the whole; and the deliberative procedures of the pluralist public sphere(s)—claim to identify an essential core that sets political life more or less apart from other modes of human behavior. But, ironically, they do so by smuggling in covert metaphors that define it in largely external terms: the political is like war, the political is like polite diplomacy, the political is like a private contractual agreement, the political is like a patriarchal family or a ship needing a captain, the political is like the religious sacrifice of the self for the greater good, or the political is like a disinterested scholarly conference devoted to rational argument. We will return to the implications of this metaphoric displacement of meaning when we look at the boundary question later in this chapter. But let me conclude this section by examining a final version of the essence of "the political," which we can call the aesthetic, which is even more explicitly metaphoric.

According to some commentators, the full "aestheticization of politics," to use Walter Benjamin's familiar phrase, was a relatively new phenomenon in the modern era, although anticipations can be found in the baroque spectacle of the absolutist monarchies of early modern Europe and even the bread and circuses of imperial Rome. Benjamin himself identified it with twentieth-century fascism and saw it as the deadly realization of the anti-ethical maxim of "art-for-art's-sake": "fiat ars, pereat mundus."[96] For the historian

Carl Schorske, who identified its role in undermining a discredited liberal, rational politics in the fin-de-siècle Vienna of Georg von Schönerer, Karl Lueger, and Theodor Herzl, it was "politics in a new key,"[97] one of demagogic irrationalism and mindless ritual. Many commentators bemoaned its ascendancy as an aberration or corruption of rational politics, for example in the following passage from the political theorist Murray Edelman's *From Art to Politics:* "The presentation of politics as a form of aesthetics includes the deliberate or unwitting use of symbols and rituals in political processes that obscure their roles in allocating values, and it enhances the ability of officials to influence and dominate the public. The prominent reliance upon spectacle, ritual, and symbol in the Third Reich is the prototypical case, but the practice is pervasive in democratic states as well."[98]

From this perspective, the collapse of the distinction between politics and aesthetics, the claim that "the political" is the making of a polity that is like a work of art or the judgment of that work in purely formal terms, is often understood to entail the sacrifice of the ethical. At its worst, so its critics charge, it allows the cloaking of violence in the garb of beauty. A frequently cited example is the infamous remark made by the Symbolist poet Laurent Tailhade after a bomb was thrown into the French Chamber of Deputies by the anarchist Auguste Vaillant in 1893: "What do the victims matter, if the gesture is beautiful."[99] Here the chilling indifference to moral concerns that marked "art for art's sake" at its most self-absorbed is transferred to the political realm, in which the imposition of beautiful form becomes more important than the human suffering that is its raw material. To privilege the aesthetic, its critics argue, is to ignore the material basis of all human life, including the political (a charge often made in particular by Marxist critics like Benjamin). It is to make politics into an end in itself, along the lines of "l'art pour l'art" anti-instrumentalism. Accordingly, anti-ethical theorists like Carl Schmitt have been accused of smuggling in an essentially aesthetic notion of "the political," despite their ardent denials of that claim.[100]

The univocal meaning of aestheticized politics, however, has never been satisfactorily settled.[101] Has it preserved or even strengthened the boundaries between "the political" and its others, or has it subverted them? One recent commentator, the political theorist Judith Squires, has claimed that postmodern approaches to politics "have tended to adopt non-topographical conceptions which are dynamic and fluid. Rather than focusing on institutions, these perspectives have highlighted discursive, linguistic, psychological and performative moments of political action. On this schema, the political is neither procedural, hermeneutic nor expressive, it is aesthetic."[102] But others have seen it as shielding the political from moral or instrumental considerations, thus reinforcing its boundaries. For them, conflating politics and art means protecting it against its becoming a mere function of some ulterior purpose, such as welfare or justice.

But even before the question of its complicity with a transferable "thing" or boundaried "domain" version of "the political" is raised, it is first necessary to sort out all the meanings that have been assigned to the metaphor itself. Several alternative interpretations have been in competition, not all of which produce the negative evaluation mentioned above. One way in which "the political" has been understood in aesthetic terms concerns the ideal of integral form, often understood according to organic models of meaningful wholeness. Whether in terms of classical models of order, balance, and harmony, or in those of the dynamic, jagged, but still holistic alternative implied by the Romantic cult of the fragment or ruin, the ideal of organic form as a way to conceptualize "the political" has been a frequent temptation. The time-honored metaphor of the "body politic," introduced by the Greeks and given its most elaborate articulation in John of Salisbury's *Metalogicon* in 1159, combined biological and aesthetic metaphors to provide a vision of the political as functional interdependence among hierarchically arranged organs. The image of the harmonious body, normally, but not always, gendered male and virile, lent itself to many different visual interpretations, but it served for a long time as a way to differentiate the "healthy" polity from the "sick" one.[103]

Even after hierarchical organic models lost their allure, the utopian belief in an "aesthetic state" in which beautiful form would harmonize what rational persuasion could not remained an intoxicating desire for many intellectuals, such as Friedrich Schiller.[104] It has, to be sure, also stimulated no less anxiety among others because of the implicit violence in the imposition of beautiful form on the messiness of political life, producing only an ideological simulacrum of real reconciliation.[105] For these critics, understanding "the political" in terms of fashioning a beautiful aesthetic state risks a soft version of the hegemonic control of otherness and difference countenanced by philosophies like Idealism, in which a metasubject is the genetic totalizer of the whole.

For commentators like Arendt, who favor a performative model of politics based on speech and action, the making of a polity that is like a beautiful artifact wrongly privileges an image of man as *Homo faber*.[106] By failing to distinguish what Aristotle called *poiesis* from *praxis*,[107] it introduces the logics of objectification, reification, exchange, and commodification into the political arena, where the only enduring residue is the glory and fame of those whose great deeds are worth remembering. Politics is a performing art, Arendt argues, not one that creates enduring objects.[108]

Rather than stressing the closed and finished work of art, the version of aesthetic politics that Arendt prefers draws on the dramatic quality of political action, which has been evident ever since the ancient Greeks wrote tragedies with political themes and Plato compared politics and the theater in the *Laws* (817b). It is not by chance that the verb "to play" is as easily applied to the political arena as to the theatrical, both of which are performative in nature. Inherent conflict, heroic protagonists and their villainous rivals, moments of crisis, ironic reversals, resolutions of one sort or another—all of these are shared by theatrical and political performances, which are often judged by spectators, actual or historical, in similar terms. From their point of view, the drama they recount can be seen as comic, tragic, melodramatic, satirical, or even as an example of the theater of the absurd. Like the historical narratives that are so often mobilized as a rationale for political action, they can be understood as expressing a finite number of tropological emplotments that recur again and again, albeit with infinite variations.[109]

Moreover, if elevating drama can descend into lurid spectacle and clear conflicts of principle or character be replaced by titillating entertainment, so too politics can become an exercise in mind-numbing distraction, even for those whose fates are decided by its impact on their lives. As the nineteenth-century British political observer Walter Bagehot noted in his celebrated study *The English Constitution*, "The mass of the English people yield a deference rather to something else than to their rulers. They defer to what we may call the *theatrical show* of society. A certain state passes before them; a certain pomp of great men; a certain spectacle of beautiful women; a wonderful scene of wealth and enjoyment is displayed, and they are coerced by it."[110]

In *The Human Condition*, Arendt also notes that theatrical action and political action are closely related, even in nondeferential democracies. The former, she contends, is itself an imitation of action and speech in the real world, revealing the character of those who act and speak, which is then rendered more meaningful by being reenacted again and again on the stage: "Only the actors and speakers who re-enact the story's plot can convey the full meaning, not so much of the story, but of the "heroes" who reveal themselves in it.... This is also why the theater is the political art par excellence; only there is the political sphere of human life transposed into art. By the same token, it is the only art whose sole subject is man in his relationship to others."[111] Those relationships, she further claims, can be both agonistic and collaborative. They can involve a struggle for greatness or glory, even for the immortality inevitably denied the anonymous common man, an immortality achievable only by the true hero. That struggle takes place in full view of spectators who know how to judge and memorialize it. Unlike Plato, who reviled both appearances and opinions, those who are really political value *doxa,* which "means not only opinion but also splendor and fame. As such, it is related to the political realm, which is the public sphere in which everyone can appear and show who he himself is."[112]

But if aesthetic politics is often a struggle for individual glory, it can be collaborative as well. "Acting in concert," to repeat Arendt's definition of power, may have as much aesthetic value—think of an orchestra playing together or a dance ensemble—as an antagonistic, or even agonal, struggle without end. It can draw on the solidaristic spirit of communitarianism against the self-regarding competitiveness of both the marketplace and the heroic narratives of individual fame. In fact, the Greeks, Arendt noted, may have been too competitive at times: "In this agonal spirit, which eventually was to bring the Greek city-states to ruin because it made alliances between them well-nigh impossible and poisoned the domestic life of the citizens with envy and mutual hatred (envy was the national vice of ancient Greece), the commonweal was constantly threatened."[113]

Nonetheless, for Arendt, "the political" at its best was realized in the Greek polis, whose spatial limits were a function as much of intersubjective interaction as of geographic locale: "The *polis*, properly speaking, is not the city-state in its physical location; it is the organization of the people as it arises out of acting and speaking together, and its true space lies between people living together for this purpose, no matter where they happen to be."[114] Because the space between players should be maintained rather than reduced, the political is always a game with many participants, a pluralist dialogue rather than the monologic unity that can be located in the interiority of the thinker. It is for Arendt, as Sheldon Wolin put it, "a mode of experience rather than a comprehensive institution such as the state. . . . The nature of the political is that it requires renewal. It is renewed not by unique deeds whose excellence sets some beings apart from others, but by rediscovering the common being of human beings. The political is based on this possibility of commonality: our common capacity to share, to share memories and a common fate."[115] Contrary to Schmitt, the essence of the political is not sovereign decision making based on the ingathering of power to one point of maximum strength: "If it were true that sovereignty and freedom are the same, then indeed no man would be free, because sovereignty, the ideal of uncompromising self-sufficiency and mastership, is contradictory to the very condition of plurality."[116]

The French post-Marxist theorist Jacques Rancière comes to similar conclusions in his recent book *The Politics of Aesthetics*. Noting that both theater and politics are visible practices carried out in public, he contrasts aesthetic politics with the philosophical hostility to the arts and democracy expressed by Plato: "From the Platonic point of view, the stage, which is simultaneously a locus of public activity and the exhibition-space for 'fantasies,' disturbs the clear partition of identities, activities, and spaces."[117] Like writing in general, which also resisted Plato's hope for organization and order, the theater is a model of sensually mediated excess, which cannot be brought under control. "This aesthetic regime of politics," Rancière adds, "is strictly identical with the regime of democracy, the regime based on the assembly of artisans, inviolable written laws, and the theatre as institution. Plato contrasts a third, good *form of art* with writing and the theatre, the *choreographic* form of the community that sings and dances its own proper unity."[118]

There are, to be sure, no less obvious differences between dramatic and political play which make the precise parallel difficult. For example, who is an actor and who a spectator is usually clearer in the theater than in politics, which can sweep all present into its drama, either as makers of history or its victims. In her last work on the implications of Kant's Third Critique for political judgment, Arendt herself struggled with the distinction between the actor on the political stage and the spectator judging the action from afar.[119] The political judgment of the latter, she argued, was similar to what Kant had called the "reflective" rather than "determinant" judgment of aesthetic taste. Instead of subsuming cases under general rules, cognitive or moral, it judged according to paradigms and analogies. But how this post facto judgment then informed the activity of the players whose actions were judged was never clear.

Moreover, as the conceptual historian Kari Palonen has noted, pure politics "is a kind of play without a pre-written manuscript, without a director, without fixed roles for the actors, who also contest with each other as regards the style of the play."[120] Thus, although Marx may have been on to something when he saw a pattern in certain instances of displaced historical repetition, "the first time as tragedy, the second as farce,"[121] *Hamlet* is always a tragedy each time it is performed, the roles are set, and the outcome foreordained. Improvisation is an occasional option in the theater; in politics it is the name of the game. The same contrast can be drawn between choreographed dance or composed music and the freer forms of political life.

It is also crucial to recognize, as Marx's statement suggests, that the genre of dramatic action that might be analogized to politics can vary widely. Tragedy, after all, has very different implications from comedy, which is not the same thing as melodrama or satire. At times each of these has seemed like the most essential form taken by "the political." It may also be useful, as the historian Michael Steinberg has suggested, to draw a terminological distinction between drama and theater rather than conflate them. In his study of the post–World War I Salzburg Festival, a monthlong musical event organized by Hugo von Hofmannstahl, he defines the difference in this way: "[Theatricality] can be said to suggest a closed system of ideas and representations; [drama] an open one. The first presents a coherent tableau in which problems of theme and plot are solved according to a predetermined set of ethical principles (the morality play is a prime example); the second presents conflict and tension that are irresolvable, even if the plot of the drama resolves itself."[122] Thus, to say that politics is theatrical implies a mystifying and ideological resolution of underlying and intractable dramatic conflicts, which is precisely the argument Steinberg makes about the function of the Salzburg Festival's ideology of the baroque as a way to paper over the crisis of the collapse of the Habsburg Empire.

The controversy over the implications of a politics modeled on aesthetic ideals of organic wholeness has lost some of its heat of late, as a different way of conceptualizing the link between the political and the aesthetic has come to the fore. In the work of a disparate group of political theorists—Claude Lefort, Pierre Rosenvallon, Jacques Rancière in France,[123] and Frank R. Ankersmit in the Netherlands, to name the most prominent—the aesthetic (or at least symbolic) quality of the political has been valorized in new ways. They trace their lineage back to several sources. One is a certain French tradition of liberalism, which set itself against the republicanism of Rousseau but was also hostile to the contractualist, economically oriented individualism of the utilitarian British tradition. Among its heroes are François Guizot, Pierre Royer-Collard, and the same Benjamin Constant we have already encountered as a critic of Kant's deontological critique of mendacity. They hark back to an even earlier figure, who was the subject of Lefort's longest study, Machiavelli.[124] For Lefort, the Republic supported by Machiavelli is opposed to a "government of a *single one*—a prince whose power is limited, a tyrant, or a despot. . . . Machiavelli is abandoning the idea of a harmonious society, one governed by the best. . . . No one has authority to decide the affairs of all, that is to say, to occupy the site of power."[125] Ankersmit echoes this appraisal in his 1996 *Aesthetic Politics*, where he goes beyond Lefort's stress on the symbolic nature of "the political" to stress its frankly aesthetic character. He notes, however, that the German tradition from Schiller to Marcuse limned in Josef Chytry's book on the "aesthetic state" is not the one he supports: "The kind of aesthetic political philosophy proposed here is . . . diametrically opposed to the German one, since aesthetics is invoked here not in order to argue for the *unity* but precisely for the *brokenness* of the political domain. The hero of this study is therefore not Schiller but Machiavelli, since the latter . . . gave us the first, and till this day the most forceful defense of the thesis of the brokenness of political reality."[126] To understand the idea of the "brokenness" of "the political" not as a problem to be solved but as a virtue to be honored, it is first necessary to make clear the role of totalitarianism as a cautionary example in the theorizing of these thinkers. From their point of view, Stalinism and fascism did not represent the primacy of "the political," but rather its antithesis. Because of the desire to politicize the totality of human relations and overcome the gap between state and civil society, public and private life, totalitarianism coercively overcame the barrier that allowed the political to thrive in its own domain. It was further characterized by a dangerous fantasy of overcoming all internal divisions within the whole, rendering it totally coherent, transparent, and controllable. Instead of accepting the inevitability of conflict and pluralism, totalitarianism forced conformity to a single, monolithic vision of virtuous unity achieved by ruthless bureaucratic organization from above backed by violent coercion. As Lefort, who exhaustively analyzed the phenomenon over his long career, put it, "At the foundation of totalitarianism lies the representation of the People-as-One. It is denied that division is constitutive of society."[127] If there is any split in the totalitarian imaginary, it is between the allegedly united internal community and an external enemy, a demonized and malevolent other.

Praising conflict within the domestic political community did not, however, mean for these thinkers reducing "the political" to an antagonistic Schmittian friend-foe existential struggle to the death. As Ankersmit put it,

> Where Machiavelli shows how to cope with the enmities and the brokenness of political reality, these enmities and brokenness had become a foundational principle for Schmitt. And this is a crucial difference. For where Machiavelli's position invites us to think how best to *deal* in a practical way with these unpleasant but inevitable aspects of political reality, Schmitt's Hobbesianism requires him to construct a political reality that is effectively *founded* on enmity and brokenness, thereby transforming enmity and brokenness into metaphysical principles.[128]

Even if their alternative did mean a certain skepticism toward a Habermasian version of political consent via communicative rationality,[129] they were careful to avoid privileging dissensus as an end in itself.

Rather than focusing on the competitive nature of political action, or reducing it to a struggle for power in the manner of, say, Michel Foucault,[130] they stressed its symbolic kernel, which they interpreted in terms largely derived from the work of the great medieval historian Ernst Kantorowicz (with an occasional nod to the distinction between the Imaginary and the Symbolic in the psychoanalytic theory of Jacques Lacan). In his classic study of medieval theology and politics, *The King's Two Bodies,* Kantorowicz had argued that the ancient idea of the body politic had to be modified to take into account the impact of the Christian doctrine of the Incarnation.[131] The double natures of Christ, both God and man, and the Eucharist, which embodies that same duality, were transferred to the monarch, whose body was at once mortal and immortal, temporal and eternal. Through the consecration of his mortal body at his coronation, which bestowed grace on him, the ruler assumed the powers of the undying institution of kingship. Like Christ, he had both a creaturely and a mystical body. Individual kings might die, but "the king" remained alive. "Le Roi est mort; vive le Roi." Ultimate power resides in the invisible body that never dies, rather than the visible one that does. A phantasmatic expression of the unity of the polity, the king's immortal body is a symbolic reality that always has a complicated relationship with its empirical double. The former is both the source of the latter's power and the limit on its absolute will. The mortal king is at once above and below "himself," the father and the son of the laws and justice, the ruler who makes the rules and their servant. In the Latin phrase from the *Liber Augustalis*, written for the Kingdom of Sicily during the reign of Frederick II in 1231, which Kantorowicz calls the founding document of the modern administrative state and Lefort cites approvingly, he is "major et minor se ipso," large and small in himself.

Carl Schmitt's version of political theology, it will be recalled, stressed the immanent power of a ruler whose will trumped any legal constraints on him.[132] Like the omnipotent God of the nominalists, who was beholden to no rational or legal constraints, even those of his own making, the sovereign for Schmitt was totally unlimited by the law. He was the embodiment of real presence in the political arena, the sovereign decider in states of emergency. Kantorowicz, in contrast, posited a transcendent institution above and beyond the actual king who occupied the throne. Invoking the medieval corporatists with their belief in a higher sacred body that is an absent but still powerful political force, he stressed the undecidability inherent in the two bodies of the king which were never perfectly fused into one.[133]

Often the arrival of a modern, fully secularized version of political authority is understood to mean the end of the king's two bodies metaphor. Charles Taylor, for example, asserts that "a doctrine like the King's Two Bodies becomes bizarre nonsense in the uniform, secular time of modernity."[134] In the case of Rousseau, as Habermas noted, the ideal of direct democracy, in which representation of any kind was anathema, meant that the sovereign had to be actually present: "The *volonté générale* as the *corpus mysticum* was bound up with the *corpus mysticum* of the people as consensual assembly. The idea of a plebiscite in permanence presented itself to Rousseau in the image of the Greek *polis*."[135] Lefort himself admits, "I am not unaware of the fact that in the eighteenth century this representation was largely undermined, that new models of sociability emerged as a result of the growth of individualism, progress in the equalization of conditions of which de Tocqueville spoke and the development of the state administration, which tended to make the latter appear as an independent, impersonal entity."[136] However, the residue of the split between symbolic and empirical reality survives the crisis of the ancien régime and Rousseauian fantasies of direct democratic presence: "But the changes that occurred did not entirely eliminate the notion of the kingdom as a unity which was both organic and mystical, of which the monarch was at the same time the body and the head."[137]

Even more fateful was the preservation of the *place* of the mystical body in a representative democratic and republican regime, although it remained vacant. That is, even after the "disincorporation" of individuals in a society lacking a symbolic center, a society in which the distinction between symbolic and real is tacitly acknowledged, the unfilled void is still significant. Although power is no longer derived from a mystical body with real presence in the empirical world, it "appears as an empty place and those who exercise it as mere mortals who occupy it only temporarily or who could install themselves in it only by force or cunning. There is no law that can be fixed, whose articles cannot be contested, whose foundations are not susceptible of being called into question. Lastly, there is no representation of a center and of the contours of society: unity cannot now efface social division."[138] Although something called "the people" will be accounted the fount of sovereign legitimacy in a modern democracy, the empirical embodiment of it is indeterminate and arbitrary, thus preserving the healthy "brokenness" of the political.[139] As Rosenvallon puts it, "There is equivocation, first of all, about the very subject of this democracy, for the people do not exist except through *approximate* successive representations of itself."[140] Or to put it differently, in a more explicitly temporal register, it remains permanently latent, never fully manifest in the actual world. Democracy, as Derrida also often pointed out, is always "to come" (*á venir*) in a future (*avenir*) that will never be fully present.[141]

The radical republican ideal of an isonomy, in which rulers and ruled are one, is, *pace* Arendt, a utopian pipedream. Even a mimetic theory of representation in which those who rule are understood to be like those they represent is mistaken, as the link is entirely arbitrary. There is no mediating higher third or *tertia comparationis*—Ankersmit explicitly denounces that idea as a monistic, realist, and rationalist legacy of Stoicism, still evident in Spinoza and other later thinkers[142]—that subtends the split between representation and represented. It is, in fact, the impossible but dangerous quest of totalitarian regimes, as we have seen Lefort claim, to try via coercion and ideological manipulation to suture the gap and create a "People-as-One, the idea of society as such, bearing the knowledge of itself, transparent to itself and homogeneous, the idea of mass opinion, sovereign and normative, the idea of the tutelary state."[143] Or as Rosenvallon puts it, "It comes down in the end to the attempt to deny and dissimulate the contradictions of the world through the illusory coherence of doctrine. It breaks free of reality in staging a phantasmatic order and in following a path in which clarity is forced."[144] Full transparency and clarity are thus the utopian goals of a nightmare politics, a contention whose implications for the issue of mendacity we will encounter again in our final section.

Expressed in the Lacanian terms that Lefort cautiously embraces, the brokenness of the political expresses the way in which the Symbolic order registers the impossibility of closure and unity, the inevitable gap between signifier and signified, whereas the totalitarian desire for complete immanence in a fully transparent regime evokes the phantasmatic corporeal wholeness of the early Imaginary stage. For Lefort, giving the first category a somewhat more positive spin than Lacan, "The symbolic makes us recognize the instauration of a system in which settled relations among groups and individuals are articulated, and in which shared notions of the real, true, and normal are established. The imaginary makes us understand that the vision of the One is supported by a frantic denial of social division and depends on a phantasm."[145]

Whether or not these psychoanalytic cum linguistic categories can be easily mapped onto political regimes, they help clarify the version of aesthetic politics that we are considering here. They help us see that "the political," especially in its democratic guise, involves a kind of benign fictionality, which no longer really believes its fictions are true, but is also unable or unwilling to give them up entirely. In fact, democracy, Rosenvallon argues, is "a regime of fictionality in a double sense. Sociologically, first, since it involves the symbolic creation of an artificial body of the people. But technically, too, for the development of a rule of law presupposes the 'generalization of the social,' its abstraction as it were, in order to make it governable according to universal rules."[146]

This insight, we have to acknowledge, is not particularly new. It was already enough of a commonplace a century earlier that it could appear in the literature of political disillusionment. In Gustave Flaubert's great novel of dashed hopes in mid-nineteenth-century France, *Sentimental Education*, Charles Deslauriers, the hero's best friend, announces his disappointment with radical politics and embrace of "scientific administration" in the following terms:

> But not a single form of government is legitimate, for all their eternal principles. You see, since *principle* means *origin*, you must always go back to a revolution, an act of violence, some transient event. Thus the principle of our state is national sovereignty, expressed in the form of parliamentary government, although our parliament doesn't agree! But why should the sovereignty of the people be any more sacred than the divine right of kings? They're both of them fictions! Let's have no more metaphysics, no more ghosts.[147]

The symbolic nature of "the political" need not, however, be understood as a mark of its spectral irrationality. As Jacques Rancière contends, "The gap between names and things, whose perversions Thucydides well knew, is precisely what defines the space of political rationality. Thus, democracy is not 'just a word' or an illusion. Rather, it is a disposition of the name and appearance of the people, a way of keeping the people present in their absence."[148] There is always a distance between the word "the people" and its concrete instantiations, and "language bears witness to this: there can be no *arche* corresponding to the *demos* as subject, no way of ruling according to some inaugurating principle; there is only a -*cracy*—a manner of prevailing."[149] A similar argument can be mobilized with regard to other general political concepts, like "the nation," "fatherland," "humanity," or "the universal class," all of which are floating signifiers that can alight on many different alleged representatives.

This means even in a democracy there is a certain limit on the power to determine our political destinies, for as Bernard Flynn puts it in describing Lefort's position, "The political (*le politique*) is not a pure construction of man."[150]

But because it is for all that no less real, it is a mistake to assume, as some nominalists and methodological individualists might, that only the empirical practices and institutions of *la politique* really exist. To draw this conclusion, Lefort argues, would be to substitute for the totalitarian fantasy of an embodied unity the liberal fantasy of particularist diversity in which every general political concept needs to be reduced to its most basic elements. Both fall back on the imaginary notion of wholeness (macro in one case, micro in the other) that the symbolic, rightly understood as valorizing the "brokenness of politics," resists.

If this can be called an aesthetic politics, it is one that draws on, to borrow the terminology of Lacoue-Labarthe and Nancy, "romantic equivocity" rather than the "eidaesthetics" of wholeness, beautiful form, and closure.[151] As a result, advocates like Schmitt of clear-cut divisions between homogeneous communities of friends and foes were its enemies. In his 1919 study *Political Romanticism*, Schmitt had, in fact, fulminated against the indecisiveness and irony of Romantic politics, which fruitlessly yearned after infinity rather than totality.[152] Liberalism, with its fetish of endless discussion was, he argued, the heir of the Romantic tradition, which preferred equivocation to decisive action. As Ankersmit has observed, inadvertently highlighting the issue that concerns us the most, "No wonder that Romantic politics gave Schmitt 'the impression of a lie.'"[153]

With this remark, we have returned to the central question of our exercise: what is the role of mendacity in the realm of politics? Or more precisely, what is the implication of each of the different claimants to the title of "the political" for the question of lying? What can we learn, to reverse the question, about these variants by exploring their affinity or lack thereof to truth-telling? But before addressing these questions, which will occupy us for the remainder of the book, we have to conclude this chapter by exploring the implications of the other great issue raised by the concept of "the political": its boundaries from what is allegedly outside or beyond it.

LIMITS: THE POLITICAL AND ITS OTHERS

How permeable are the boundaries separating "the political" from what is outside its territorial limits, whether we define that putative exterior in moral, legal, technical, economic, social, or aesthetic terms? Are these spaces mutually exclusive, or do they overlap like the circles in a Venn diagram? What are the dangers of going too far in the opposite direction, favoring the view that the political is "a thing" and not "a domain," and thus allowing infinite transferability? Can we efface all boundaries, collapsing the political entirely into the larger ensemble of human relations, call it society or the totality? Is there perhaps a cost to be paid by asserting, in the catchphrase of the 1960s, that "the personal is the political"?[154] Is the radical "deterritorialization" of the political, to borrow a term from Gilles Deleuze and Félix Guattari, necessarily an advance over the restriction of "the political" to its own, proper domain?

To begin to address these questions, we need first to examine what might be called an internal limit or boundary, the categorical distinction between the political and politics, *le politique* and *la politique*. If Mouffe is right, it roughly parallels Heidegger's ontological/ontic opposition, which separates Being from mere beings. These terms themselves, of course, come with a great deal of baggage and have stirred considerable philosophical controversy. As some of Heidegger's critics have warned, bracketing the messiness of impure ontic reality in the search for a more profound level of Being can lead to an indifference, even hostility, to the mundane world in which most of our normal lives are led. Not every action we undertake needs to be performed while contemplating our finitude or motivated by a search for authentic ontological truth. Not every immersion in everyday life is a mark of superficiality or distraction.

Similarly, it may be worth lingering in the impure world of mundane politics before we seek the ultimate reality of "the political," understood as a life-risking high seriousness or a space for the accomplishment of great and immortal deeds or the realization of freedom. Those theories that tacitly turn "the political" into a normative rather than merely descriptive category may be splitting the political world into a hierarchy of noble and ignoble or profound and trivial acts and motives, with the result that much of what passes for politics in our normal understanding of the phenomenon is stigmatized as inherently inferior.

In fact, it may well be acknowledging the creative tension between the two levels, *le politique* and *la politique,* that helps us avoid the biases that so often bedevil discussions of the issues. That is, if we deny that there is an unbridgeable gap between a pure notion of the political—however we define it—and the often grubbier practices and institutions of politics in everyday life, we can avoid some of the more questionable dicta of certain theorists who want to legislate what is genuine and what is fraudulent in the region of human endeavor they are discussing. We can avoid such problematic assertions as Schmitt's claim that liberalism is inherently antipolitical or Badiou's assertion that the state is never the locus of "real" politics. Instead, we can recognize that pollution of "the political" by mere "politics," *le politique* by *la politique,* is far more likely than the unequivocal separation of one from the other.

Nor should we be tempted to pursue the absolute conflation of the two. In fact, to return to the implications of the argument about the king's two bodies that informed the version of aesthetic politics defended by Lefort, Ankersmit, and Rosenvallon, we might say the very distinction between them is a healthy check on the fantasy that the "return of the political" might ever mean a restoration of the normative notion to complete hegemony over its less exalted alternatives. That is, as in the case of popular sovereignty, where the people are never identical with their representations, so too *le politique* remains at some distance—to be sure, historically variable—from *la politique* in all its motley variety.

When we descend from the lofty heights of "the political" as a timeless essence, we may also note that in historical terms the categorical boundary asserted by Aristotle between it and its external others, and then revived by twentieth-century theorists like Schmitt and Arendt, was not very solid to begin with. As the literary historian Michael McKeon has argued, the antithesis between *polis* and *oikos* was itself based on "a confusion of two distinct 'family' categories: the *oikos,* the household of persons and property; and the *genos,* the cult-oriented blood kin or clan. When the tension between ancestral *genos* and emergent *polis* in preclassical Greece is taken to bespeak also a historical estrangement of *polis* from *oikos,* the ongoing correlation of the latter two entities becomes obscured."[155] Before Aristotle imposed a strict opposition in his *Politics,* there was both a metaphoric and metonymic relationship between city-state and household: "The *polis* was conceived and arranged on the model of the family, that is the *oikos,* whose economic management was also seen to be functionally inseparable from the financial relations of the *polis,* or state."[156] Even Aristotle, McKeon points out, admitted an analogical relationship between head of state and head of family. And in the Roman period, both private and public law, family and state, were often inextricably intertwined.

Certainly, in the modern state, it has been rare indeed that the separation of the political and its various others has approached anything that could be called complete. Schmitt himself acknowledged that the politicization of all realms of social life was possible— a prudent admission for an opportunist to make during the Nazi years, when totalitarianism was doing precisely that—although he resisted the reverse process in which the political was invaded by economic or religious values.[157] Even in nontotalitarian societies, efforts to distinguish "the political" categorically from adjacent domains of human practice have had to be fought again and again. As Benhabib has rightly observed,

> For the moderns public space is essentially porous; neither access to it nor its agenda of debate can be predefined by criteria of moral and political homogeneity. With the entry of every new group into the public space of politics after the French and American revolutions, the scope of the public gets extended. . . . The distinction between the "social" and the "political" makes no sense in the modern world, not because all politics has become administration and because the economy has become the quintessential "public," as Hannah Arendt thought, but primarily because the struggle to make something public is a struggle for justice.[158]

Even Mouffe agrees that, contrary to attempts by Schmitt and Arendt to build an impermeable barrier, "every order is the temporary and precarious articulation of contingent practices. The frontier between the social and the political is essentially unstable and requires constant displacements and renegotiations between social agents."[159] Looking at it from the other perspective of the erosion of state sovereignty from the outside in an increasingly globalized world—where nongovernmental organizations proliferate, capital and labor mobility defies attempts at autarky, and issues like climate change know no boundaries—the local place of politics becomes increasingly dissolved into deterritorialized (cyber?) space.

Looking at some of the alleged "others" of "the political" reinforces this conclusion for even earlier periods of history. Take, for example, the relationship between politics and religion or theology. Machiavelli's autonomization of politics, it will be recalled, has often been understood as the rejection of theological constraints on political action, including, of course, those that stigmatize mendacity as sinful. But if we take seriously Schmitt's claim that modern concepts of politics such as the idea of sovereignty are secularized versions of earlier religious notions, then the shadow of the theological can be said still to fall over the political realm.[160] As Pierre Manent has pointed out, when the ancient models of the city-state and the empire ceased to be effective and feudal decentralization was reversed, Europe invented the monarchy, which drew its legitimacy from divine right theory.[161] When it faltered in turn, it was necessary to find a surrogate for religious legitimation, and many political theorists confronted this challenge. For example, Leo Strauss acknowledged that after his early study of Spinoza's *Theologico-Political Treatise*, written from 1925 to 1928, "the theologico-political problem has remained, from that time on, *the* theme of my inquiries."[162] Jacques Derrida would likewise argue that "the fundamental concepts that often permit us to isolate or to *pretend* to isolate the *political* . . . remain religious or in any case theologico-political."[163]

In a recent essay entitled "The Permanence of the Theological-Political," Lefort noted that from the standpoint of political science, which concerns itself only with *la politique*, the modern divorce between religious and political spheres can be acknowledged as objectively true, even if at times their practical entanglement is conceded.[164] But when it comes to political philosophy and *le politique*, such a distinction cannot be maintained, for both religion and the political partake of the symbolic in the ways that have been described above. Insofar as the two bodies of the king can be traced to the dual nature of Christ, even the democratic empty place substituted for the no longer divine king cannot be fully understood without reference to the religious underpinnings of the symbolic order. Although the traditional notion of "real presence" is denied and the gap between symbol and reality is a fundamental tenet of democratic politics, the residual importance of a transcendent point of reference, one that cannot be realized in concrete embodiments, bespeaks the continuing power of the theological origins of "the political."

Even a more resolutely Enlightenment political theorist like Habermas, who denies the prehumanist sources of legitimacy and resists the claim that we live in a "post-secular society," can acknowledge that the content of many of the categories that animate political discourse are ultimately religious in origin. "This work of appropriation," he writes, "crystallized in strongly charged, normative conceptual networks, such as responsibility, autonomy and justification, history and memory, beginning anew, innovation and return, emancipation and fulfillment, externalization, internalization and incorporation, individuality and community. This work indeed transformed the originally religious meaning, but it did not deflate and expend in such a way as to empty it out."[165]

It would, of course, be possible to multiply other examples of the ways in which religion remains interpenetrated with "the political" without their being fully collapsed into each other. But the main point is simply that at least this boundary is relatively porous, even at times when politics seems to be most autonomous. When it comes to the question of lying in politics, it may therefore be impossible to disentangle entirely the religious considerations of the issue from political ones strictly speaking. Paradoxically, to be sure, the results may not necessarily be what one would likely expect. For as Steven Shapin has noted in his *Social History of Truth*, "One sign of a gap between dominant Christian and secular ethical postures in early modern Europe was the contrast between the relatively judicious and temperate attitude toward truth-telling adopted by many theologians and the obsession with the purity of truth-telling manifested in the secular canon. So far as civil society was concerned, the connection of truth-telling with external concepts of honor was evidently more powerful than its link with piety and the imitation of God."[166] But whatever the implication, the point is that in the real world, religious attitudes toward lying are very hard to separate entirely from political ones.

A similar conclusion can be drawn about the attempt to separate politics radically from the legal arena, made by theorists like Schmitt and Arendt. From Schmitt's point of view, it will be recalled, political legitimacy is ultimately more important than legality and cannot be decided by prior legal principles. "Legal indeterminacy" means that there are no higher tribunals than the decision of a judge when it comes to deciding how to interpret the law, and that of a political leader when it comes to carrying it out.[167] Will, in short, trumps reason; legal decisions cannot be made by submitting cases under general rules or by following precedents, nor *a fortiori* can political ones. The executive function of government, where ultimate sovereign power lies, is more fundamental than the legislative; the liberal model of what the nineteenth-century Germans called the *Rechtstaat,* a state circumscribed by the rule of law, is thus inherently antipolitical.

According to Arendt, the mistaken promulgation of legislation as the essence of "the political" derives from the image of man as *Homo faber* rather than political actor: "The Greeks, in distinction from all later developments, did not count legislating among the political activities. . . . To them, the laws, like the wall around the city, were not results of actions but products of making."[168] The Platonic tradition, however, ignored *praxis* in favor of *poiesis,* leading to a mistaken overvaluing of lawmaking ever since. Despite her respect for the American Constitution as the founding document of the political space in which action might take place, a respect absent in Schmitt,[169] Arendt always gave priority to actions over fabrication. Although resisting his emphasis on the sovereign will, which she damned for its monologic indifference to plurality, Arendt shared Schmitt's distrust of the priority of law over action and speech. Against the normative proceduralism of the liberal tradition, she stressed the power to initiate action *ex nihilo,* which she called "natality" and analogized from the birth of new people into the world. Law is necessary, to be sure, to set limits on the arbitrary abuse of power characteristic of totalitarianism, but it is not an engine of political innovation. As James Bohman has remarked, for Arendt, "law is quite limited in its function: it guarantees the equal freedom of all citizens and nothing else. It is not a means to promote greater justice or to compensate for economic disadvantages, such as those of class."[170]

But as in the case of the divide between politics and religion, that between politics and legality reveals itself time and again as less than watertight. As we have noted, Arendt herself acknowledged that constitutional fabrication was the foundation on which stable institutions could be erected that provided the stage on which political theater can take place. The initial act of foundation was itself often in need of renewal, which meant that political action was often aimed at fabrication (e.g., in amending a constitution). Likewise, Schmitt's attempt to make legitimacy inherently prior to legality comes up against the objection that the very notion of legitimacy implies more than just naked power or the bald assertion of a right; it entails the presupposition of that right having a normative force, which in turn implies some principle or rule by which it is endowed with that authority.[171] The sovereign, after all, is not only the one who decides *in* a state of emergency but also the one who has the legitimacy to decide *that* a state of emergency exists. If this formulation is to avoid circularity, it is only if the sovereign is assumed to have some legitimate authority to declare that the state of emergency exists (as in the famous case of Article 48 of the Weimar constitution, which gave that authority to the president).

Virtually any theory of universal and transcendent human rights, moreover, introduces an inevitable limit on the unchecked power of political action, one that requires an appeal to legal safeguards against the tyranny of majorities or elites or single rulers. Even if the appeal to nature is unpersuasive, the rights that have accrued historically—helping to constitute that "world" of institutions, practices, and habits that Arendt saw as the integument of human interaction—are often expressed in the language of legality. And with the proliferation of international bodies that can be seen to constrain the absolute sovereignty of nation-states established by the Peace of Westphalia, the constraints of legality are even felt to at least some extent in the agonistic realm of international relations.

It would be possible to multiply other examples of the porosity of the boundaries that have been erected by theorists between "the political" and its various—and heteroclite—others, such as morality, science, the market, or violence. But having thus called into question the categorical distinctions between both an "ontological" notion of "the political" and an "ontic" notion of politics and "the political" and its other alleged conceptual others, we should not conclude by going to the opposite extreme and claiming that no distinctions at all can be maintained and that "everything is political." Positing the radical deterritorialization of the domain of the political may have its costs, both theoretical and practical. For as Cornelius Castoriadis has noted,

> The gains to be made by calling the overall institution of society "the political" are hard to see, the damages are obvious. Either, in calling "the political" that which everybody would naturally call the institution of society, one merely attempts a change in vocabulary without substantive content . . . or one attempts to preserve in this substitution the connotations linked with the word "political" since its creation by the Greeks, that is, whatever pertains to explicit and at least partially reflective decisions concerning the fate of the collectivity; but then, through a strange reversal, language, economy, religion, representation of the world, family, etc., have to be said to depend upon political decisions in a way that would win the approval of Charles Maurras as well as Pol Pot. "Everything is political" either means nothing, or it means: everything ought to be political, ought to flow from an explicit decision of the Sovereign.[172]

That is, as the totalitarian experiments of the twentieth century made manifestly clear, entirely effacing the boundary between "the political" and its others, demanding that private life be conflated with public, and expecting absolute transparency of citizens who have to reveal their actions, even confess their innermost thoughts, can be a recipe for disaster. As the political theorist Michael Halberstam notes, "Totalitarianism confronts liberalism with the challenge to individual autonomy that the artificial construction of meaning harbors. . . . The distinction between the political and the nonpolitical is undermined where the possibility of an artificial construction of shared meanings is granted."[173] However much the "personal is the political" could be understood as a liberating slogan in the struggle to take seriously the ways in which power relations invade everyday life, it could also function as a license to abolish the protections provided by keeping up the wall, however porous, between personal and political realms. Even if the space of the political—or more precisely, if Lefort is right, the space of the modern political sovereign—is an empty space, which is filled at our peril, it may be wise to maintain the distinction between the void and what surrounds it.

To conclude this chapter with a salient example of the ways in which maintaining that boundary has been a mark of democratic polities, let me refer to a critical passage in the American Constitution. Article I, Section 6 says of senators and representatives: "They shall in all Cases, except Treason, Felony and Breach of the Peace, be privileged from Arrest during their Attendance at the Session of their respective Houses, and in going to and returning from the same; and for any Speech or Debate in either House, they shall not be questioned in any other Place." The purpose of this clause seems to have been to assure unfettered political debate without fear of lawsuits, to effect in other words that separation of the political from the legal whose absolute difference we have seen is so hard to maintain.

It has also had another, perhaps unintended consequence, which the liberal journalist Eric Alterman has noted in his book *When Presidents Lie:* "The result, as in the case of Senator McCarthy, has been the assertion of the right to lie with impunity."[174] That is, when inside the confines of the explicitly political space of Congress, no charge of perjury can be brought against a member of either house. Outsiders testifying in front of Congress can, to be sure, be prosecuted for perjury when speaking under oath. But the oath that politicians take when they assume office is not "to tell the truth, the whole truth, and nothing but the truth," as in a court of law. Swearing to uphold and defend the Constitution is not the same thing, although it is worth noting that the old Protestant suspicion of Catholic casuistry is preserved in the phrase "without any mental reservation" included in oaths taken for public office.[175] When perjury entered the English common law, as it did in 1563, the crime, originally confined to jurors, was extended to witnesses testifying under oath, but not to statements made outside that framework.[176] Attempts to criminalize political lying, at least in the United States, have not been very successful.[177]

The penalty that members of Congress and other politicians may suffer for lying can indeed be severe, but it is a political not legal punishment. And as the case of Bill Clinton's impeachment trial of 1998 shows, a trial in the Senate in which he was acquitted by a vote along party lines, political decisions can trump legal ones even when it comes to convictions for legal perjury in another venue. Not all political activity takes place, of course, within the confines of a privileged space like that of the floor of the American Congress, but in providing that immunity from prosecution for perjury, the Founding Fathers were acknowledging the special nature of political speech. Is mendacity, we now have to ask, implicitly protected by that immunity, broadly speaking? But if it is, does it matter which version of "the political" is in play in deciding the type of mendacious speech to protect? What are the implications of each of our salient versions for affirming or denying the imperative to tell the truth in the political arena, however porous its boundaries? Our final chapter will be devoted to addressing these deeply troubling questions.

3
ON LYING IN POLITICS

POLITICAL PSEUDOLOGY

> Now from the chamber all are gone
> Who gazed and wept o'er Wellington
> Derby and Sis do all they can
> To emulate so great a man.
> If neither can be quite as great,
> Resolved is each to LIE in state.
>
> —WALTER SAVAGE LANDOR, 1852

> In a certain way, "ruling" and "lying" are synonyms. The truth
> of rulers and the truth of servants are different.
>
> —PETER SLOTERDIJK, *CRITIQUE OF CYNICAL REASON*

Despite the recent furor over the apparent increase of lying in politics, the two have long been intimately intertwined. Ever since Machiavellianism was identified with a group simply called the Politiques, they have indeed seemed almost synonymous. Satirists throughout the ages have accordingly found the link an inviting target. To take a typical example, in 1710 Jonathan Swift wrote "An Essay upon the Art of Political Lying" for *The Examiner,* which began by acknowledging the widespread belief that "the Devil is the father of lies." But what is even more important, Swift quickly added, is that "his first essay of it was purely political, employed in undermining the authority of his Prince, and seducing a third part of his subjects from their obedience."[1] Although admitting, with tongue firmly planted in cheek, that "who first reduced lying into an art, and adapted it to politics, is not so clear from history, though I have made some diligent enquires," Swift went on to say that it had been steadily refined in the modern era. Whereas its earliest usage may have been to provide post facto relief for those who lost a rebellion, abetting their posthumous fame through false rumor, "the moderns have made great addition, applying this art to the gaining of power, and preserving it, as well as revenging themselves after they have lost it."[2]

Two years later, the British physician and wit John Arbuthnot published a mock proposal for printing a two-volume "curious discourse" entitled "ΨΕΥΔΟΛΟΓΙΑ ΠΟΛΙΤΙΚΗ; or, A Treatise of The Art of Political Lying, With an Abstract of the First Volume of the said Treatise."[3] Pretending to summarize the arguments of its unnamed author, Arbuthnot produced a lesson in "the sound rules of pseudology," which he defined as "the art of convincing the people of salutary falsehoods, for some good end."[4] After giving several different categories of political lies and tactics for disseminating them most effectively, he cautioned against their excessive use, "glutting the market, and retailing too much of a bad commodity at once: where there is too great a quantity of worms, it is hard to catch grudgeons."[5] To avoid this outcome, an official corporation of liars, exceptionally gifted in their invention and telling, would be useful to manage the level of mendacity permitted in politics. But the antidote to excessive lies, he warned, is not speaking the truth. "The author says that, considering the large extent of the cylindrical surface of the soul, and the great propensity to believe lies in the generality of mankind of late years, he thinks the properest contradiction to a lie is another lie."[6]

In the late nineteenth century, Oscar Wilde joined Mark Twain in lamenting the decay of lying, but doubled the irony when it came to politics. When one of the protagonists in Wilde's dialogue of 1889 announces that he is writing an essay called "The Decay of Lying: An Observation," the other responds, "Lying! I should have thought that our politicians kept up that habit." His friend replies,

I assure you that they do not. They never rise beyond the level of misrepresentation, and actually condescend to prove, to discuss, to argue. How different from the temper of the true liar, with his frank fearless statements, his superb irresponsibility, his healthy, natural disdain of proof of any kind! After all, what is a fine lie? Simply that which is its own evidence. If a man is sufficiently un-imaginative to produce evidence in support of a lie, he might just as well speak the truth at once. No, the politicians won't do.[7]

But for those with a less exalted notion than Wilde of the artistic value of a "fine lie," politicians have indeed routinely served as the supreme examples of mendacious actors. The adjective "cunning," it would sometimes seem, was made to modify the noun "politician."[8] It would, however, be mistaken to collapse the two and conclude cynically that politics means by definition nothing but "dirty hands."[9] As Agnes Heller has pointed out, "Defining the concept of the polit-ical in terms of 'a routine of cheating or lying' or as 'mere manipula-tion' is meaningless because it disregards the existence of rules of the game without which the term 'cheating' or 'bending the rules' is empty."[10] As we saw in examining the issue of language and lying, the default position has to be veracity as a norm if lying can function at all. What varies, of course, is the proportion of truthful to menda-cious speech acts, with political speech arguably more prone to the latter than other language games. Although there have been occa-sional attempts to banish lying from politics as much as possible—Gandhi's doctrine of *Satyagraha* is a salient example; another is Václav Havel's campaign promise to "live in truth"[11]—by and large politics has been generally acknowledged as a natural game preserve for the preservation of the lie.

However, as we have noted, there is no consensus about "the political" itself, which suggests that simple arguments about the uni-versality and permanence of any one essential proportion will be suspect. What, we have to ask, is the probable relationship between distinct versions of "the political" and the prevalence of mendacity? As we saw in the previous chapter, it is no simple business to discern its essential nature, despite efforts to assign one or another meaning to its singular "concept." Rather than forcing a resolution to the question of the allegedly proper "concept of the political," it would be more productive to explore the affinities between the major contenders and the propensity to lie they betray.

But before we turn our attention to those contenders, one other vital point needs to be made. In most discussions of political mendacity, the focus is on rulers who lie to those they govern or represent, or at best, on equals in an adversarial power struggle, either benign or lethal. But what if political lying goes in the other direction? What if it is used by the relatively powerless to protect themselves against those in authority? In the "hidden transcripts" of what the anthropologist James C. Scott calls the "arts of resistance" practiced by the oppressed against their oppressors, duplicity and dissembling are normal strategies employed to subvert the compliant "public transcripts" demanded by the powers that be.[12] Although sometimes this tactic has led to naturalizing attributions of mendacity to those forced to use it—Scott cites several sexist assertions of women's intrinsic propensity to lie in the misogynist writings of Arthur Schopenhauer and Otto Weininger—historical explanations are far more persuasive.

Evidence comes in particular from the history of oppression for heterodox religious beliefs. As students of that history like Perez Zagorin have shown, many religions have come to tolerate lying, despite their normal condemnation of it as sinful, when it is a matter of resisting persecution by another faith then in power.[13] Medieval Waldensians and other heretics, for example, were famous dissimulators. During the Reformation, Catholics were permitted falsely to proclaim their allegiance to a Protestant prince, but with mental reservations that allowed them to tell God their true beliefs. A split between mouth and heart was justifiable if martyrdom was the likely consequence of absolute candor. Despite the disdain of Calvin for "Nicodemites," Protestants often did likewise. Much earlier, the Shiite minority in Islam developed a doctrine called "taqiya," justified by certain passages in the Koran, which permitted outward expressions of Sunni fidelity to hide their inward beliefs when revealing the truth about them would be dangerous.[14] And the still observant crypto-Jews called Marranos during the era of the Spanish Inquisition could keep their true faith hidden for the same reason.[15]

Especially in circumstances of desperate repression, guile and deception have seemed the only weapons left to those with few other tools at their disposal. As popular literature like Jurek Becker's 1969 Holocaust novel *Jacob the Liar* demonstrates, it is sometimes necessary to lie even to those who are fellow victims in order to provide some hope against the unendurable realities of political horror.[16] Other novels, like Louis Begley's semiautobiographical *Wartime Lies* of 1991, which depicts the necessity and cost of disguising one's ethnic identity, depict the extent to which survival justifies violating taboos against hypocrisy.[17]

Not only in clearly oppressive circumstances but also in modern democracies there may be some warrant for resisting the imperative always to tell the truth to those in power. As the political theorist Franz Neumann noted, "Every political system impresses the mores of the ruling group upon its population. The greater the tensions, the more stringent the impositions become. The individual then resorts to many forms of dissimulation; and, in certain periods of history, it is the liar who becomes the hero. The lie (in its many forms) becomes the protection of the individual against a universalized system of propaganda."[18] A salient manifestation of the resistance to governmental intrusion concerns the role of secrecy, which, to be sure, is not precisely the same as lying.[19] Although we often insist on transparency and openness, especially in democratic polities, the protective value of secrecy against the prying eyes of government surveillance is now widely acknowledged. The idea of a secret ballot only became widespread in the late nineteenth century, although it had been introduced in the French constitution of 1795. Australia was the first to adopt it in the English-speaking world in 1856 in Tasmania and Victoria, where the influence of Chartism was strong (one of the six points of the Charter had been the secret ballot). Secret ballots were often called "Australian ballots" as a result. In Britain it was instituted in the Ballot Act of 1872. In America most states adopted secret ballots soon after the presidential election of 1884, with Kentucky holding out until 1891. However much publicity might be a feature of the democratic ethos, privacy became the norm for the casting of votes to avoid bribery, intimidation, and retaliation. It was now possible, if pressed, to lie about one's choices and not be held accountable, a practice that has bedeviled opinion polling before and after elections ever since. In short, it has sometimes seemed both prudent and justifiable to reverse the now reigning cliché—which was fresh and powerful when first popularized by the Quakers in the 1950s[20]—and "speak lies to power" in order to resist intolerance, coercion, and intrusive surveillance either religious or political.

But if the right to dissemble in order to survive political oppression seems unimpeachable, what of those cases when the arrow is pointing in a different direction, with lies being told by those in authority to those below or equal in the game of power? Can one justify mendacity when it is used by the strong against the weak (even for their putative benefit)? Let us begin our discussion with the variant of politics that is most often seen as hospitable to—indeed, dependent on—deliberate deception: totalitarianism. As noted in our introduction, the so-called big lie denounced in Hitler's *Mein Kampf* quickly became identified with his own practices, despite his introducing the idea in order to defame his enemies. It soon was detected in other totalitarian regimes, once that concept gained momentum as a way to differentiate the most rabidly antidemocratic, antiliberal polities from their less extreme authoritarian, despotic, or tyrannical cousins.[21] As early as the 1938 publication of *Au pays du grand mensonge* by the Croatian Trotskyist Ante (Anton) Ciliga, the Soviet Union was damned for its systematic distortion of the truth.[22] In his 1945 essay "The Political Function of the Modern Lie," Alexandre Koyré, the Russian-born philosopher and historian of science then in American exile, contended that "modern man—*genus* totalitarian—bathes in the lie, breathes the lie, is in the thrall to the lie every moment of his existence. . . . The totalitarian regime is founded on the *primacy of the lie*."[23]

Popularized by Orwell's depiction of the ironically named Ministry of Truth in *Nineteen Eighty-Four*, the claim that totalitarianism completely falsified the past as well as the present, destroying collective memory and replacing it with an entirely fabricated alternative reality, soon became widely accepted. A generation later, Leszek Kolakowski, the lapsed Marxist Polish philosopher, could still argue that whereas normal political mendacity honors the difference between true and false, in totalitarian states, "the lie really becomes truth or, at least, the distinction between true and false in their usual meaning has disappeared. This is the great cognitive triumph of totalitarianism: it cannot be accused of lying any longer since it has succeeded in abrogating the very idea of truth."[24] That classical totalitarianism had, in fact, decayed in the post-Stalinist era was registered, so Cornelius Castoriadis claimed at the same time, by the fact that "the official propaganda produces an incoherent stream of petty lies—it is incapable of engineering a grandiose and paranoiacally watertight fictitious world."[25] Or to put it in the terms of the aesthetic politics we have discussed in the previous chapter, its attempt to suture the symbolic gap between represented and representation in an imaginary totality—which may be the biggest lie of all—comes undone. Although denunciations of the "big lie" could survive totalitarianism's decline, at least as a term of opprobrium—in, for example, paranoid rants like the French journalist Thierry Meyssan's attempt to blame 9/11 on right-wing conspirators[26]—its heyday has passed.

Classical totalitarian states were, moreover, relatively few in number, with historians rarely agreeing on candidates beyond Stalin's USSR, Nazi Germany, and Mao's China. Some commentators—Arendt and Lefort come immediately to mind—have also argued that politics, rightly understood, was precisely what totalitarianism suppressed.[27] The alternative it presented might better be called "metapolitics," as it once was in a book on Nazism by Peter Viereck,[28] which suggests the overweening extension of politics to all aspects of human existence, overrunning the boundaries that we have seen are so often drawn between politics and its others. Terminology, however, is less important than the fact that totalitarianism developed an attitude toward lying that suspended whatever ethical considerations make lying a contested and reviled tactic in virtually all other political contexts, where the vice of hypocrisy still has to pay homage to the virtue of sincerity. It is to these more frequent alternatives that we must turn to assess the ambiguous affinity between mendacity and politics.

In the previous chapter, we identified several salient candidates for "the political" understood as the ontological, rather than merely ontic, dimension of political life (*le politique* as opposed to *la poli-*

tique, as the French define that opposition): an existential antagonism between friend and foe, the less confrontational agonism in a nonlethal, diplomatic dance of shifting alliances and rivalries, the forging of compacts or contracts based on trust and mutual benefit, the benign rule of rational philosopher-kings, the republican virtue of self-sacrifice for the good of the whole, and the deliberative procedures of pluralist public sphere(s). We also focused on a version that stressed the aesthetic dimension of all political life, understood largely in terms of the symbolic, perhaps illusory nature of collective identities.

THE POLITICAL AS ANTAGONISM: ON WAR AND LYING

The first model we examined, following Carl Schmitt's controversial coinage of "the concept of the political," was the existential struggle between friend and foe, a struggle that was unbeholden to moral constraints or material interests. It involved an antagonistic, life-and-death conflict that found its ultimate expression in outright war fought between states (not the individual war of all against all posited by Hobbes's notion of the state of nature). "To the enemy concept," Schmitt argued, "belongs the ever present possibility of combat."[29] Although Schmitt may not have wished for that outcome, he argued that a world without war would be a world without politics. According to Robert Howse, "The radical implication of Schmitt's move is to allow the possibility of war to determine the whole content of politics, even under conditions of peace, thereby eroding any possible moral meaning in the distinction between the requirements of normal politics and those of an extreme situation such as an emergency."[30]

The enemy in wartime should be understood as an emotionally neutral public foe, not a hated private adversary, a *hostis* not an *inimicus.* Because war has no normative meaning beyond the existential struggle between friend and foe, the idea of a just war is incoherent, since justice is not an issue when existential survival is at stake. There are no universal standards by which the political can be judged, including humanitarian concerns. "The concept of humanity is an especially useful ideological instrument of imperialist expansion," Schmitt cynically warned, "and in its ethical-humanitarian form it is a specific vehicle of economic imperialism."[31] All genuine political theories assume that man is inherently evil (Schmitt's Catholic background made it hard for him to abandon the idea of original sin). All political decisions are made without recourse to universal ethical standards or even general rules of procedure. No Kantian categorical imperative or other moral principle provides a check on arbitrary decisions.

Schmitt did not, however, explicitly conclude that the nonnormative, existential struggle between friend and foe necessarily justified mendacity. One of his defenders could in fact go so far as to talk of "Schmitt's high esteem for *honesty* and *visibility* in politics."[32] In this sense, Schmitt was not Machiavelli, arguing for the necessity of playing the sly fox by the clever ruler. In fact, in *The Concept of the Political* he argued that "one could just as well the other way around define politics as the sphere of honest rivalry and economics as a world of deception. The connection of politics with thievery, force, and repression is, in the final analysis, no more precise than is the connection of economics with cunning and deception. Exchange and deception are often not far apart."[33] Liberal contractualism with all its talk of trust is no guarantee against political mendacity. Nor is there any virtue in construing politics as an open discussion of different opinions leading to a consensus via persuasion. It is more honest and sincere to confront the dark truth about the antagonistic essence of "the political."

But by so closely identifying "the political" with a life-and-death existential struggle, always containing the possibility of real combat between enemies, Schmitt opened the door for an apparently natural affinity between political speech and mendacity. In military affairs, after all, the role of deception has always been recognized and indeed often explicitly taught as a potent weapon. In his famous *Art of War*, written circa 500 BCE, Sun Tzu observed that "all warfare is based on deception. When able to attack, we must seem unable; when using our forces, we must seem inactive; when we are near, we must make the enemy believe we are far away; when far away we must make him believe we are near. Hold out the bait; entice the enemy. Feign disorder and crush him."[34] In his *Memorabilia*, Xenophon also acknowledged that deceiving an enemy in wartime and lying to a dispirited army to rally their morale were valid tactics.[35] Despite its negative connotations, contemporary observers continue to claim that "strategic deception, far from being either ungentlemanly or random, is a systematic and consistent process in which success may bring substantial benefits."[36] According to Koyré, "One may lie to an adversary. There are few societies that, like the Maoris, are chivalrous enough to ban trickery in war. And fewer still are those, like the Quakers and the Wahabis, which are religious enough to the point of prohibiting any lie to an outsider under any circumstances."[37] The example often given of the deliberate misleading of the Nazis concerning the likely landing places for the D-day invasion of Normandy is very convincing. Although there are limits to the moral transgressions that can be committed during wartime— at least most combatants agree there are—lying is not prohibited by the Geneva Convention or any other protocol aimed at minimizing atrocities. Even Sissela Bok in her across-the-board denunciation of lying acknowledges that cases like the D-day invasion are hard to condemn.[38] Indeed, they may not even be examples of lying strictly speaking, since enemies do not share a basic initial trust in the truthfulness of their foes.

Still, the history of propaganda during wartime does raise an important question, since it may be directed not only against the enemy but also against one's own population. The classic example here are the stories made up to scare the British population during the First World War about the horrors committed by the Germans in Belgium and France (e.g., a crucified Canadian soldier, a mutilated British nurse, an executed French boy), some of which (though not all) turned out to be exaggerations.[39] Although later denounced by critics, such as the antiwar British peer Lord Arthur Ponsonby in his 1928 tract *Falsehood in War-Time*,[40] the practice had been defended during the war by politicians like Arthur Bonar Law as a necessary ploy to bolster hatred of the enemy. So one might conclude that a version of "the political" that identifies it with existentially decisive friend/foe relations has little defense against including mendacity as a weapon in the struggle to survive, a weapon that can be turned just as easily on domestic "friends" as on alien "foes."

THE POLITICAL AS AGONISM: ON DIPLOMACY AND LYING

What of the second model of foreign politics, which stresses the shifting alliances and rivalries between states in an international system that seeks to avoid solidification of binary oppositions and the descent into armed struggle? What is the role of lying in international relations as the essential model of "the political"? According to the political theorist John Mearsheimer, lying "is an accepted practice in international politics, mainly because there are sometimes compelling strategic reasons for a state's leaders to lie either to other states or their own people. These practical logics almost always override moral arguments against lying."[41] Lying in this situation involves not only outright lying between states but also fearmongering aimed at mobilizing one's own population (as we have seen is characteristic as well of wartime) and the idealizing of motives and creation of virtuous nationalist myths that hide a more cynical agenda of *Realpolitik*. Although a certain amount of embarrassment can accompany the revelation of a lie—think of President Eisenhower's situation when the U2 spy plane was shot down over the Soviet Union in 1960—the actual penalties are often modest, at least in terms of internal politics. As Mearsheimer notes, "Inter-state lying does not have a significant downside. There is not much danger of blowback into the domestic arena. Most people understand that states sometimes have to lie and cheat in international politics, especially if they are dealing with a dangerous opponent."[42]

The niceties of diplomacy among states are also based on a delicate mutual understanding of the inevitability of stretching the truth by all parties. Here the link between politics and the dissembling skills of *politesse* developed in the early modern court is most apparent. As was once noted by the German philosopher Alfred Bäumler, who was a serious scholar of aesthetics before he turned into a craven apologist for Nazism, the idea of taste first developed by Gracian in the early modern period "does not yet show an immediate relationship to the problem of aesthetics. It belongs to ethics and politics rather than to aesthetics. The man of taste is the consummate cosmopolitan. . . . [In Germany] the *discreto* here becomes the '*politicus*,' the man who knows how to conduct himself at court, who is equal to every situation and has that certain *je ne sais quoi*."[43] What was first practiced within aristocratic courts was soon perfected in the interaction of diplomats representing their countries at the courts of other countries. By the early seventeenth century, it was possible for the British diplomat Sir Henry Wotton, James I's envoy to the Venetian republic, to make the often cited remark that "an ambassador is a man of virtue sent abroad to lie for his country."[44] Secrecy is likewise valued for governmental business that is justifiably classified as confidential, involving diplomatic relations as well as domestic negotiations and the counsel given by advisers to those in power. Here too, the public has come to expect only a modified and often delayed access to the truth of what happens behind closed doors. It is not for nothing that we still often call our ministerial leaders "secretaries," the keepers of secrets, or insignificant that the word "diplomat" is derived from a folded-over document, whose contents are not public.[45]

In the most extreme version of the tradition that came to be called *raison d'état*, the claim that states were ethical entities in themselves, unbeholden to higher norms of conduct, meant that whatever they might do in order to protect their interests was by definition morally justifiable. But no matter how intrinsically ethical a state might conceive itself to be, it normally operated in a context in which the comparable and competing claims of other states made paying at least lip service to general ethical values difficult to avoid. A certain level of hypocrisy in forging and maintaining fragile international alliances is, it has often been noted, virtually inevitable. As Machiavelli understood, even the most hardheaded and cynical political realism requires a façade of moral idealism. Summarizing this insight, Ruth Grant writes: "The actions of states take place within a particular moral horizon and are always subject to ethical judgment. Rulers must attend to the way their actions will appear, they must speak a moral language, and they should exploit the opportunities to advance their aims that public moral discourse offers."[46]

Acknowledging the larger moral horizon within which international relations take place, even when they are at their most "realistic," introduces the issue of the porosity of the boundary of the political, which we will treat later in our discussion. It also suggests that there is a strong inclination to speak untruthfully, at least to some extent, when conducting diplomacy. Once again, an example from the Second World War comes readily to mind: the alliance between the Soviet Union, the United States, and the United Kingdom forged to fight the common threat of fascism. The alliance was possible, of course, only after the earlier Nazi-Soviet Pact, which allowed Hitler and Stalin to collaborate in carving up Eastern Europe, was undermined by the German invasion of Russia. In order for the Allies to work together, such fundamental differences as attitudes toward the maintenance of the British Empire or the struggle between communism and capitalism were conveniently forgotten, only, of course, to revive once the Allies went their separate ways. As Grant has argued, the dependency of one state on another in a pluralist world where no single country can enjoy unique hegemony necessitates their willingness to speak a common language, even if their values and interests are ultimately at odds.

As for governmental lying to a domestic audience in order to bring about a desired change of foreign policy, credibility gaps can widen to the point that basic confidence in leadership is eroded. But the price is much lower when the outcome is favorable—think, for example, of Franklin Roosevelt's duplicity in getting America into World War II—than when it is not, as Lyndon Johnson discovered in Vietnam, Ronald Reagan during the Iran-Contra scandal, and George W. Bush in the case of Iraq. But with wartime domestic propaganda, the manufacturing of consent through deception and fearmongering leaves a very bad taste in the mouths of those who insist that at least liberal, democratic polities needs to be accountable and transparent.

Here we are entering a different territory, that of domestic rather than foreign relations, in which the concept of the political is identified variously with contracts or compacts among individuals based on trust in those who govern them, the ideal of wise rulership by the benevolent, paternalistic leader, or the discursive rationality of republican virtue. All have different implications for the issue of political mendacity. Let us take each in turn.

THE POLITICAL AS CONTRACTUALISM: ON LIBERALISM AND LYING

There is no easy way to generalize about the diverse and dynamic body of political theory that has called itself liberal ever since the term was first introduced at the beginning of the nineteenth century by Spanish defenders of constitutional monarchy.[47] National versions are not fully equivalent and developments over time led to many differences even within a single national tradition. We have also seen some critics like Carl Schmitt claim that liberalism was inherently antipolitical because of its stress on market relations, faith in legal procedures, and reliance on rational discourse rather than existential decisions by sovereigns who make the law. The contemporary political theorist Ruth Grant concurs, arguing that "liberal theory does not take sufficient account of the distinctive character of political relations, of political passion, and of moral discourse and so underestimates the place of hypocrisy in politics."[48] On the question of justifying lying, we have already encountered two founding fathers of liberal politics, Immanuel Kant and Benjamin Constant, on opposite sides of the fence.

There are, nonetheless, certain prevailing attitudes that make liberalism a coherent enough phenomenon to allow us to ask what its implications are for the issue of mendacity in politics. One of the most typical elements of liberal politics is a faith in the rights of man as opposed to those merely of citizens in a specific polity. Deciding which rights are to be included is, of course, an enormously difficult task, and there has been no consensus even among liberals, let alone the larger community of theorists of rights about a definitive list. Is the right not to be lied to among them? According to the political theorist Michael Walzer, who in some of his moods is more a social democrat than a liberal, there is a "thin" list of human rights "to which all societies can be held—negative injunctions, most likely, rules against murder, deceit, torture, oppression and tyranny."[49] But this is clearly an eccentric and untenable claim, since it fails to register all the myriad ways in which lies are part of daily social life, as we have noted in the first chapter.

Another fundamental attitude of liberalism involves the founding fiction of a contract or compact, which is based on the alienation of individual sovereignty to a social or political community. As Bernard Williams has noted, this emphasis on trust has clear implications for the issue of lying in general and lying in politics in particular: "Truth, and specifically, the virtues of truth, are connected with trust. The connections are to be seen in the English language. The word 'truth' and its ancestors in Early and Middle English originally meant fidelity, loyalty, or reliability. . . . Truthfulness is a form of trustworthiness, that which relates in a particular way to speech."[50] Broadly speaking, one might say that a definition of the political that stressed its cooperative nature and believed in the goal of rational consensus, often identified with modern liberalism,[51] was one in which truthfulness was highly valued (although in the complicated case of Hobbes, as Kinch Hoekstra has shown,[52] not as a value higher than maintaining the peace or security).

Some liberals, to be sure, were unconvinced by the conceit of an original contract, following Bentham and the Utilitarian tradition in distrusting conceptual fictions of any kind. If one takes John Stuart Mill as exemplary of this tradition, then a concern for truth and the ways to protect it against a variety of tyrannies, including the state and majority opinion, remains, however, a prominent element in it. The Utilitarian tradition out of which Mill came, and against which he in part rebelled, had already been concerned with the role of political and legal fictions, with Jeremy Bentham rejecting notions like "natural rights" and "social contracts" as untenable nonsense.[53] Rather than rely on them as truths, it was better to acknowledge frankly that they were contrivances that may or may not have utility in promoting human progress. In *On Liberty* (1859), Mill provided the classic defense of a fallibilist search for truth in which no single opinion could claim a monopoly of wisdom, thus preventing others from being heard. In a "free marketplace of ideas,"[54] there was a greater likelihood for the truth to emerge, especially the truths of ethics and values which any society needed to encourage.

Although Mill did not stress truthfulness as distinct from the search for truth, he strongly implied that it was entailed in the process he hoped to promote. The claim that there are "useful" lies, those for example that help maintain public order and the continuity of institutions, is mistaken, for "the usefulness of an opinion is itself a matter of opinion: as disputable, as open to discussion, and requiring discussion as much, as the opinion itself. . . . The truth of an opinion is part of its utility."[55] Whether Mill ever entirely lost his Benthamite reverence for the superiority of scientific knowledge over mere opinion or flirted with the idea of a Platonic class of benevolent guardian rulers,[56] he never countenanced "noble lies" as a tactic of their wise rule. Although he justified despotism as "a legitimate mode of government in dealing with barbarians, provided the end be their improvement, and the means justified by actually effecting their end,"[57] he did not specifically defend well-intentioned lying as a tool of that improvement.

For Mill, transparency and accountability were essential aspects of public life. In his later years, under the influence of the great love of his life, Harriet Taylor, Mill even abandoned his initial enthusiasm for the secret ballot, which had been fervently supported by his Philosophical Radical colleagues like George Grote.[58] Believing that the threat of coercion and intimidation had passed, he argued that publicity would prevent voters from voting their personal interests instead of the general good, an especially urgent issue when disenfranchised women were allegedly represented by men. Open ballots meant no one could lie about his or her actions in the voting booth, even if it might occasionally lead to anxiety about the consequences of voting against the majority.

Mill's earnest defense of a politics of transparency and integrity was elaborated with various nuances in the work of such disciples as John Morley, journalist, biographer, leading member of William Gladstone's government, and author of *On Compromise* of 1874, and Henry Sidgwick, utilitarian ethicist and author of *The Elements of Politics* of 1891.[59] Common to their position was an understanding of the political in terms of the power of rational discourse—in Habermasian terms, communicative interaction seeking a consensus based on the better argument—rather than the exercise of will, either that of the tyrant or that of the people.[60] At its most idealist, liberalism seeks to subordinate factional interests and hopes to generate agreement about the general good through discursive argumentation rather than strategic, negotiated compromise among interests that remain at odds. When someone like Morley did admit that compromise might be necessary, it was based on the premise, to quote David Runciman, that "when principled Liberals compromise, you can trust to their compromises precisely because they take their compromises so seriously."[61] Although it often explicitly or implicitly limits access to the public realm, including only those deemed rational enough to participate, liberalism's self-understanding is that of a politics of abstract equality in which who you are is less important than what you say. As a result, it has sometimes been accused of tacitly countenancing the very hypocrisy it claims to overcome, because political reality involves competing factions, partial interests, and perpetual dissensus rather than rationally achieved consensus. Thus a contemporary American right-wing critic of liberalism, Andrew Klavan, can boast:

> The thing I like best about being a conservative is that I don't have to lie. I don't have to pretend that men and women are the same. I don't have to declare that failed or oppressive cultures are as good as mine. I don't have to say that everyone's special or that the rich cause poverty or that all religions are a path to God. I don't have to claim that a bad writer like Alice Walker is a good one or that a good writer like Toni Morrison is a great one. I don't have to pretend that Islam means peace.[62]

With less malice and reversing the condemnation of hypocrisy, Ruth Grant makes a similar point:

> Liberal politics needs a certain kind of hypocritical speech. Because the theorists are right that people are often self-interested, they are wrong that politics can be conducted through the rational adjudication of interests without hypocrisy. . . . The practice of liberal politics is improved by a certain sort of hypocrisy, even though liberalism understands itself as an alternative to hypocritical politics.[63]

There is also another dimension of liberalism that works against its equation with rational deliberation, that derived from the commercial tradition associated with laissez-faire economics. Although *Homo economicus* is rational in terms of his private self-interest, he pursues it with no direct regard for public outcomes. The belief that the indulgence of private interests, even private vices, can somehow translate into the public good via the market was infamously developed by Bernard de Mandeville in his *Fable of the Bees* (1714).[64] Attacking moralism in politics as itself a form of hypocrisy—here Oliver Cromwell was his favorite cautionary example—Mandeville sought to find a way to justify a more benign version of hypocritical behavior. In the beehive he introduced as an analogy of society, self-interest ruled and "all trades and places knew some cheat, no calling was without deceit."[65] Although more a defense of the positive effects of luxury, pride, vanity, and fickleness in stimulating prosperity than of lying per se, *Fable of the Bees* concluded that "fools only strive to make a great an honest hive."[66] At least one strain of liberalism thus countenanced a selfish individualism, harmonized to be sure by the occult rationality of what Adam Smith would later make famous as an "invisible hand" into the general good. In this quasi-Leibnizian universe, moral prohibitions against deceit were relaxed and deliberate consideration for the common good rendered otiose.[67]

THE POLITICAL AS GOOD GOVERNANCE: ON NOBLE LYING BY WISE ELITES

Broadly speaking, the ancient world bequeathed to posterity two competing political traditions, one descending from Plato's *Republic* (and his other dialogues *The Laws, The Statesman,* and *Gorgias*) and the second derived from the practice of the Greek polis and the Roman Republic. With the modern theorists Leo Strauss and Hannah Arendt serving as our major representatives of these two classical models, let us now turn to the implications of each for the issue of political mendacity.

In his struggle with Sophists like Gorgias, Plato was at pains to denounce mendacity.[68] His well-known denunciation of the arts, motivated by many different considerations, was fueled in part by his contention that the poets mislead their readers about the true virtues of the gods.[69] But in the early dialogue called *Hippias Minor,* an argument over the superiority of the honest Achilles to the wily Odysseus in Homer, Plato came to the unexpected, perhaps even ironic, conclusion that the man who lies—or errs willingly—is superior to the one who makes mistakes involuntarily.[70] For to lie is a cognitive achievement, not merely speaking falsely, but knowing that one is doing so, whereas merely making a mistake is based on ignorance. Insofar as the false man is thus knowledgeable, he is not so different from the true man. Socrates' reasoning against Hippias in the dialogue is a brilliant example of *reductio ad absurdum,* which concludes by asking the rhetorical question, "So one who errs and does disgraceful things voluntarily, Hippias, if indeed there is such a man, would be none other than the good man?"[71] Although he admits he himself balks at this unsettling conclusion, as does Hippias, Socrates confesses that he has no logical way to avoid it.

Plato's ingenious defense of lying in *Hippias Minor* may not be fully convincing, but it alerts us to the fact that he did not have a principled hostility to mendacity, as would Augustine and Kant. Although the dialogue doesn't concern politics, when it came to conceiving a perfect republic, a "splendid city" (*kallipolis*), Plato had no qualms about arguing for the virtue of lying under certain circumstances. In *The Republic* 414b–c, he discusses the myth of the metals originated by Hesiod, in which God had made the golden race to rule, men of silver to be soldiers, and people of iron and bronze workers. Plato has Socrates wonder, "How, then, said I, might we contrive one of those opportune falsehoods [*pseudon*] of which we were just now speaking, so as by one noble lie [*gennaion ti en pseudomenos*] to persuade if possible the rulers themselves, but failing that the rest of the city?"[72] For the sake of political stability based on allegedly natural hierarchies of talent and function, Plato allows the telling of falsehoods—or, if *pseudon* is more liberally translated, fairy tales like those told to children, containing a kernel of symbolic truth—for the city's own good. Thus the lie is not only told for a noble purpose but also justifiable because it is told by a noble leader, well bred and of superior moral character. One commentator, D. Dombrowski, goes so far as to claim that "for Plato it is right for the ruler to tell the *gennaion pseudos* not because it is for the public good—even a crude utilitarian could do this—but rather because of the kind of individual the ruler is. . . . They are truth-loving agents and possess noticeably superior intellectual and moral abilities to those of the general population."[73] In other words, the ultimate justification for benign lying is the trust that the ruled have in the virtue and rationality of their rulers, the Guardians of the Republic who have the common good in mind. Like the harmless myths told to children for educational purposes, lies are useful in manipulating the gullible masses to follow their best interests. Ultimately, they will thank the rulers, who will reveal their ruse as a necessary expedient in an educational process. Although it is sometimes argued that because *The Republic* candidly reveals the need to tell "noble lies," Plato really intended to expose and diminish their power,[74] this result would follow only if those gullible masses actually read the text, not a likely prospect.

Later in *The Republic* Plato reasserts the point that rulers will have to concoct "a throng of lies and deceptions for the benefit of the ruled," for example encouraging marriage only among the elite in order to maximize the chance for the procreation of superior children for the state.[75] Although unfriendly to the "lies" of rhetoricians and artists, whose fictions distract humankind from the truth, Plato accepted the necessity of the political lie as a useful expedient—like the moderate use of poison to cure (a *pharmakon*)—in the effort to secure the just and virtuous republic among men. Or more precisely, he accepted mendacity only from those who deserved to rule and explicitly denied it to their inferiors:

> And if any citizen lies to our rulers, we shall regard it as a still graver offence than it is for a patient to lie to his doctor, or for an athlete to lie to his trainer about his physical condition, or for a sailor to misrepresent to his captain any matter concerning the ship or crew, or the state of himself or his fellow sailors . . . and so if anyone else is found in our state telling lies "whether he be craftsman, prophet, physician or shipwright," he will be punished for introducing a practice likely to capsize and wreck the ship of state.[76]

Only experts, after all, know how to use a dose of poison to cure; others are likely to produce disastrous results.

For a long while Plato's defense of the noble lie slid into relative obscurity. The religious tradition stemming from Augustine, promoting a deontological rather than consequentialist ethics, ignored or tacitly denounced it. Although Machiavelli rejected the Augustinian tradition, he was far more influenced by Xenophon than by Plato. As Lefort has noted, he abandoned "the idea of a harmonious society, one governed by the best, whose constitution would be conceived as a way of warding off the dangers of innovations and would proceed from the knowledge of the ultimate ends of man and of the city."[77] And with that abandonment went the logic of appealing to the nobility of a disinterested liar who knew the rationally best way to organize a society. Satirists like Swift, Arbuthnot, and Twain never invoked it, even in mock support. Ralph Waldo Emerson, a great admirer of Plato, mentioned it only in passing and with regret.[78] Oscar Wilde, while noting and turning in a positive direction Plato's linkage of poetry and lying, did not remark on the *gennaion pseudos* in "The Decay of Lying."

There were, to be sure, sometimes indirect defenses of a comparable position in the politics of those who understood the power of duplicity in maintaining public order. Thus, for example, Edmund Burke, in his *Reflections on the Revolution in France,* could warn that the revolutionary's zeal for utter transparency and honesty threatened the loss of healthy political mystification:

> All the pleasing illusions which made power gentle and obedience liberal, which harmonized the different shades of life, and which, by a bland assimilation, incorporated into politics the sentiments which beautify and soften private society, are to be dissolved by this new conquering empire of light and reason. All the decent drapery of life is to be rudely torn. All the super-added ideas, furnished from the wardrobe of a moral imagination, which the heart owns and the understanding ratifies as necessary to cover the defects of our naked, shivering nature, and to raise it to dignity in our own estimation, are to be exploded as ridiculous, absurd and antiquated fashion.[79]

Others, arguing for the ethical value of the state, unbeholden to external moral constraints, could also warn against the expectation that popular opinion could be made utterly free of mendacity. Hegel, for example, could write, "In public opinion all falsehood and all truth is contained, but to find the truth is the task of the great man.

He who says and accomplishes what his time wants and desires is the great man of his time. He does what is the inner essence of his time, he realizes it, and yet he who does not know how to despise public opinion as one hears it here and there will never accomplish anything great."[80] With such leaders at the helm, the state can take on a tutelary role and help guide a populace that is not always able to discern the difference between truth and falsehood. Rationalists, even those like Hegel who stress the immanence of reason in history, can find ways to disdain the imperfect reasoning of the common man, who sometimes needs to be helped by whatever means necessary to see his true interest. The explicitly antirationalist and elitist Nietzsche could less apologetically invoke *The Republic* in the third of his *Untimely Meditations,* "Uses and Disadvantages of History for Life," where he argued with his characteristically provocative brio that what he called "necessary lies" (*Notlüge*) were the fictions on which all politics is based.[81]

But it was perhaps only in the twentieth century that the explicit idea of the "noble lie" once again attracted significant widespread attention. In the denunciations of Plato as proto-totalitarian by critics like Richard Crossman and Karl Popper, it played a prominent role.[82] Sisella Bok would concur: "We cannot take for granted either the altruism or the good judgment of those who lie to us, no matter how much they intend to benefit us. We have learned that much deceit for private gain masquerades as being in the public interest."[83] But not all the attention was negative. For example, the philosopher Loyal Rue concludes *By the Grace of Guile* (1993) with a chapter on "the saving grace of noble lies," in which he defends the need for new myths, like the "life-lies" extolled by Ibsen, to combat the nihilism he sees as the major threat in the modern world.[84] It was, however, in the work of Leo Strauss and his alleged neoconservative followers that the "noble lie" found its most ostensible support, especially after they were often held accountable for the mendacity of the Bush administration's Iraq policy.[85]

To interpret Strauss's legacy is no easy task, since he wrote in an oblique and often gnomic style, commented on other figures rather than revealed his own beliefs, and couched his ideas in ways that defy easy understanding. It may even have been the case, as Shadia B.

Drury has speculated, that he deliberately taught different things to different disciples.[86] Or his difficulty might have resulted from what he called "pedagogical reserve," a salutary method of making his readers think for themselves. Or maybe he was just a miserable communicator unable—rather than intentionally unwilling—to present his ideas with straightforward clarity. Even the most devoted keepers of his flame have quarreled bitterly over the content of his teachings, with separate schools—East Coast Straussians vs. West Coast Straussians—emerging to claim his mantle. Some interpreters have identified him as a defender of ancient Athens, while others claim instead his allegiance was to Jerusalem, and still others see a complicated mixture of the two.[87] New materials periodically surface, such as his shocking assertion in a letter of 1933 to Karl Löwith that Nazism can be fought "only from the principles of the right, that is from fascist, authoritarian and imperialist principles . . . without resort to the ludicrous and despicable appeal to the *droits impre-scriptibles de l'homme,*"[88] which throws his critics into a frenzy of denunciation and his followers into ever more ingenious defenses. As a result, an increasingly large cottage industry has developed in the effort to get his ideas right, but with no consensus in sight.

Significantly, one of the few characterizations that all can agree on is that Strauss believed that great philosophy has often been presented esoterically because of the frequent threat of religious or political persecution.[89] His readings of the medieval Jewish philosopher Maimonides and the medieval Islamic Aristotelian al-Fārābī had convinced him of the wisdom of this approach. Thus obscurity, indirection, and secrecy are vital tools of the philosopher's art. The modern project of universal enlightenment was a pipe dream, and a dangerous one at that. Unlike Foucault, Strauss never made a hero out of the courageous truth-teller, the *parrhesiastes* who tells truth to power even at the risk of his life. The best one can say for Strauss is that because he did tell the truth about esoteric writing, he wasn't always committed to secrecy, although, of course, he did so when he was safely in exile from modern tyranny and the only penalty he would face would be the possible scorn of other theorists.

But did his position amount to an elitist brief for necessary mendacity on the part of philosophers under all circumstances, including liberal democracy? One of Strauss's defenders, Steven B. Smith, answers negatively:

> Philosophy does not engage in the kind of systematic deception characteristic of the liar, but the responsibility to speak the truth must always be balanced with other ends such as the desire for self-preservation and the philosopher's sense of responsibility to the society in which he lives. . . . Philosophers may thus write in ways that deliberately conceal or obscure through the use of secrecy and obfuscation, that may not amount to lies but fall somewhere short of full disclosure.[90]

That is, although Strauss was no Kantian when it came to the deontological imperative to tell the truth no matter the consequences, he did not counsel the opposite position in a principled way. As in the case of heterodox religious figures in danger of persecution for their beliefs, the philosopher in his eyes was given permission to obfuscate in order to survive. This is not to say, of course, that philosophers were wrong to desire the truth, to seek knowledge of the timeless order of things—indeed he called it their "dominating passion"[91]—just that they didn't always have to be truthful in their communicating it to others. As he put it admiringly in his essay "How Fārābī Read Plato's Laws," the Arab philosopher, like Plato, "presented what he regarded as the truth by means of ambiguous, allusive, misleading, and obscure speech."[92] Why this was just as necessary in an open society like the America *to* which he fled, as in a closed one like the Nazi Germany *from* which he fled, Strauss did not clearly explain.[93]

What was Strauss's specific attitude toward lying in the realm of politics, rather than in philosophy per se? Or did he perhaps combine the two, following Plato's model of a philosopher-king, ruling, if behind the scenes, over a utopian *kallipolis*, a city of justice and truth? Could politics be made philosophical rather than remaining hostage to opinion and prejudice, the rule of sophistry?[94] Did Strauss believe in the imposition of reason and natural right on the world of politics or was he more of a skeptic acknowledging his own ignorance—in the terminology he adopted in his debate with Alexandre Kojève on tyranny, a nondogmatic "zetetic"?[95] Did he conclude that the philosopher and the politician should be separate vocations? Is Michael Roth right in arguing that "*the* lesson of political philosophy, for Strauss, is that the conflict between politics and philosophy is irremediable; to forget this conflict is to invite disaster in both domains"?[96]

This is not the place to hazard a definitive answer to these questions, which continue to generate as much heat as light in the scholarship on Strauss. Whatever the precise relationship he imagined between philosophy and the city, Strauss was always an ardent defender of the centrality of the political, in dialogue with other theorists we have encountered like Schmitt and Arendt and in writing books on others like Machiavelli and Plato. What he shared with them, however, is not certain; even the disdain for liberalism it has been normally assumed they all espoused has been called into question in his case in a recent interpretation.[97] Despite his friendship with Schmitt before his exile to America in the wake of the Nazi seizure of power, he had no use for an antagonistic concept of the political. According to one observer, commenting on his complicated relationship with Schmitt, "Whereas the political does have central significance for the thought of Leo Strauss, the enemy and enmity do not."[98] Although as Lefort has noted with regard to Strauss's position on esoteric writing and the dangers of speaking the truth, "For the philosopher, to proceed politically presupposes that one take into account the friend-enemy opposition,"[99] Strauss never accepted the contention that politics itself must always be antagonistic. Nor like Arendt was he a strong believer in the agonism characterizing a participatory democracy of plural opinions. A single, teleological model of virtue and the good, the authority of one correct *nomos*, trumps the pursuit of individual or group liberty and happiness. Unlike Schmitt or Arendt, he believed that man was inherently a rational animal, or at least that some men could obtain the wisdom to act according to reason.[100]

Strauss's position was thus closer to Plato's than to Machiavelli's— or Arendt's or Lefort's—in its faith in the single truth that reason could provide those in power, a truth that transcends the vagaries of time and place. Nature, understood teleologically, rather than history was the ground of valid political insight; historicism led to debilitating relativism, which was one step away from nihilism. Machiavelli was to blame for debasing the ancient political wisdom that had looked to nature for guidance in choosing the good life, putting in its place instrumental rationality designed to promote mere security and stability. Strauss read Machiavelli, the father of modern political theory, as defending a strategic use of deception in politics for reasons other than a Platonic idea of the "noble lie." As he wrote in his *Thoughts on Machiavelli,*

> Machiavelli is far from denying that man's dependence on man compels most members of a society in their intercourse with one another to comply with certain simple and crude rules of conduct (the prohibitions against murder, fraud, theft and so on) and to cherish such qualities as gratitude, kindness, faithfulness and gentleness; but he contends that the same needs which make man dependent on other men compel him to form political societies the very preservation of which requires the transgression of those simple rules no less than their observation, as well as the practice of those virtues no less than that of their opposites.[101]

This argument, as we will see shortly, could be applied in many different contexts, including liberal democracy, but it was not the argument Strauss found in Plato. In *The City and Man,* he devoted a chapter to *The Republic* in which he notes that the "noble lie" is introduced "with special regard to the ruled, or more precisely to the soldiers, the strongest part of the city . . . that noble lie is to bring about the maximum of caring for the city and for one another on the part of the ruled (415d3–4). The good city is not possible then without a fundamental falsehood; it cannot exist in the element of truth, of nature."[102] That fundamental falsehood for Plato, Strauss suggested, has two parts. The first blurs the difference between art and nature, seducing the citizens to think that their placement in the hierarchy is natural rather than cultural. The second tells them that the inequality they endure is caused by a beneficent god, and therefore is itself good. "It is the second part of the noble lie, which, by adding divine sanctions to the natural hierarchy, supplies the required incentive for the soldiers to obey the rulers and thus to serve the city wholeheartedly."[103]

Strauss also cited with no evident disapproval the defense of noble lies by other ancient writers like Xenophon, whose advice to tyrants he discussed in *On Tyranny*. We have already cited his essay on the Greek thinker called "The Spirit of Sparta or the Taste of Xenophon," where he apparently endorses the philosopher's claim that it was for a wise elite "a matter of duty to hide the truth from the majority of mankind."[104] Was Strauss advocating the same obligation on the part of wise tyrants, understood in the ancient sense of being guided by natural right—although not natural law[105]—rather than modern Machiavellian relativism? Whereas the former led to a healthy moderation and restraint, the latter, he claimed, spawned the endless "conquest of nature."[106] Although Strauss never explicitly identified himself with one of the positions in Xenophon's imagined dialogue between the philosopher Simonides and the tyrant Hiero, even one of Strauss's sympathetic readers has admitted that "the question left hanging by the end of the commentary is why Strauss devotes an entire book intended to lay bare the roots of modern tyranny to the examination of an ancient work that appears to conclude with the praise of 'beneficent' tyranny. This hardly seems like condemnation, much less like identifying a political cancer for what it is."[107]

Whether Strauss fully endorsed the "noble lie" is still a bone of contention. Most of his critics claim he did and decry it,[108] while his defenders often come up with ingenious ways of defusing the charge.[109] But the correct answer, if indeed there really is one, is not something of great consequence to determine except for the devotees and detractors who squabble over his legacy. What is crucial to note is that the elitist tradition that descended from Plato had a rationale for its defense if its advocates so desired. Believing in a single truth about the good society based on natural right, but one whose candid dissemination might be dangerous to the stability of the state, meant that mendacity could be justified by the guardians of that truth for the benefit of the whole. Full transparency and honesty could be a threat to order, as conservatives ever since Burke with his celebrated defense of the value of "veils" and "drapery" have known.

POLITICS AS REPUBLICAN VIRTUE: COUNTERFACTUALITY AND MENDACITY

A very different rationale underpinned the defense of lying in the republican tradition, which we have identified with Machiavellian relativism and the critique of Platonic notions of natural right. Perhaps its most eloquent modern advocate was Hannah Arendt, whose two essays "Truth and Politics" of 1967 and "Lying in Politics: Reflections on the Pentagon Papers" of 1971 are among the most profound considerations of the question we have. Whereas Strauss was an absolutist, believing that "philosophy is the attempt to replace opinions about the whole with genuine knowledge of the whole,"[110] Arendt remained a committed pluralist, valorizing different opinions over coercive knowledge, especially in the realm of politics. She decried the authoritarian Platonic fantasy of an "ideocracy,"[111] ruled by the idea of the Good, in favor of an endless Socratic dialogue among contesting beliefs. "The search for truth in the *doxa*," she warned, "can lead to the catastrophic result that the *doxa* is altogether destroyed, or that what had appeared is revealed as an illusion. . . . Truth therefore can destroy *doxa*; it can destroy the specific political reality of the citizen."[112] Whereas Strauss was a believer in natural hierarchy, she was a fervent defender of the egalitarian premises of democracy produced in the artificial space of politics, a space between men called "the world," not inherent in them prior to the creation of that space. Whereas he made a fetish out of esoteric writing and public secrecy, she argued for appearing in the public realm and the disclosure of opinions through speech designed to persuade rather than manipulate. Whereas he argued that rulership was the essence of "the political," she replied that it was instead "action and speech." Privileging good governance, she argued, was in fact a mistaken extrapolation from the private household to the public realm. And while she preferred dialogic agonism to monologic uniformity, she believed, *pace* Schmitt, that men "acting in concert"[113] could nonetheless overcome the eternal antagonism of "friend and foe," which erroneously elevated foreign affairs to the essence of "the political."

Not only did Arendt's discussion of lying in politics derive from different premises than those informing the defense of the "noble lie," she went so far as to challenge the whole tradition of seeing it as endorsed by Plato:

> I hope no one will tell me any more that Plato was the inventor of the "noble lie." This belief rested on a misreading of a crucial passage (414C) in *The Republic,* where Plato speaks of one of his myths—a "Phoenician tale"—as a ψεῦδος. Since the same Greek word signifies "fiction," "error," and "lie," according to context—when Plato wants to distinguish between error and lie, the Greek language forces him to speak of "involuntary" and "voluntary" ψεῦδος—the text can be rendered with Cornford as "bold flight of invention" or be read with Eric Voegelin (*Order and History: Plato and Aristotle,* Louisiana State Press, 1957, vol. 3, p. 106) as satirical in intention; under no circumstances can it be understood as a recommendation of lying as we understand it.[114]

Arendt's reading of the Greek may be open to debate, but it nonetheless signaled her deep dissatisfaction with the defense of lying by well-intentioned rulers who know the truth but prudently withhold it from those on whose behalf they rule. Her own more nuanced defense of the virtues of mendacity rested on very different grounds.

"Truth and Politics" was occasioned by her controversial book *Eichmann in Jerusalem,* for which she had been accused of believing "fiat veritas, pereat mundus" (let there be truth, even if the world perishes) because in it she reported uncomfortable facts about the role of the Jewish councils in enabling the Holocaust.[115] Struck by the number of distortions and lies told about her own position during the controversy, she was compelled to think more reflectively about the role they play in politics in general. Her second essay, "Lying in Politics," was a response four years later to the furor unleashed by the publication of the Pentagon Papers during the Vietnam War.[116] It rehearsed and deepened her reflections on the questions raised in the first essay.

These essays were not, to be sure, the first time Arendt considered the question of mendacity. In *The Human Condition,* published in 1958, she had commented on the effect of the loss of certainty about the truth in the modern age, which "ended in a new, entirely unprecedented zeal for truthfulness—as though man could afford to be a liar only so long as he was certain of the unchallengeable existence of truth and objective reality, which surely would survive and defeat all his lies."[117] "It certainly is quite striking," she continued in a footnote, "that not one of the major religions, with the exception of Zoroastrianism, has ever included lying as such among the mortal sins. Not only is there no commandment: Thou shalt not lie (for the commandment: Thou shalt not bear false witness against thy neighbor, is of course of a different nature), but it seems as though prior to puritan morality nobody ever considered lies to be serious offenses."[118] And in *On Revolution*, which appeared in 1963, she had discussed the role the campaign against hypocrisy had played during the French Revolution, whose target was the corruption of the ancien régime court: "It was the war against hypocrisy that transformed Robespierre's dictatorship into the Reign of Terror. . . . And if it became boundless, it did so only because the hunt for hypocrites is boundless by nature."[119] Although Arendt recognized the dangers of hypocrisy, she warned that the ruthless quest to purge it from the public realm, the insistence on tearing away all masks to reveal the "true self," had the effect of dissolving the distinction between the natural self and the public persona, a distinction— based on the theatrical tradition of dramatis personae—that had provided legal protections unwisely abandoned in the hunt for absolute transparency.[120]

The same suspicion of unqualified truthfulness animated her two later essays on the theme. "Truth in Politics" begins with what she called the "commonplace" assertion, which we've already had occasion to cite in the introduction, that "no one has ever doubted that truth and politics are on rather bad terms with each other, and no one, as far as I know, has ever counted truthfulness among the political virtues. Lies have always been regarded as necessary and justifiable tools not only of the politician's or the demagogue's but also of the statesman's trade."[121] The first justification for lying in politics Arendt considered is that which sees politics in terms of means and ends, the consequentialist position that has been juxtaposed, as we saw earlier, to a deontological one. From this point of view, it may

seem that "lies, since they are often used as substitutes for more violent means, are apt to be considered relatively harmless tools in the
arsenal of political action" (546). In other words, if survival is the
goal, then lying might be justified. Arendt, however, quickly distanced herself from this position, noting that no society that lacks a
reverence for the truth can last for long: "No permanence, no perse-
verance in existence, can even be conceived of without men willing
to testify to what is and appears to them because it is" (547).

Following a brief discussion of the conflict between truth-telling
and politics in Plato and Hobbes, Arendt distinguished rational
truths—those of mathematics, science, and philosophy—from factual truths, arguing that "although the politically most relevant truths
are factual, the conflict between truth and politics was first discovered and articulated with respect to rational truth." The Greeks, she
argued, had been more concerned to contrast rational truth with
either error or ignorance, in the case of science, or opinion and illusion, in the case of philosophy, than with outright lies. "Only with
the rise of Puritan morality, coinciding with the rise of organized
science, whose progress had to be assured on the firm ground of the
absolute veracity and reliability of every scientist, were lies considered serious offenses" (549).

The crucial issue for the political realm is not that of rational
truth, which is monologic and hostile to plurality, but factual truth,
which involves other people and is dependent on testimonials and
witnessing. Facts and opinions are thus both in the political realm.
But ultimately there is a tension between them, for "all truths—not
only the various kinds of rational truth but also factual truth—are
opposed to opinion in their *mode of asserting validity.* Truth carries
with it an element of coercion, and the frequently tyrannical tendencies so deplorably obvious among professional truthtellers may
be caused less by a failing of character than by the strain of habitually living under a kind of compulsion" (555). Politics always keeps
open the possibility of future persuasion, whereas truth demands to
be recognized once and for all. Thus, "seen from the viewpoint of
politics, truth has a despotic character," which makes both tyrants
who see it as competition and governments based on consent uneasy about it. The reason truth is problematic for the latter, Arendt

averred, is that factual truth, like rational truth, "peremptorily claims to be acknowledged and precludes debate, and debate constitutes the very essence of political life. The modes of thought and communication that deal with truth, if seen from the political perspective, are necessarily domineering; they don't take into account other people's opinions, and taking these into account is the hallmark of all strictly political thinking" (556). Although what Kant had called "enlarged mentality" meant that other opinions can be taken into account, the goal of a single truth is counterpolitical. Any attempt to discover and follow a singular ethical position will also spell disaster for politics. Democracy can only thrive, Arendt continued, when this quest is abandoned. Thus, although the American Declaration of Independence spoke of self-evident truths, it prefaced the assertion of their self-evidence by saying "*We hold* these truths to be self-evident," which implied that "equality, if it is to be politically relevant, is a matter of opinion, and not 'the truth'" (560). Even Jefferson tacitly admitted that he was basing the Declaration on opinion not truth.

There is also a positive implication that one can draw from the role of mendacity in politics, which is connected to the fundamental principle of "the political" for Arendt: the power to act, to interrupt the apparent causality of fate and start a new chain of consequences, a new narrative of meaning. Rahel Varnhagen, the German Jewish salonnière whose biography Arendt had written years before, argued that introspection inspired mendacity because

> lying can obliterate the outside event which introspection has already converted into a purely psychic factor. Lying takes up the heritage of introspection, sums it up, and makes a reality of the freedom that introspection has won. "Lying is lovely if we choose it, and is an important component of our freedom." . . . Whatever is not proved by thinking is not provable—therefore, make your denials, falsify by lies, make use of your freedom to change and render reality ineffective at will.[122]

Lying, Arendt now echoed Varnhagen in arguing, "is clearly an attempt to change the record, and as such it is a form of *action*. . . . While the liar is a man of action, the truthteller, whether he tells rational or factual truth, most emphatically is not" (563). Whereas the truth-teller often tries to accommodate the cause of truth to the interests of the collective, "the liar, on the contrary, needs no such doubtful accommodation to appear on the political scene; he has the great advantage that he always is, so to speak, already in the midst of it. He is an actor by nature; he says what is not so because he wants things to be different from what they are—that is, he wants to change the world." Truth-telling is thus in a fundamental sense conservative, preserving what is the case, except in those instances— and here totalitarian polities are implied—when daily life is as a whole a lie.

There is, however, an important distinction between traditional political lies, told by diplomats and statesmen, and modern ones, most explicitly employed by totalitarian regimes. Whereas the former involved secrets or intentions, "modern political lies deal efficiently with things that are not secrets at all but are known to practically everybody. This is obvious in the case of rewriting contemporary history under the eyes of those who witnessed it, but it is equally true in image-making of all sorts" (564). Because the modern lie harbors a certain violence, it has a powerful destructive force: "The difference between the traditional lie and the modern lie will more often than not amount to the difference between hiding and destroying" (565). The latter—and here Arendt was talking about the "big lie" of totalitarianism—threatens to become an entirely new "reality," which often fools the teller himself. In fact, self-deception, she argued, is fundamental to the modern lie, in which even the liar is caught up in the falsehood. Although the spread of global communication networks makes it hard to sustain the "big lie" for very long, there is a danger in our losing our bearings in a reality whose ground is not easy to ascertain.

There is, however, so Arendt continued, a basic difference between lies concerning the past and those that involve the future. Only the latter can be genuinely changed by lies: "Not the past—and all factual truth, of course, concerns the past—or the present, insofar as it is the outcome of the past, but the future is open to action" (569). Such action can only take place against the relatively stable background of a past that is stubbornly factual. But ultimately, there is a conflict between the imperative to tell the truth and the realm of politics, because the former is monologic rather than dialogic: "Outstanding among the existential modes of truthtelling are the solitude of the philosopher, the isolation of the scientist and the artist, the impartiality of the historian and the judge, and the independence of the fact-finder, the witness, and the reporter" (570–71). Although there are public institutions, like the judiciary and the university, whose telos is the truth and whose impartial findings impinge on the public realm—an issue to which we will later return when addressing the implications of the boundaries of "the political"—it is necessary to acknowledge that such a boundary does exist. If we examine politics only from the external perspective of truth-telling, Arendt warned, we will miss what makes politics so valuable in itself: "the joy and the gratification that arise out of *being* in company with our peers, out of acting together and appearing in public, out of inserting ourselves into the world by word and deed, thus acquiring and sustaining our personal identity and beginning something entirely new." However much we may try to hold the realm of the political to the high moral standards of the truth-teller, however much we may want to resist the modern totalitarian "big lie's" destruction of even factual truth, "it is only by respecting its own borders that this realm, where we are free to act and to change, can remain intact, preserving its integrity and keeping its promises" (574). In short, while it would be disastrous to politicize everything, it would be no less a loss to human freedom to extirpate the uncertain realm of opinion, rhetoric, and, yes, mendacity that we call "the political."

"Lying in Politics" picked up where "Truth and Politics" left off: "Secrecy—what diplomatically is called 'discretion,' as well as *arcana imperii*, the mysteries of government—and deception, the deliberate falsehood and the outright lie used as legitimate means to achieve political ends, have been with us since the beginning of recorded history. Truthfulness has never been counted among the political virtues, and lies have always been regarded as justifiable tools in political dealings."[123] Arendt then spelled out even more clearly than in her earlier essay the link between action and deception. Because the former always involves a negation of what is the case, it always has a certain destructive force, removing what is in its way. "In other words," she wrote, "the deliberate denial of factual truth—the ability to lie—and the capacity to change facts—the ability to act—are interconnected: they owe their existence to the same source: imagination" (5). It is thus not an accident that politics and mendacity are so closely intertwined and that "moral outrage, for this reason alone, is not likely to make it disappear" (6). Whatever one may feel about the compelling power of deontological prohibitions on lying, they do not work in the realm of "the political." Contingent facts are never necessarily true, but always a function of the opinions of those who hold them and based on the testimony of witnesses, who may or may not be trustworthy.

But, stepping back from the abyss, Arendt then noted that deception is easy, but only "up to a point. . . . [For] under normal circumstances the liar is defeated by reality, for which there is no substitute" (6–7). One of the lessons of totalitarianism, or rather of its defeat, is the limits of the "big lie," which always becomes counterproductive when it undermines entirely the boundary between truth and falsehood. There are, to be sure, other variants of less extreme lying that characterize the modern era—unlike in "Truth and Politics," she no longer identified the "modern lie" with the totalitarian destruction, rather than mere hiding, of truth—such as the increased use of public relations techniques of manipulation.

A second new variant Arendt identified with the officials who promulgated the Pentagon Papers, the controversial report on the status of the Vietnam War leaked to the press by Daniel Ellsberg. Not only were they normal makers of images, but they also prided themselves on being rational problem solvers, men of theory, who were willing to adjust the facts to fit their pet ideas. "That concealment, falsehood, and the role of the deliberate lie became the chief issues of the Pentagon Papers, rather than illusion, error, miscalculation, and the like," she wrote, "is mainly due to the strange fact that the mistaken decisions and lying statements consistently violated the astoundingly accurate factual reports of the intelligence community" (14). Rather than exercising political judgment, they arrogantly calculated based on a flawed notion of rational truth. It is not even right to call the leaders of the war effort the victims of self-deception, for "self-deception still presupposes a distinction between

truth and falsehood, between facts and fantasy, and therefore a conflict between the real world and the self-deceived deceiver that
disappears in an entirely defactualized world" (36). In short, they
suffered from an excessive certainty about their command of the
rational truth, which, although Arendt didn't spell out the comparison, was similar to that displayed by the Platonic defenders of the
"noble lie."

The upshot of Arendt's complicated animadversions on lying in
politics was that there were benign and injurious versions of it.
When it was done by rulers who thought they were in command of
a rational, absolute truth and were able to exercise their will over the
contingent facts, it could lead to disaster. When it tried to create an
entirely alternative world, it came up against the resistance of reality,
especially that of past facts, and undermined the trust necessary to
"act in concert." Because she acknowledged and condemned these
drawbacks, some commentators have come to argue that Arendt
ultimately valued both truth and truthfulness, despite appearances
to the contrary, even in politics.[124]

But when lying was a weapon in the endless struggle of plural
opinions, in which there was no strong claim to a singular truth and
rhetoric rather calculation prevailed, Arendt praised it as an expression of imagination, action, even freedom to change the world. In
the service of a counterfactual denial of what is, she speculated, it
might point to an alternative world of what might be (the French
word for lie [le mensonge], as Jean-Michel Rabaté later pointed out,
contains the word for dream [le songe]).[125] Whereas the "big lie" was
an expression of man in his guise as *Homo faber*, the fabricator of a
world that was like a finished object, more modest lies were the sign
of man as free actor, with the world still open to change.[126] As such,
they were inextricably bound up with the essence of "the political,"
as Arendt defined it, the arena in which monologic truth and coercive reason were tyrannical intruders. In moderation and within the
boundaries of "the political," mendacity was thus for Arendt not an
unequivocal evil to be denounced. Indeed, as the case of the anti-
hypocritical Robespierre and the Terror showed, the wholesale denunciation of it might well produce worse results than its opposite.

One additional point needs to be made about the relationship between opinion and mendacity, which Arendt herself did not elaborate, but whose implications Harry Frankfurt discusses in his now celebrated analysis of bullshit.[127] Although careful to distinguish the latter from deliberate lying, he notes that in a situation where people are expected to have opinions on virtually all issues before them, they inevitably base them on prejudices, imperfect knowledge, and fallacious understandings of the complexities of the choices. Democratic politics is particularly inclined to sponsor this outcome beause it claims that every responsible citizen should have opinions, which are allegedly "well-informed." But since no one has the time and few have the inclination to inform themselves on all the bewildering and often technically obscure issues they are expected to opine about, the result is a kind of collective phoniness in which people pretend their opinions are grounded in reason, logic, and evidence. It may not be outright mendacity, but it certainly falls short of the high standard of rational decision making underlying much liberal theory.

The most eloquent current defender of that standard, albeit from a position that goes beyond both traditional liberalism and republicanism, is Jürgen Habermas, whose discourse theory of law and politics is grounded, as we noted, in a universal pragmatics claiming language has an inherent normative telos of "comprehensibility, truth, truthfulness, and rightness." The ideal of perfect communicability leading to a rational consensus provides the transcendental norm that motivates political action in the public sphere, which allows opinion, *pace* Frankfurt, to become more than just arbitrary whim or prejudice.[128] As Amanda Anderson has observed, the value of sincerity has been elevated by Habermas from a personality trait into an impersonal communicative presupposition, which underpins his proceduralist defense of a political ethos of argumentation.[129] Thus from a Habermasian point of view, it would seem that mendacity could never be construed as a political virtue.

There is, however, a realistic appreciation in Habermas that the norm of rational consensus based on the better argument is still a counterfactual ideal that is only approached asymptotically in the public sphere, which has been debased from its high point in the eighteenth and early nineteenth centuries through the influence of manipulated mass communications. In fact, he acknowledges that, even during that period, there was a fundamental deception at the heart of the matter, which involved the claim that the bourgeoisie, whose members were the primary constituents of the public sphere, were above narrow partisan interest and could represent the whole. In a sentence significantly italicized in *The Structural Transformation of the Public Sphere,* he writes, "The fully developed bourgeois public sphere was based on the fictitious identity of the two roles assumed by the privatized individuals who came together to form a public: the role of property owners and the role of human beings pure and simple."[130] Fueling the fictional basis of the identity of bourgeois and human was a prior counterfactual reality, that of the world of the novel, especially in its epistolary form. Here the conjugal family as a community of reciprocal love could be taken as a model of human relations based on equality, sympathy, and mutuality rather than hierarchy, a kind of training grounds for the subjectivity needed in the public sphere. Habermas acknowledges the ambivalent nature of this new cultural formation, at once an expression of yearning and an illusion. The reality as illusion that the new genre created received its proper name in English, "fiction," "as it shed the character of the *merely* fictitious. The psychological novel fashioned for the first time the kind of realism that allowed anyone to enter into the literary action as a substitute for his own, to use the relationship between the figures, between the author, the characters, and the readers as substitute relationships for reality."[131]

In other words, at the heart of even the Habermasian version of the political as discursive rationality is a realization that it is based on a founding duplicity—or at least a counterfactual ideal that resists disclosing itself as such—which goes against the telos of total transparency, accountability, and honesty. Neither the bourgeois family nor the bourgeois public sphere was fully what it claimed to be, even if its aspiration to become what it was not might have a critical force. Although the result was by no means tantamount to an endorsement of deliberate mendacity in politics, it did suggest that a policy of full disclosure could be a problem for a proceduralist politics of pure sincerity.

POLITICS AND THE AESTHETIC: ON HYPOCRISY AND THE SYMBOLIC

Lying as the fabrication of alternative worlds, imagining as stating as true what is not the case, the "fictionality" of a particular class pretending to speak for the whole, or a conjugal family idealizing its internal relations as egalitarian—all of these raise the inevitable question of the relationship between "the political" understood in largely aesthetic terms and mendacity. As we noted in our previous chapter, there have been many critics of the aestheticization of politics, especially among those who hold out hope for rationality, either administrative or communicative, as the antidote to political mystification and demagoguery. From their perspective, a politics of false images and misleading rhetoric is a politics in which the naked struggle for power is shrouded in garments of deception. The ethical moment in political life, which can be understood in many ways—the search for justice, the preservation of rights, the protection of the innocent, to name a few—is undermined, these critics worry, if aesthetics is allowed to trump ethics. To the extent that the aesthetic dimension of political life abets illusion and prevents the truth from being told and is indifferent to moral considerations, they argue it must be vigorously resisted.

In addition, other critics point out, there is the danger of a politics based on the aesthetics of organic wholeness that analogizes from the work of art to the community. Like the imaginary unity nurtured in what Lacan made famous as the "mirror stage" of infant development, fantasies of organic wholeness give rise to monolithic ideologies of totality. The latter appear, as we have seen, in the totalitarian "big lie," in which the agonistic and pluralistic messiness of normal political life is at least temporarily overcome through a forced harmony based on a mixture of coercion and mystification. And even if this more extreme version of aesthetic politics can be avoided, the taint of falsification remains. In democracies, where many worry politics has become excessively theatrical, we routinely chastise our opponents for "playing politics," as if that were somehow a betrayal of what they should be doing. (Would, for example, a natural scientist ever accuse an opponent in a scientific debate of "playing science" or an attorney damn a rival for "playing law?").

There have, however, been several recent theorists—Lefort, Rosenvallon, Ankersmit, and Rancière were the names we cited—who have revised the generally negative image of aesthetic, or at least symbolic, politics, even in its modern, democratic guise. Drawing, as we saw, on Ernst Kantorowicz's analysis of the king's two bodies, they argue that even in modern democracies there is an inevitable distinction between a symbolic and real notion of "the people." Despite the efforts of totalitarian governments to fuse the two in an imaginary unity, they remain stubbornly irreconcilable, producing that healthy "broken" symbolic politics we have seen Ankersmit praise.[132] Rosenvallon identifies this gap with the fundamental distinction between and yet entanglement of le politique and la politique: "It is first of all thanks to the impossibility of dissociating *the political* from *politics* that a certain kind of disappointment with the modern regime comes about. For it is never simple to separate the noble from the vulgar, the great ambitions from the petty egotistical calculations, the trenchant language of truth from the sophistry of manipulation and seduction. . . . There grows up around the political, as a result, a longing that in a certain sense is impossible to fulfill."[133]

That longing for an unbroken politics of full transparency, integrity, honesty, and truthfulness—a kind of nostalgia for an imaginary wholeness that never existed—is doomed to fail because at the very heart of political life is an often unacknowledged tension between ideal unity and real dissensus, which can never be overcome, even through totalitarian phantasmatic means. Representation, in both political and aesthetic terms, involves a substitution that never produces a "real presence" in the theological sense of full unity between universal and particular. In short, there is a fundamental affinity between politics and aesthetics understood as the healthy role of the symbolic, rather than the imaginary. No matter how much we strive to make it the arena for the triumph of rational argumentation over coercion, manipulation, and mystification, there will always be some resistance to a regime of transparent truth-telling. For even in a democracy, the ultimately fictional quality of the sovereign people is impossible to overcome. But it would also be wrong to shatter the illusion. Even Jeremy Bentham, so often the anti-aesthetic scourge of linguistic fictions such as natural rights, admitted that when it came to such ideas as the "court of public opinion" or "the infallibility of the people," there were benefits that accrue from keeping the pretense undisturbed.[134]

Of course, there are always dangers in that pretense when its illusory side is entirely forgotten, leading to forced attempts to fill the empty space of "the people" with a concrete embodiment, which risks the transformation of agonistic democracy into totalitarianism. As Habermas notes with reference to Rousseau's dangerous notion of the general will and fantasy of direct democracy, "The *volonté générale* as the *corpus mysticum* was bound up with the *corpus physicum* of the people as a consensual assembly. The idea of a plebiscite in permanence presented itself to Rousseau as the image of the Greek *polis*."[135]

No less ominous are the consequences when the operative unit of uniform solidarity is understood in ethnic or national terms, as imagined communities struggle to create unified identities through inclusion and exclusion. All types of myths of origin or blood or destiny have been generated to justify what in fact are contingent and mutable collective entities.[136] There is, in other words, a delicate balance that has to be maintained between preserving the symbolic myth of unity and refraining from trying to make it fully incarnate in a positive way. The space of the eternal king and his postmonarchical surrogates must always be kept empty, however much we pretend to know who fills them.

Even in a self-consciously pluralist polity that eschews the goal of homogeneity and valorizes agonism, there is often a fictional quality to more fragile coalitions of partners, whose interests and values may well clash, despite their protestations of unity. As Ruth Grant has noted, building solidarity requires a certain dissembling about the basis on which it is built. Machiavelli and Rousseau were correct in noting the inevitability in politics of dependency in creating coalitions of partners with different interests. "Politics," she argues, "is characterized by relationships of mutual need among parties with conflicting interests. To enlist the support of the other party requires flattery, manipulation, and a pretence of concern for his needs."[137] That is, because there is no fully homogenous majority in which a total congruence of values and interests creates complete solidarity, it is necessary to build coalitions on the basis at least in part of imagined, fictional commonalities. This involves inevitable hypocrisy, which means the public proclamation of shared values and interests combined with a private acknowledgment of their hollowness. Often this end requires the invocation of high-minded ideals. "Machiavelli and Rousseau," she explains, "appreciate the necessity of political hypocrisy, which is to say, they appreciate the importance of appeals to genuine public moral principles. Hypocrisy requires moral pretense, and that pretense is necessary because politics cannot be conducted solely through bargaining among competing particular interests."[138] Moral values, such as the prescription of lying, can therefore be neither abandoned nor fully observed. For, as Rochefoucauld famously remarked, "hypocrisy is the homage vice pays to virtue."

In democracies in particular, where fragile coalitions need to be created to avoid coercive minority rule, the function of hypocrisy is especially important, despite the rationalist hope that the better argument can rally disparate factions around the common interest. That hope is not entirely misplaced, but it cannot be fully realized. The liberal faith in trust in a pluralist society is not enough to overcome the stubborn persistence of real differences in values, passions, and interests. The wholesale moralistic condemnation of hypocrisy can in fact mask a partial interest that pretends to be a universal one, and therefore has the potential to employ violence to enforce its will on others. "Political relations," Grant argues, tacitly against both Schmitt and Habermas, "are neither enmities nor friendships but friendly relations sustained among nonfriends."[139] As such, they require the fiction of greater common interest and values than is actually the case.

A parallel argument based on the often unacknowledged social underpinnings of political life is made by the political theorist Judith Shklar in her discussion of hypocrisy in *Ordinary Vices*: "The paradox of liberal democracy is that it encourages hypocrisy because the politics of persuasion require, as any reader of Aristotle's *Rhetoric* knows, a certain amount of dissimulation on the part of all speakers. . . . The democracy of everyday life, which is rightly admired by egalitarian visitors to America, does not arise from sincerity. It is based on the pretense that we must speak to each other as if social standings were a matter of indifference in our views of each other."[140] That is, we dutifully observe the fiction that egalitarian blindness to distinction is already a reality, rather than a desideratum to be sought, albeit never fully achieved. To the extent that democracy is always a condition to come rather than a state of being already realized, we cannot avoid a certain duplicity—and perhaps a necessary and even healthy one—in our claim that we live in one in the present.[141]

Moreover, as David Runciman notes, "Any politics founded on the idea of equality will produce politicians of a type with the people they rule, and yet recognizably different, given the fact that they also have to rule them. All political leaders in these circumstances will need to put on the appropriate mask that allows them to sustain this tricky double act."[142] In the place of the king's two bodies, we have the president's two faces, as brilliantly exemplified by the figure of George W. Bush, at once the privileged scion of a powerful eastern political dynasty and the "good ole boy" Texan with plebeian tastes and the crude sensibility of a frat boy. Whether or not Bush was consciously crafting his second persona or somehow came to believe he really was what he seemed to be, he was clearly living a role that persuaded a lot of people that it was authentic.

Does that mean that politics understood aesthetically is inherently based on a mendacious premise? It is, of course, important to avoid conflating fictionality and the symbolic with outright mendacity. Ever since Aristotle's *Poetics,* most commentators have realized that aesthetic fictions were in a realm of discourse with its own protocols and markers of distinction. From time to time the lesson was lost, thus compelling a writer like Sir Philip Sydney to write *The Defense of Poesie* in 1595 in order to reestablish the boundary by stressing the distinction between what Wittgenstein would have called different language games: "Now for the Poet, he nothing affirmeth, and therefore never lieth: for as I take it, to lie, is to affirme that to bee true, which is false." It was not perhaps until the time of the modern novel that the full power of fictionality was registered, and then ironically through the device of "formal realism," which dispensed with the earlier emblems of explicit fabulation in fairy tales, epic poems, romances, fables, and the like.[143] Although dogged antinaturalists like Oscar Wilde could still insist that art and lying were virtual synonyms, echoing Plato both in the substance and the dialogic form of his argument while reversing his evaluation of its implications,[144] the audiences at his plays and readers of his novel had come to know the difference.

But if on a metalevel of understanding, fictionality involves suspending the language game of asserting the truth in a way that the intentional lie does not, we must nonetheless acknowledge the cumulative effect of the aesthetic moment in politics in creating an environment in which a premium is not placed on veracity. That is, a great deal of what passes for politics in virtually all of its guises contains an irreducible element of aesthetic play, understood to various extents by the participants involved, which makes the issue of truth-telling marginal, if not irrelevant. Whether we see the essential core of "the political" as aesthetic or merely concede that the latter has a meaningful role, the inevitable presence of this element makes it very hard to hope for a politics fully purged of looseness toward the truth. Playing politics is, in other words, what politicians necessarily do in the inevitably theatricalized arena of the political, and there is no way we can overcome it short of imposing the standards of the nonpolitical on their behavior.

To put this conclusion in somewhat different terms, it will be useful to recall Arendt's claim about the parallels between aesthetic and political judgment in her posthumously published *Lectures on Kant's Political Philosophy*.[145] Here she argued that the reflective judgments Kant famously distinguished from their determinant counterparts in the *Critique of Judgment* were a better model for political judgment than those exercised in the first two Critiques, which were, respectively, epistemological and moral. Whereas these involved universal, binding categories of understanding or transcendental norms applicable under all circumstances, aesthetic and political judgments relied on analogies from specific cases and paradigmatic exemplars. Although one might debate the implications of casuistry for a theologian or moralist, for a politician, it provides a far more useful training than deontological absolutism. Thus, the unqualified prohibition on lying we have seen Kant uphold might be plausible in terms of categorical moral judgments—although utilitarian moralists would demur—but when it comes to political judgments, it is inappropriately imposed.

In one important sense, however, it should be conceded that the parallel between aesthetic fabulation and political mendacity breaks down. For, although W. H. Auden may have exaggerated when he famously claimed that "poetry makes nothing happen,"[146] the performative effects of artistic fabulation are different from those of political lies. That is, a lie told by a character in a novel has no consequences in the real world, nor at least in principle does the reading of a fictional narrative, even if our sensibilities can be genuinely affected by the experience. Pinocchio's nose doesn't really grow outside the aesthetic frame, nor was his creator, Carlo Collodi—his real creator, that is, not the fictional shoemaker Geppetto—in danger of being accused of perjury for having written that it did.

But lies told in the political realm do, of course, often have real consequences; indeed, they are intended to have them, whether or not the intentions are "noble." The performative function of deception, as we have noted in our discussion of the linguistics of lying, is even more important than its constative function, insofar as sometimes saying what is factually true can be intended to deceive, as evidenced by the famous Jewish joke about train destinations. Whereas on a metalevel, everyone is in on the nonperformative nature of aesthetic assertions—they are illusions that are understood as such, semblances that are not mistaken for reality—political lies sometimes split the world into those in the know and those deceived (although in a situation of hypercynicism, everyone may be in on the game).[147] So as in all the other attempts to define "the political," here too we have to be careful about concluding that we have somehow found an essential and normative answer, applicable in all cases, in privileging the aesthetic.

THE BOUNDARIES OF THE POLITICAL AND THE LIMITS
OF MENDACITY

Much of the argument for the special status of "the political," however it is defined, is based on the premise that it occupies, either literally or metaphorically, a room of its own. Although it is clear that it can colonize new spaces or vacate older ones, thus expanding or contracting its boundaries, the conclusion that there can be a meaningful distinction between the realm of politics and other realms of human endeavor is difficult to gainsay. It may not be, *pace* Schmitt and Arendt, a transcendental, ontological distinction valid for all cultures at all times, nor necessarily a normative one worth defending when it is in danger of being weakened. But at least in much of the experience of complex societies such as ours, it has achieved a functional significance that cannot be ignored.

Moreover, as noted in the previous chapter, utopian versions of (meta-)politics—those that dream of a purified realm of action unsullied by compromise or dissensus—are often set in imaginary heterotopias or even more likely, no-places at all (thus the etymology of u-topos). As William Morris tellingly put it in the title of his great utopian romance, their news comes "from nowhere." Not surprisingly, they tend to privilege the value of absolute truth-telling and decry mendacity as a falling off from their ideal of perfect political behavior. Perhaps the most explicit version of that credo appeared in William Godwin's celebrated *Political Justice* of 1793, which included a ringing endorsement of unflinching sincerity in all human relations, political or otherwise, from a utilitarian point of view. For Godwin, "the only species of sincerity which can in any degree prove satisfactory to the enlightened moralist and politician is that where the frankness is perfect, and every degree of reserve is discarded."[148] For a utopian like Godwin, there was no distinction between an enlightened moralist and a politician because politics was not a realm apart from other spheres of human interaction.

For nonutopian political theory, as we have seen, the space of the political has meant that at least to some degree it is segregated off into a special realm of its own. Such a conclusion is, in fact, hard to deny. It would, however, be problematic to construe the boundary surrounding it as so watertight that leakage cannot occur between inside and outside. No other spaces, after all, have shown themselves to be permanently off-limits to its permeating power. Art, religion, law, science, culture, family life, even the interior of the individual subject, have all shown themselves capable of being politicized, however one construes "the political." Although the claim that the personal is inherently indistinguishable from the political may be untenable as a universal truth, the two, we have come to appreciate, are not categorical and impenetrable opposites.

What is important to acknowledge, however, is that the infiltration can go in both directions. That is, despite efforts of purists like Carl Schmitt or Hannah Arendt to keep the walls high and tight, political life cannot prevent its own permeation by its various others. Perhaps most obviously, although politicians are often encouraged to suspend their normal moral scruples, and have been faulted by commentators at least since Machiavelli if they fail to do so,[149] it is very difficult for them to cast off entirely their prior socialization in conventional morality. Insofar as this education normally stigmatizes lying and calls into question the character of the liar and the hypocrite, it is very hard to dirty one's hands without ultimately feeling remorse, as even Lady Macbeth discovered to her great chagrin.[150] The Platonic "noble liar" might strive to justify his actions not only by the nobility of his intentions but also by the nobility of his intrinsic character, which was virtuous by definition, but for those who understand character as itself the cumulative effect of actions, no such consolation is available. You don't have to be a Hegelian "beautiful soul," fastidiously avoiding even petty compromises with an imperfect world, to worry about the results of choosing tainted means to achieve a laudable goal, as goals are rarely unaffected by the means used to attain them.

Perhaps the best that can be hoped for in politics is a utilitarian moral calculus, akin to the probabilistic casuistry that so outraged Jansenist and Puritanical rigorists, which weighs one transgression against another, and allows the politician consciously and courageously to take on the weighty burden of getting his hands soiled for a higher cause. Constant's response to Kant's absolute prohibition of mendacity, whether or not it can be applied across the board, is nonetheless valid for the politician, who cannot easily, if at all, separate the noumenal from the phenomenal world, the world of principles from the world of effects. This interaction goes, of course, in both directions. As many commentators have noted, the very resort to hypocritical protestations of moral rectitude indicate the power that social codes of moral conduct have over any public transaction. The internalization of those codes cannot be entirely escaped, no matter how imperfect or conflict-ridden the results. Honest men sent abroad to lie for their country cannot easily suppress the moral training they have brought with them. The role of the diplomat and the character of the person occupying it can, as history abundantly shows us,[151] even come into conflict, with the latter winning out.

If the boundary between the politician qua political actor and qua moral agent is not watertight, neither are the ones differentiating formal institutions or informal spheres of human behavior from the realm of politics. Who, after all, could deny that economic considerations impinge on politics in a wide variety of ways, even if one resists the reduction of one to the other along the lines of rational choice theory? But it is perhaps three institutions in particular that are most relevant for our argument, at least in their ideal form: a free press, an independent judiciary, and an open academic culture. Although it would be naïve to think that any of these is untouched by politicization and therefore escapes the pressures to practice mendacity we have been outlining in this book, they all follow a logic that goes in a different direction.

A free press can seek to uncover the truths hidden or denied by politicians, testing their claims against independent standards, offering evidence to undercut deliberate obfuscations of the facts. As in the case of the Pentagon Papers, it can make known what is secret, revealing to all what is intended for the eyes of the few, those soi-disant noble liars whose motives may not, after all, be as pure as they claim. The tradition of what has come to be called muckraking has been especially vigilant in exposing political duplicity, following the celebrated edict of I. F. Stone that "all governments lie." Journalism, of course, can itself perpetuate lies, as we know from the various scandals that have exposed false stories and given offenders like Janet Cook and Stephen Glass their notoriety. And the zeal for exposure can violate the privacy of public figures in ways that cause considerable unease in a society that has not yet abandoned its ambivalence about utter transparency and full disclosures. But at least as a check on the spins, dissimulations, deliberate ambiguities, and outright falsehoods of political rhetoric, the fourth estate provides a vital service for a public that wisely resists accepting at face value the claims of those who would sway their opinions.

Similarly, an independent judiciary dedicated to the fair and impartial implementation of the laws promulgated by the political process is, at least when that process can no longer directly influence it, able to follow procedures that seek to determine the truth about a case before it. Of course, those procedures are themselves merely formal rather than substantive, and can sometimes be manipulated to prevent the truth from being ascertained and avoid responsibility for violating it, with the guilty getting off, as we say, on "a technicality." And in an adversarial system in which lawyers represent defendants no matter what their guilt or innocence might be, advocacy can overwhelm disinterestedness. But at least there are penalties for a sworn witness who violates the oath to "tell the truth, the whole truth, and nothing but the truth," and perjury is a crime that can be punished in a court of law, if not the court of public opinion. Moreover, when they are admitted to the bars of American states and elsewhere, attorneys are required to swear an oath themselves, which typically includes the promise: "I will employ for the purpose of maintaining the causes confided to me such means only as are consistent with truth and honor, and will never seek to mislead the judge or jury by any artifice or false statement of fact or law."[152]

Politicians who are compelled to testify in court or in front of political bodies like the American Congress, which can compel sworn testimony, are vulnerable to the legal penalties they will face if they violate perjury laws in a way they are not in the political arena per se. As Bill Clinton discovered to his chagrin, such testimony can provide the basis for severe political repercussions, even if in his case the ultimate judgment was made in the political realm, with party-line voting in the Senate—with some Republicans breaking ranks to vote against the two articles of impeachment—preventing a conviction.

The Clinton case also illustrates another boundary issue, that between science or the realm of professional academic life and politics. Although here too it would be easy to offer examples of mendacity in the scientific and academic worlds, their normative procedures come far closer to the ideal model of a perfect speech situation posited by Habermas as the telos of the public sphere. That is, they are postulated on the grounds of the better argument winning out over the authority of the person making it, and professional judgment being based on openness, transparency, and the replicability, especially in the case of science, of experimental data. Although there are critics, such as Stanley Fish, who have tried to question these ideals, claiming they are more ideological than realizable in practice,[153] most observers resist the folding of the academic realm entirely into the political (as Fish tacitly advocates). As the scientific evidence of DNA samples of presidential semen on Monica Lewinsky's dress demonstrated, that boundary can, however, be undone in the opposite direction, and mendacity in the political realm exposed by techniques developed in the scientific.

The implications of the porous boundaries between the political and its others (as well, we might add, between the political and mere politics) are clear: whatever the claims that can be made for the special affinity between mendacity and the political, they are relativized by the inevitable imbrication of it with other realms of human endeavor where truth-telling is more normative and perhaps more frequently observed in practice. For all the attempts to isolate the political as an utterly autonomous realm, however its essential characteristics may be defined, it cannot be utterly differentiated from its various others. And as a result, no unequivocal defense of political hypocrisy or mendacity will ever be fully convincing. For no matter what hat he or she may wear in his role as a politician, the person underneath is still a product of the moral and social norms he or she absorbed before entering the space of the political. Even Lady Macbeth had trouble sleeping at night.

Still, however leaky its boundaries, within the realm of the political the search for perfect truthfulness is not only vain but also potentially dangerous. For ironically, the mirror image of the "big lie" may well be the ideal of "big truth," the absolute, univocal truth, which silences those who disagree with it and abruptly terminates discussion. Both are the enemy of the pluralism of opinions, the ongoing vigor of debate, and the bracing clash of values and interests. Both reduce politics, as Arendt would have it, to the monologic fabrication of man as *Homo faber,* rather than the give and take of men in their motley variety. Instead, it may be healthier to foster lots of little countervailing lies or at least half-truths, as well as the ability to test and see through them, rather than hold out hope for ending mendacity once and for all. It may well be wise to beware the pharisaical politician who loudly proclaims his own purity of intention and refusal ever to lie, the self-congratulating paragon of authenticity who damns all his opponents as opportunists or worse. It may be prudent to relax our outrage against hypocrisy under any circumstances, and concede that there are many necessary fictions at the heart of even the most transparent and accountable of political systems.

For ironically, truth-telling can under certain circumstances be a weapon of the powerful, while lying is a tactic of the weak.[154] And the politician who doggedly follows his moral convictions, embracing what Weber famously called a *Gesinnungsethik* (ethic of ultimate ends), may ultimately do more harm than one who practices a *Verantworthungsethik* (ethic of responsibility). Conviction, after all, is an ambivalent virtue when compromise and flexibility may better serve the common good. For it may be fueled more by the desire— dare we call it self-serving?—to save one's soul than to save the world. This is not a brief for cynicism or immorality, nor a justification of winning "by any means necessary," let alone an exhortation to give up entirely the desire to know what is the truth (at least to the extent politics includes that quest). It is just a sober recognition that politics, however we chose to define its essence and limit its contours, will never be an entirely fib-free zone of authenticity, sincerity, integrity, transparency, and righteousness. And maybe, I hope it will be clear by now, that's ultimately a good thing too.

NOTES

PREFACE

1. The title was, of course, a play on the popular game "Truth and Consequences" and was liberally employed in other writings on the theme, e.g., David MacMichael's March 2004 column for CommonDreams.com and Carl M. Cannon's essay for the January/February issue of the *Atlantic*.

2. Nicholas von Hoffman, *Hoax: Why Americans Are Suckered by White House Lies* (New York, 2004), 3.

3. George Stephanopolous, *All Too Human: A Political Education* (Boston, 1999); Christopher Hitchens, *No One Left to Lie To: The Triangulations of William Jefferson Clinton* (London, 1999).

4. Cited in Hitchens, *No One Left to Lie To*, 24.

5. Martin Jay, *Songs of Experience: Modern American and European Variations on a Universal Theme* (Berkeley, 2004).

INTRODUCTION

1. Adolf Hitler, *Mein Kampf*, trans. Ralph Mannheim (Boston, 1943), 231–32.

2. Hitler continued, "The foremost connoisseurs of this truth regarding the possibilities in the use of falsehood and slander have always been the Jews; for after all, their whole existence is based on one single great lie, to wit, that they are a religious community while actually they are a race—and what a race! One of the greatest minds of humanity [Schopenhauer] has nailed them forever as such in an eternally correct phrase of fundamental truth: he called them 'the great masters of the lie.' And anyone who does not recognize this or does not want to believe it will never in this world be able to help the truth to victory" (*Mein Kampf*, 232).

3. See Jeffrey Herf, "The 'Jewish War': Goebbels and the Antisemitic Campaigns of the Nazi Propaganda Ministry," *Holocaust and Genocide Studies* 19.1 (Spring 2005).

4. Theodor W. Adorno, *Minima Moralia: Reflections from Damaged Life,* trans. E. F. N. Jephcott (London, 1974), 108.

5. Alexandre Koyré, "The Political Function of the Modern Lie," *Contemporary Jewish Record* 8.3 (June 1945): 296–97.

6. As Harald Weinrich put it in a new preface to his classic essay "The Linguistics of Lying": "I doubt even more now than in 1965 that the corruption of political consciousness caused by this lying can ever be fully described in linguistic means. Public discussion of the day was dominated by the question of whether the German language shared in the disgrace, perhaps even in the guilt, of the crimes that were later identified with terms like *Holocaust* and *Shoah.*" *The Linguistics of Lying and Other Essays,* trans. Jane K. Brown and Marshall Brown (Seattle, 2005), 6.

7. Judith N. Shklar, *Ordinary Vices* (Cambridge, Mass., 1984), 83.

8. For a thorough rehearsal of the debate, which canvasses other places in Plato's writings where similar ideas are discussed, see Carl Page, "The Truth about Lies in Plato's *Republic,*" *Ancient Philosophy* 11 (1991).

9. Hans Sluga, *Heidegger's Crisis: Philosophy and Politics in Nazi Germany* (Cambridge, Mass., 1993), 175.

10. The most infamous example is the October 4, 1943, speech Heinrich Himmler gave to the SS in Poznan justifying the Holocaust by saying even later generations would have to be protected from the terrible knowledge of what was being done for their own good.

11. Leo Strauss, *On Tyranny,* rev. and expanded ed., ed. Victor Gourevitch and Michael S. Roth (New York, 1991).

12. Leo Strauss, "The Spirit of Sparta or the Taste of Xenophon," *Social Research* 6.4 (November 1939): 535.

13. Niccolò Machiavelli, *The Prince: With Related Documents,* trans. and ed. William J. Connell (Boston, 2005), 93.

14. Ibid, 94. The classic treatment of the idea of *raison d'état* and its development is Friedrich Meinecke, *Machiavellism: The Doctrine of Raison d'État and Its Place in Modern History,* trans. Douglas Stark (London, 1957).

15. Machiavelli, letter to Luigi Guicciardini, May 17, 1521, *The Letters of Machiavelli: A Selection* (Chicago, 1988), 200.

16. Machiavelli, *The Prince,* 134–40.

17. Leo Strauss, *Thoughts on Machiavelli* (Chicago, 1958), 173. He then adds, more controversially, that "Machiavelli breaks with the Great Tradition and initiates the Enlightenment. We shall have to consider whether that Enlightenment deserves its name or whether its true name is Obfuscation."

18. William J. Bouwsma, *The Waning of the Renaissance* (New Haven, 2000), 220.

19. J. A. Fernández-Santamaria, *Reason of State and Statecraft in Spanish Political Thought, 1595–1640* (Lanham, Md., 1983), chap. 2. It should be noted that the reputation of politicians was not uniformly negative in the period after Machiavelli. At the beginning of the nineteenth century in Great Britain, for example, it enjoyed a relatively high status, based on identifying the role

with the statesman and parliamentarian. The change occurred with the growth of mass party machines after the Reform Bill of 1867, which turned politicians into electioneering specialists and party managers. See the discussion in Kari Palonen, *Re-Thinking Politics: Essays from a Quarter-Century* (Jyväskylä, Finland, 2007), chap. 14.

20. Claude Lefort, *Le travail de l'oeuvre Machiavel* (Paris, 1972); for a discussion, see Bernard Flynn, *The Philosophy of Claude Lefort: Interpreting the Political* (Evanston, 2005), 77–78. The term "disenchantment of the world," coined by Friedrich Schiller, was made famous by Max Weber in his treatment of modernist secularization.

21. The attempt to adopt a modified version of Machiavellianism for religious purposes was already underway in the writings of Spanish ethicists at the end of the sixteenth century. See Fernández-Santamaria, *Reason of State and Statecraft*, chap. 3.

22. David Livingstone Smith, *Why We Lie: The Evolutionary Roots of Deception and the Unconscious Mind* (New York, 2004), chap. 4.

23. Benedetto Croce, *Elementi di politica* (Bari, 1925), 60.

24. For these and other nuanced evaluations of Machiavelli, see Sheldon Wolin, *Politics and Vision: Continuity and Vision in Western Political Thought* (Boston, 1960), chap. 7.

25. Maureen Ramsey, "Justifications for Lying in Politics," in *The Politics of Lying: Implications for Democracy*, ed. Lionel Cliffe, Maureen Ramsay, and Dave Bartlett (New York, 2000), 6.

26. Strauss, *Thoughts on Machiavelli*, 13.

27. J. G. A. Pocock, *The Machiavellian Moment* (Princeton, 1975).

28. Bernard Wishy, *Good-bye, Machiavelli: Government and American Life* (Baton Rouge, 1995), 1.

29. Lionel Trilling, *Sincerity and Authenticity* (Cambridge, Mass., 1974), chap. 1.

30. Jonas Barish, *The Anti-Theatrical Prejudice* (Berkeley, 1981). It should be remembered that it was Polonius, not one of Shakespeare's heroes, who advised his son "to thine own self be true." Shakespeare's own attitude toward sincerity was never so straightforward.

31. Sissela Bok, *Lying: Moral Choice in Public and Private Life*, 2nd ed. (New York, 1999), 84.

32. There were, of course, significant exceptions to the hostility to theatricality in early American history, with figures like William Dunlap (1766–1839) producing many plays. But it is telling that in 1774 the Continental Congress outlawed all theatrical entertainments as a corrupting luxury imported from England. The Old American Company, the leading professional troupe, left for Jamaica and did not return until ten years later.

33. See Lester Gilbert Crocker, "The Problem of Truth and Falsehood in the Age of Enlightenment," *Journal of the History of Ideas* 14.4 (1953). He shows that there was a full spectrum of attitudes toward the value of truth-telling in politics during the Enlightenment, which ranged from the elitist defense of

the *mensonge officieux* by enlightened despots like Frederick the Great to the defense of the social utility of truth by *philosophes* like Helvétius and the imperative to tell the truth for the sake of the law in Kant.

34. The famous passage from Mason L. Weems, *The Life of Washington*, ed. Marcus Cunliffe (Cambridge, Mass, 1967), reads:

> "George," said his father, "do you know who killed that beautiful little cherry-tree yonder in the garden?"
>
> This was a tough question; and George staggered under it for a moment; but quickly recovered himself; and looking at his father, with the sweet face of youth brightened with the inexpressible charm of all-conquering truth, he bravely cried out, "I can't tell a lie, Pa; you know I can't tell a lie. I did cut it with my hatchet."—Run to my arms, you dearest boy, cried his father in transports, run to my arms; glad am I, George, that you killed my tree, for you have paid me for it a thousand fold. Such an act of heroism in my son is worth more than a thousand trees, though blossomed with silver and their fruits of purest gold. (12)

35. Lincoln's legendary honesty was expressed in a series of apparently real anecdotes, stretching back to his days as a clerk in a store, when he realized he had overcharged a customer 6.25¢ and walked a considerable distance to return the right change. American children were often regaled with these exemplary anecdotes, including by Horatio Alger Jr. in his *Abraham Lincoln: The Backwoods Boy* (New York, 1883). Only much later would a less ingenuous historian like Richard Hofstadter refer to him as "among the world's greatest propagandists." *The American Political Tradition and the Men Who Made It* (New York, 1973), 110.

36. See David Vincent, *The Culture of Secrecy: Britain, 1832–1998* (Oxford, 1999). Bernard Williams also notes that "in the British Parliament, there is a convention that ministers may not lie when answering questions or making statements, but they can certainly omit, select, give answers that reveal less than the whole truth, and generally, give a misleading impression." *Truth and Truthfulness: An Essay in Genealogy* (Princeton, 2002), 108.

37. Whether or not Freud's own attitude toward truth and lying was simply a straightforward exhortation to confess the truth is another question. For a subtle analysis of the ways in which psychoanalysis can be called "the science of lying," see John Forrester's "Lying on the Couch," in *Dismantling Truth: Reality in the Postmodern World,* ed. Hilary Lawson and Lisa Appignanesi (London, 1989), in which he argues that

> first, it is the *only* science that does not find the prospect that the "object" of its enquiry may intentionally deceive the scientific investigator subversive of the truth. Secondly, the verbal material upon which it *concentrates* its attention (although everything the subject says has *some* significance) is very much akin to methodical deviations from the truth: fantasies and dream-texts. . . . Instead . . . of seeking the truth criterion *outside* their ut-

terances, he discarded the *necessity* for finding a criterion of truth. What matters is the fact that they *said* it, not whether it is true or not. (156, 159)

See also Jean-Michel Rabaté, *The Ethics of the Lie,* trans. Suzanne Verderber (New York, 2007), chap. 5. He argues that the psychoanalyst searches for the *proton pseudos,* the mythic origin of the current symptom, such as childhood seduction.

38. Michael T. Gilmore, *Surface and Depth: The Quest for Legibility in American Culture* (New York, 2003), 12.

39. Kenneth Cmiel, *Democratic Eloquence: The Fight over Popular Speech in Nineteenth-Century America* (New York, 1990).

40. Ibid., 260.

41. James W. Cook, *The Arts of Deception: Playing with Fraud in the Age of Barnum* (Cambridge, Mass., 2001).

42. The fictional version of this new sophistication, immersed in wonder and yet ironically distanced from it, in several Western countries at the end of the nineteenth century, is discussed by Michael Saler, "Modernity and Enchantment: A Historiographic Review," *American Historical Review* 111.3 (June 2006).

43. Lawrence W. Levine, *Highbrow Lowbrow: The Emergence of Cultural Hierarchy in America* (Cambridge, Mass., 1988).

44. Mark Twain, "On the Decay of the Art of Lying" (1882), in *The Complete Humorous Sketches and Tales of Mark Twain,* ed. Charles Neider (New York, 1985), 505. For what it is worth as an indication of the popularity of this point of view, it should be noted that Twain wrote this piece for a thirty-dollar prize awarded by the Historical and Antiquarian Club of Hartford, which he did not win.

45. The official use of the motto did not begin, in fact, until 1843, some time after Yale had adopted "Lux et Veritas" for its motto. See the discussion in http://www.yalealumnimagazine.com/issues/01_03/seal.html.

46. See David A. Hollinger, "Science and Anarchy: Walter Lippmann's *Drift and Mastery,*" in *In the American Province: Studies in the History and Historiography of Ideas* (Bloomington, 1985). He argues that Lippmann's version was less technocratic and more democratic than Bernard's. See also Dorothy Ross, "Modernist Social Science in the Land of the New/Old," in *Modernist Impulses in the Human Sciences, 1870–1930,* ed. Ross (Baltimore, 1994), who argues that "mainstream sociologists developed a technocratic conception of science aimed at prediction and control" (187).

47. Walter Lippmann, *Public Opinion* (New York, 1922), 358.

48. See the discussion in Garett S. Jowett and Victoria O'Donnell, *Propaganda and Persuasion* (Thousand Oaks, 1999), 2. Lippmann argued that propaganda had been used by both sides in the First World War (*Public Opinion,* 42).

49. Geoffrey C. Bunn, "Constructing the Suspect: A Brief History of the Lie Detector," *Borderlines* 40 (1996); Bunn, "The Lie Detector, *Wonder Woman*

and Liberty: The Life and Work of William Moulton Marston," *History of the Human Sciences* 10.1 (February 1997); Ken Alder, "To Tell the Truth: The Polygraph Exam and the Marketing of American Expertise," *Historical Reflections* 24 (1998); Adler, "A Social History of Untruth: Lie Detection and Trust in 20th-Century America," *Representations* 80 (2002). Despite a ruling against the use of Marston's device in a case in 1923 involving an African American named Frye in Washington, D.C., the device continued to have avid defenders both in legal and in lay circles. Often it has been used to settle cases without trial. In the early twenty-first century, it is apparently regaining some of its prestige in the realm of law enforcement. The scientific quest for lie detection remains a powerful imperative, for example in the work of Daniel Langleben and Paul Ekman. For a popular recent survey of the state of the field, see Robin Marantz Henig, "Looking for the Lie," *New York Times Magazine*, February 5, 2006.

50. Adler, "A Social History of Untruth," 11.

51. Bunn, "The Lie Detector," 112.

52. For discussions of Orwell's enthusiastic reception in America, which extended from left to right, see John Rodden, *George Orwell: The Politics of Literary Reputation* (New Brunswick, 2002); *Scenes from an Afterlife: The Legacy of George Orwell* (Wilmington, 2003); and Thomas Cushman and John Rodden, eds., *George Orwell: Into the Twenty-First Century* (Boulder, 2004). Interestingly, the essay was taught more frequently in America than in Britain because of its use in college composition readers adopted in freshman English classes. According to Rodden (*George Orwell*, 392), its popularity only began to wane in the 1980s and 1990s, when the left attacked the "Orwell myth" and the "plain style" seemed to some ideologically suspect.

53. George Orwell, "Politics and the English Language," in *A Collection of Essays* (New York, 1953), 166, 171.

54. Lionel Trilling, "George Orwell and the Politics of Truth" (1955), reprinted in *Orwell's* Nineteen Eighty-Four: *Text, Sources, Criticism*, ed. Irving Howe (New York, 1963), 226. Trilling's first paean to Orwell was his 1952 introduction to *Homage to Catalonia*. The abiding importance of Orwell for the New York intellectuals, even when they broke up into radical and neoconservative factions, is detailed by Rodden, *George Orwell*, 73–84, 336–62.

55. Stefan Collini, *Absent Minds: Intellectuals in Britain* (Oxford, 2006), 355.

56. Cited from an unpublished talk in David Lloyd and Paul Thomas, *Culture and the State* (New York, 1998), 175.

57. Christopher Hitchens, *Why Orwell Matters* (New York, 2002); Michael P. Lynch, *True to Life: Why Truth Matters* (Cambridge, Mass., 2004), 161–62.

58. Jacques Derrida, "'Le Parjure,' Perhaps: Storytelling and Lying," in *Without Alibi*, ed. and trans. Peggy Kamuf (Stanford, 2002), 171–72.

59. Trilling, *Sincerity and Authenticity*, 16.

60. Harold D. Lasswell, "The Vocation of Propagandists," in *On Political Sociology* (Chicago, 1934); and George E. Gordon Catlin, "Propaganda as a

Function of Democratic Government," in *Propaganda and Dictatorship*, ed. Harwood L. Childs (Princeton, 1934).

61. For an attempt to outline some of them, see Martin Jay, "The Ambivalent Virtues of Mendacity: How Europeans Taught (Some of) Us to Learn to Love the Lies of Politics," in David Hollinger, ed., *The Humanities and the Dynamics of Inclusion since World War II* (Baltimore, 2006). A more recent example of this pattern can be found in Jean-Michel Rabaté, *The Ethics of the Lie*, trans. Suzanne Verderber (New York, 2007).

62. George Orwell, *The Road to Wigan Pier* (1937), in *The Complete Works of George Orwell*, ed. Peter Davidson, 20 vols. (London, 1998), 5:152.

63. For a discussion of Adorno's critique of the jargon, see Martin Jay, "Taking on the Stigma of Inauthenticity: Adorno's Critique of Genuineness," *New German Critique* 97 (Winter 2006).

64. See, for example, Timothy Bewes, *Cynicism and Postmodernity* (London, 1997), 50–52.

65. See, for example, Lionel Cliffe, "Explanation: Deception in the US Political System," in *The Politics of Lying*, 56. The alleged increase in political lying has been detected in other contexts as well. For a recent account that focuses on political falsehood during the Major and Blair governments in the United Kingdom, see Peter Osborne, *The Rise of Political Lying* (London, 2005), which claims that "Britain now lives in a post-truth political environment" (6).

66. Mark Morford, "Who Knew Bush's Lies Had a Finite Number," *San Francisco Chronicle*, January 30, 2008.

67. Rabaté, *The Ethics of the Lie*, 3.

68. Christopher Hitchens, *No One Left to Lie To: The Triangulation of William Jefferson Clinton* (New York, 2000); Ann Coulter, *Slander: Liberal Lies about the American Right* (New York, 2002); Al Franken, *Lies and the Lying Liars Who Tell Them: A Fair and Balanced Look at the Right* (New York, 2003); Joe Conason, *Big Lies: The Rightwing Propaganda Machine and How It Distorts the Truth* (New York, 2003); Sheldon Rampton and John C. Stauber, *Weapons of Mass Deception: The Uses of Propaganda in Bush's War on Iraq* (New York, 2003); David Corn, *The Lies of George W. Bush: Mastering the Politics of Deception* (New York, 2003); Nicholas von Hoffman, *Hoax: Why Americans Are Suckered by White House Lies* (New York, 2004); Paul Waldman, *Fraud: The Strategy behind the Bush Lies and Why the Media Didn't Tell You* (Napervillle, 2004); and Eric Alterman, *When Presidents Lie: A History of Official Deception and Its Consequences* (New York, 2004).

69. Joel Best, *Lies, Damned Lies and Statistics: Untangling Numbers from the Media, Politicians, and Activists* (Berkeley, 2001); Best, *More Damned Lies and Statistics: How Numbers Confuse Public Issues* (Berkeley, 2004).

70. Bok, *Lying*, 174.

71. Harry Frankfurt, *On Bullshit* (Princeton, 2005). Frankfurt claimed that whereas liars were still able to acknowledge that what is true still matters, bullshitters had given up even that concern and were thus an even greater

enemy to truth. For responses to his argument, see Gary L. Hardcastle and George A. Reich, eds., *Bullshit and Philosophy* (Chicago, 2006).

72. Jocelyn Noveck, "Hedging Truth Not Bad," *San Francisco Chronicle,* July 12, 2006; see also Gordon S. Livingston, "Culture of Lying Swamps the U.S.," in the same newspaper, August 13, 2006.

73. Hannah Arendt, "Truth and Politics," in *The Portable Hannah Arendt,* ed. Peter Baehr (New York, 2000), 545. For a similar position, see Pierre Lenan, *Le mensonge politique* (Paris, 1988), which begins: "At the center of the political game is the lie: that is, deliberate, organized, regulated, calculated, necessary deception: reasoning about politics while excluding the lie leads to an abusive, naïve vision, to an error of evaluation. To believe that there can be a politics without lying would seem illusory: political life, the way it is practiced, supposes an elevated rate, a tight *web* of lies of different forms and degrees" (7).

74. Alain Badiou, *Metapolitics,* trans. Jason Barker (London, 2005), 97.

75. The phrase was used as the title of Myra MacPherson's biography *All Governments Lie: The Life and Times of Rebel Journalist I. F. Stone* (New York, 2006).

76. Jürgen Habermas, *The Structural Transformation of the Public Sphere,* trans. Thomas Burger and Frederick Lawrence (Cambridge, Mass., 1991); see also Craig Calhoun, ed., *Habermas and the Public Sphere* (Cambridge, Mass., 2002).

77. As Jenny Davidson notes, "It should not be surprising that explicit defenses of hypocrisy still tend to be affiliated with the conservative end of the political spectrum." *Hypocrisy and the Politics of Politeness: Manners and Morals from Locke to Austen* (Cambridge, 2004), 172.

78. Bok, *Lying,* 169–70.

79. Alterman, *When Presidents Lie,* 22.

80. Ibid, 314.

81. This is not to say, to be sure, that those who stress consequences as opposed to principles always defend lying as a necessary expedient. Examining four cases of presidential mendacity—Roosevelt after Yalta, Kennedy and the Cuban missile crisis, Johnson and the Gulf of Tonkin incident, and Reagan and the Iran-Contra scandal—Alterman tries to demonstrate in *When Presidents Lie* that lying produces unanticipated negative political consequences.

82. This is not to claim utter originality. Among the recent political theorists and critics whose work I will draw on to make a case for political mendacity are Hannah Arendt, Judith Shklar, Ruth Grant, and Jenny Davidson. More general, if nuanced, defenses of lying can be found in the work of David Nyberg, Loyal Rue, John Vignaux Smyth, and David Livingstone Smith. For illuminating arguments on both sides of the question, see the symposium in *Theory and Event* 94 (2006), with articles by Andrew Norris, Linda Zerilli, Richard Flathman, Tracy Strong, and Jeremy Elkins.

1 ON LYING

A note on the epigraphs: The passage from Psalms, to be sure, reads in full "I said in my haste, all men are liars," which implies that the psalmist thinks that some men in fact are not and that lying can be avoided. The Petronius saying is sometimes also attributed to Sebastian Franck or Quintus Mucius Scaevola Pontifex.

1. See, for example, Ernst Bloch, *Natural Law and Human Dignity*, trans. Dennis J. Schmidt (Cambridge, Mass., 1986).

2. It has long been recognized that defining "nature" is a daunting task. For recent discussions of its different usages around the world, see Nadia Tazi, ed., *Keywords/Nature: For a Different Kind of Globalization* (New York, 2005).

3. Martin Buber, *Good and Evil: Two Interpretations* (New York, 1952), 7.

4. For a discussion, see Loyal Rue, *By the Grace of Guile: The Role of Deception in Natural History and Human Affairs* (New York, 1994), 108–9.

5. Charles Darwin, *The Descent of Man* (New York, 1936), 666.

6. For an array of examples, see David Livingstone Smith, *Why We Lie: The Evolutionary Roots of Deception and the Unconscious Mind* (New York, 2004), chap. 2. For still others, see Rue, *By the Grace of Guile*, chap. 2.

7. The issue of nature's alleged cunning, which inspired Lamarckian challengers to Darwin like Samuel Butler, is discussed in Jeremy Campbell, *The Liar's Tale: A History of Falsehood* (New York, 2001), chap. 2. Rue suggests that "the rejection of intentionality as an essential feature of deception does not, however, prevent us from speaking of deceit as purposeful behavior. All living organisms manifest purpose and design in their strategies for survival and reproduction, even though few of them (primarily humans) may be said to act with explicit intentions or self-conscious motives" (*By the Grace of Guile*, 90).

8. Some commentators, however, have argued that a scale of different kinds of deception both unites and divides us from the plants and other animals. See, for example, the four-part typology suggested by Robert Mitchell, which begins with deception by unwilled appearance (e.g., butterflies and plants), continues through involuntary responses to stimuli (birds feigning injuries) and learned behavior (dogs faking injuries based on past experience), and concludes with planned deception to treat novel threats (some primates and humans). Robert W. Mitchell, "A Framework for Discussing Deception," in *Deception: Perspectives on Human and Nonhuman Deceit,* ed. Mitchell and Nicholas S. Thompson (Albany, 1986), 21–29.

9. Hanna Rose Schell, *Hide and Seek: Camouflage, Photography and the Media of Reconnaissance* (New York, 2009).

10. Dario Maestripieri, *Macachiavellian Intelligence: How Rhesus Macaques and Humans Have Conquered the World* (Chicago, 2007).

11. Self-deception raises the fundamental questions of the integrity of the self and the locus of intentionality. For an unexpected critique of the concept, see Jacques Derrida, "History of the Lie: Prolegomena," *Without Alibi,* ed. and

trans. Peggy Kamuf (Stanford, 2002), where he claims that it "remains confused in the 'psychology' it implies. It is also logically incompatible with the rigor of any classical concept of the lie and with the 'frank' problematic of the lie. To lie will always mean to deceive *intentionally* and *consciously*, while *knowing* what it is that one is deliberately hiding, therefore while not lying to oneself. And the addressee must be other enough to be, at the moment of the lie, an enemy to be deceived in his belief. The *self*, if this word has a sense, excludes the self-lie" (67).

12. On reading the facial expressions that give away lies, see Paul Ekman, *Telling Lies: Clues to Deceit in the Market Place, Politics and Marriage* (New York, 2001).

13. Smith, *Why We Lie*, 76.

14. Friedrich Nietzsche, *Human, All Too Human*, trans. R. J. Hollingdale (Cambridge, 1986), 40.

15. Jean Piaget, *The Moral Judgment of the Child* (New York, 1965), 139.

16. Smith, *Why We Lie*, 18.

17. Campbell, *The Liar's Tale*, 260.

18. Friedrich Nietzsche, "On Truth and Lie in an Extramoral Sense" (1873), in *The Portable Nietzsche*, ed. Walter Kaufmann (London, 1968), 43.

19. Friedrich Nietzsche, *The Gay Science*, trans. Walter Kaufmann (New York, 1974), 38.

20. Ibid., 172. The issue of truth and truthfulness in Nietzsche has consumed commentators for a very long time. For recent attempts to sort it out, see Maudemarie Clark, *Nietzsche on Truth and Philosophy* (Cambridge, 1990); Simon Blackburn, *Truth: A Guide* (Oxford, 2005), chap. 4.

21. Friedrich Nietzsche, "L'art pour l'art," from *Twilight of the Idols*, in *The Portable Nietzsche*, 529.

22. Ironically, there has always been a question of Descartes' own deception in presenting his real views of God. See Hiram Caton, "The Problem of Descartes' Sincerity," *Philosophical Forum* 2.3 (Spring 1971).

23. J. A. Barnes, *A Pack of Lies: Toward a Sociology of Lying* (Cambridge, 1994), 154.

24. Arnold Gehlen, *Der Mensch: Seine Natur und seine Stellung in der Welt* (Frankfurt, 1971).

25. Bernard Williams, *Truth and Truthfulness* (Princeton, 2002), 28.

26. For exemplary attempts to unpack its meanings, see Raymond Williams, *Keywords: A Vocabulary of Culture and Society* (London, 1976); and Tony Bennett, Lawrence Grossberg, and Meaghan Morris, eds., *New Keywords: A Revised Vocabulary of Culture and Society* (Malden, 2005).

27. See Rue, *By the Grace of Guile*, chap. 1, for an extensive record of the historical denunciation of lying.

28. Are animals always ruled by monarchs, like the bees with their queen? Alternative fictional versions, of course, abound, for example in George Orwell's *Animal Farm*. Plants never seem to be granted political status of any kind (sorry, the Banana Republic doesn't count).

29. For a general consideration of the issue of trust, see Peter Johnson, *Frames of Deceit: A Study of the Loss and Recovery of Public and Private Trust* (Cambridge, 1993).

30. See, in particular, the work of Axel Honneth, *The Struggle for Recognition: The Moral Grammar of Social Conflicts,* trans. Joel Anderson (Cambridge, Mass., 1995).

31. Georg Simmel, "The Secret and Secret Society," in *The Sociology of Georg Simmel,* ed. and trans. Kurt H. Wolff (London, 1950), 313.

32. John Vignaux Smyth, *The Habit of Lying: Sacrificial Studies in Literature, Philosophy, and Fashion Theory* (Durham, 2002), 155.

33. Karl E. Scheibe, "In Defense of Lying: On the Moral Neutrality of Misrepresentation," *Berkshire Review* 15 (1980): 19.

34. Barnes, *A Pack of Lies,* 195, citing the work of Michael Lewis, Catherine Stanger, and Margaret S. Sullivan, "Deception in 3-year-olds," *Developmental Psychology* 25 (1989).

35. There are, to be sure, significant differences between tact, politeness, and outright lying as variants of intentional deception, with gradations of moral implication. For a subtle discussion, see Jonathan E. Adler, "Lying, Deceiving, or Falsely Implicating," *Journal of Philosophy* 94.9 (September 1997). He concludes that the seeming moral superiority of tactful and polite deception over deliberate lying may be illusory, for "it encourages deviousness and a legalistic attempt to get away with what one can. One may be less blameworthy for deceiving than lying, but still have acted worse by seeking to be less blameworthy" (452).

36. Ruth W. Grant, *Hypocrisy and Integrity: Machiavelli, Rousseau, and the Ethics of Politics* (Chicago, 1997), 31.

37. Williams, *Truth and Truthfulness,* 94. The link can still be heard in the archaic word "troth," which is pledged in marriage.

38. David Nyberg, *The Varnished Truth: Truth-Telling and Deceiving in Ordinary Life* (Chicago, 1993), 145.

39. Harald Weinrich, "Politeness, an Affair of Honor," in *The Linguistics of Lying and Other Essays,* trans. Jane K. Brown and Marshall Brown (Seattle, 2005); Jean-Michel Besnier et al., eds. *Politesse et sincérité* (Paris, 1994).

40. Jean-Pierre Cavaillé, "De la dissimulation honnête," *Sigila* 8 (Autumn–Winter 2001).

41. Pascal, *Pensées,* trans. W. F. Trotter (New York, 1958), 32.

42. Domna C. Stanton, *The Aristocrat as Art: A Study of the Honnête Homme and the Dandy in 17th- and 19th-Century French Literature* (New York, 1980).

43. Dena Goodman, *The Republic of Letters: A Cultural History of the French Enlightenment* (Ithaca, 1994).

44. Julia Abramson, *Learning from Lying: Paradoxes of Literary Mystification* (Newark, 2005).

45. Lawrence E. Klein, *Shaftesbury and the Culture of Politeness: Moral Discourse and Cultural Politics in Early Eighteenth-Century England* (Cambridge, 1994).

46. See Jenny Davidson, *Hypocrisy and the Politics of Politeness: Manners and Morals from Locke to Austin* (Cambridge, 2004)

47. Steven Shapin, *A Social History of Truth: Civility and Science in Seventeenth-Century England* (Chicago, 1994), 83–84.

48. Jean-Jacques Rousseau, "Fourth Walk," from *The Reveries of the Solitary Walker,* in *The Collected Writings of Rousseau,* vol. 8, ed. Christopher Kelly, trans. Charles E. Butterworth (Hanover, 2000). As Ruth W. Grant has argued, Rousseau often relativized his critique of hypocrisy and support for integrity in politics as well. See her *Hypocrisy and Integrity,* chaps. 3–5.

49. For a discussion of the war against hypocrisy during the French Revolution, see Hannah Arendt, *On Revolution* (New York, 1965), 92–101.

50. Goodman, *The Republic of Letters,* chap. 6; and Margaret C. Jacob, *Living the Enlightenment: Freemasonry and Politics in Eighteenth-Century Europe* (New York, 1991).

51. Jürgen Habermas, *The Structural Transformation of the Public Sphere: An Inquiry into a Category of Bourgeois Society,* trans. Thomas Burger and Frederick Lawrence (Cambridge, Mass., 1991); Craig Calhoun, ed., *Habermas and the Public Sphere* (Cambridge, Mass., 1992); and Johanna Meehan, ed., *Feminists Read Habermas: Gendering the Subject of Discourse* (New York, 1995).

52. Mary Wollstonecraft, *A Vindication of the Rights of Woman,* ed. Carol H. Poston (New York, 1975), chap. 7.

53. Whether Wollstonecraft fully escaped the genre of conduct books is examined in Ruth Bernard Yeazell, *Fictions of Modesty: Women and Courtship in the English Novel* (Chicago, 1991).

54. Mary Wollstonecraft, *A Short Residence in Sweden, Norway, and Denmark,* and William Godwin, *Memoirs of the Author of "The Rights of Women,"* ed. Richard Holmes, Penguin Classics (New York, 1987).

55. Lionel Trilling, *Sincerity and Authenticity* (Cambridge, Mass., 1971); Charles Guignon, *On Being Authentic* (London, 2004).

56. Johann Wolfgang Goethe, *Faust,* part 2, act 2, verse 6671.

57. John Morley, *On Compromise* (London, 1874).

58. Kenneth Cmiel, *Democratic Eloquence: The Fight over Popular Speech in Nineteenth-Century America* (New York, 1990).

59. Scheibe, "In Defense of Lying," 23.

60. Norbert Elias, *The Civilizing Process: Sociogenetic and Psychogenetic Investigations,* trans. Edmund Jephcott (Oxford, 1994).

61. Barnes, *A Pack of Lies,* 67. In Russian, a distinction is made between *vranyo* and *lozh,* which involves a more deliberate attempt to mislead.

62. Erving Goffman, *Interaction Ritual: Essays on Face-to-Face Behavior* (New York, 1982).

63. Helmut Lethen, *Cool Conduct: The Culture of Distance in Weimar Germany,* trans. Don Reneau (Berkeley, 2002). In Weimar, the anthropologist Helmut Plessner attacked the cult of authenticity and directness in favor of coldness and distance.

64. Jean-Paul Sartre, "Existentialism Is a Humanism," in *Existentialism from Dostoyevsky to Sartre,* ed. Walter Kaufmann (New York, 1963), 216–62. For a discussion of the recent debate over outing homosexuals, see Paul Robinson, *Queer Wars: The New Gay Right and Its Critics* (Chicago, 2005).

65. Talleyrand, cited in Weinrich, *The Linguistics of Lying,* 10. Weinrich mentions that the expression has also been attributed to Fouché and Metternich.

66. Smyth, *The Habit of Lying,* 3.

67. Simmel, "The Secret and the Secret Society," 315–16.

68. Ibid, 316.

69. Bernard Williams, *Ethics and the Limits of Philosophy* (London, 1985), 200.

70. For a subtle consideration of the implications of the Cretan Liar's paradox for the question of lying in general, see Jean-Michel Rabaté, *The Ethic of the Lie,* trans. Suzanne Verderber (New York, 2007), chap. 4. He argues that the lie "always obeys a paradoxical logic. On the one hand, it is everywhere in social life, and we learn to lie very early in order to obtain little favors or evade punishment, or fulfill everyday obligations such as being nice to annoying neighbors or to gruff distant relatives. On the other hand, it is violently rejected as soon as it is discovered" (26).

71. Ludwig Wittgenstein, *Philosophical Investigations,* ed. G. E. M. Anscombe and G. H. von Wright (New York, 1968), 249.

72. St. Augustine, "Lying," in *Treatises on Various Subjects,* ed. Roy J. Deferrari, trans. Mary Sarah Muldowney (New York, 1952), 58–59. Weinrich emends this description to read: "Linguistics, however, considers it a lie if behind the (spoken) lying sentence there stands an (unspoken) true sentence, which differs by contradiction, that is by virtue of the assertion morpheme *yes/no*" (*The Linguistics of Lying,* 39).

73. David Simpson, "Lying, Liars and Language," *Philosophy and Phenomenological Research* 52.3 (September 1992): 625.

74. Jacques Lacan, *Écrits: A Selection,* trans. Alan Sheridan (New York, 1977), 172–73. Lacan's debt to Jean-Paul Sartre's description of lying in *Being and Nothingness* is obvious: "The ideal description of the liar would be a cynical consciousness, affirming truth within himself, denying it in his words, and denying that negation as such. Now this doubly negative attitude rests on the transcendent; the fact expressed is transcendent since it does not exist, and the original negation rests on a *truth;* that is, on a particular type of transcendence. As for the inner negation which I effect correlatively with the affirmation for myself of the truth, this rests on *words;* that is, on an event in the world." *Being and Nothingness,* trans. Hazel E. Barnes (New York, 1966), 57–58.

75. Jacques Derrida, "And Say the Animal Responded?" in *Zoonotologies: The Question of the Animal,* ed. Cary Wolfe (Minneapolis, 2003), 135. He claims that animal pretence also takes into account the existence of the Other.

76. Joseph Kupfer, "The Moral Presumption against Lying," *Review of Metaphysics* 36.1 (September 1982): 118.

77. Alasdair MacIntyre, *Truthfulness, Lies and Moral Philosophers: What Can We Learn from Mill and Kant?* The Tanner Lectures on Human Values (Salt Lake City, 1994), 311. For other considerations of the issue from the perspective of prototype semantics, which understands meanings not through positing categorical boundaries but by investigating their prototypical, central applications, see Linda Coleman and Paul Kay, "Prototype Semantics: The English Word *Lie*," *Language* 57.1 (March 1981); and Eve E. Sweester, "The Definition of Lie: An Examination of the Folk Models Underlying a Semantic Prototype," in *Cultural Models in Language and Thought,* ed. Dorothy Holland and Naomi Quinn (Cambridge, 1987).

78. Jürgen Habermas, "What Is Universal Pragmatics?," in *Communication and the Evolution of Society,* trans. Thomas McCarthy (Boston, 1979), 58.

79. Ibid., 64 (italics in original).

80. Jacques Derrida, "Faith and Knowledge: The Two Sources of 'Religion' at the Limits of Reason Alone," trans. Samuel Weber, in *Religion,* ed. Jacques Derrida and Gianni Vattimo (Stanford, 1998). Derrida's larger point here is that both science and religion depend on a similar faith in truthfulness.

81. Christopher Ricks, "Lies," *Critical Inquiry* 2 (1975): 124.

82. Albert Carr, "Is Business Bluffing Ethical?," in *Ethical Issues in Business,* ed. Thomas Donaldson and Patricia Werhane (Englewood Cliffs, 1979). According to Sissela Bok, 60 percent of students are routinely classified in the top 10 percent of their class! See Bok, *Lying: Moral Choice in Public and Private Life,* 2nd ed. (New York, 1999), 72.

83. See, for example, Bella M. DePaulo and Audrey Jordan, "Age Changes in Deceiving and Detecting Deceit," in *Development of Nonverbal Behavior in Children,* ed. Robert St. Feldman (New York, 1982).

84. For a discussion, see Nyberg, *The Varnished Truth,* chap. 8.

85. Simpson, "Lying, Liars and Language," 633.

86. Weinrich, *The Linguistics of Lying,* 12.

87. For a full consideration of this issue, see Ricks, who argues that "the importance of the *lie/lie* pun is that it concentrates an extraordinarily ranging and profound network of truth-testing situations and postures: it brings mendacity up against those situations and postures which constitute the great moments or endurances of truth: the child-bed, the love bed, the bed of sleep and dreams, the sickbed, the death-bed, the grave. . . . And even perhaps the modern secular counterpart to the confessional's kneeling: the psychiatrist's couch" ("Lies," 131).

88. See W. J. Verdenius, "Gorgias' Doctrine of Deception," in *The Sophists and Their Legacy,* ed. G. B. Kerferd (Wisebaden, 1981).

89. Plato, *The Republic,* 597e.

90. Bertrand Russell, *An Inquiry into Meaning and Truth* (London, 1962), 277.

91. Oscar Wilde, "The Decay of Lying," in *Aesthetes and Decadents of the 1890's,* ed. Karl Beckson (Chicago, 1981), 193.

92. Weinrich, *The Linguistics of Lying*, 46.

93. Ibid., 71.

94. Mary Catherine Gormally, "The Ethical Root of Language," in *Logic and Ethics*, ed. Peter Geach (Dordrecht, 1991), 66.

95. For the now canonical account of its emergence in the novel, most notably written by women, see Catherine Gallagher, *Nobody's Story: The Vanishing Acts of Woman Writers in the Marketplace, 1670–1820* (Berkeley, 1994). Words spoken on a stage, of course, were normally understood to be playacting rather than lying much earlier. For other discussions of this issue, see Barnes, *A Pack of Lies*, chap. 9; and Patricia Waugh, *Metafiction: The Theory and Practice of Self-Conscious Fiction* (London, 1984).

96. Derrida, "History of the Lie," 36.

97. However, for some commentators, fiction ironically tells a kind of inadvertent truth by revealing more explicitly than other uses of language that words are never transparent representations of the prior thoughts of an intentional consciousness. J. Hillis Miller discerns in writers like Proust the frequent use of the trope called "anacoluthon," which entails the uneasy coexistence of two or more syntactical voices (e.g., first and third person) in a single text. He argues that it reveals that language often defies reduction to a unitary narrative consciousness, the assertion of which is itself a kind of lie. "Language," he concludes, "may be a mindless machine that has as one of its effects the generation of a false appearance of some mind as source." J. Hillis Miller, "The Anacoluthonic Lie," in *Reading Narrative* (Norman, 1998), 152. The implication of this speculation is that language always betrays intentions and that the desire for a sincere expression of interior thoughts is inevitably doomed to fail. This conclusion is too sweeping for a discussion of lying, however, because it removes all personal responsibility from the equation and undermines the deliberation entailed by the choice to lie.

98. Bok, *Lying*, 207.

99. Walter Benjamin, "The Work of Art in the Age of Mechanical Reproduction," in *Illuminations*, ed. Hannah Arendt, trans. Harry Zohn (New York, 1968), 244. For my own gloss on this issue, see "'The Aesthetic Ideology' as Ideology; or, What Does It Mean to Aestheticize Politics?,'" in *Force Fields: Between Intellectual History and Cultural Critique* (New York, 1993).

100. Miller, "The Anacoluthonic Lie," 154.

101. George Steiner, *After Babel: Aspects of Language and Translation* (London, 1975), 217–18 (italics in original). For a critique, see Max Black, *The Prevalence of Humbug and Other Essays* (Ithaca, 1983).

102. Michel de Montaigne, "Of Liars," in *The Complete Essays of Montaigne*, trans. Donald. M. Frame (Stanford, 1958), 24.

103. Henrik Ibsen, *The Wild Duck*, trans. Stephen Mulrine (London, 2006), 117–18.

104. Derrida, "History of the Lie," 29.

105. For a discussion of Nietzsche's defense of truthfulness even as he criticizes the ideal of truth, see Williams, *Truth and Truthfulness*, 12–18.

106. Sartre, *Being and Nothingness*, 58.

107. Simpson, "Lying, Liars and Language," 637.

108. Axel Honneth, *The Struggle for Recognition: The Moral Grammar of Social Conflicts*, trans. Joel Anderson (Cambridge, Mass., 1995).

109. Bok, *Lying*, 18.

110. Smyth, *The Habit of Lying*, chap. 1. Foucault, he reminds us, had pointed out that since the Middle Ages, torture and the Church's demand for confessing the truth were "the dark twins." Michel Foucault, *The History of Sexuality*, vol. 1, *An Introduction*, trans. Robert Hurley (New York, 1978), 59.

111. Rousseau, "Fourth Walk," 28.

112. For an account of the deontological position, see Arnold Isenberg, "Deontology and the Ethics of Lying," *Philosophy and Phenomenological Research* 24.4 (June 1964). The word comes from the Greek τὸ δέον, "that which is proper").For a useful sample of different consequentialist positions on all moral questions, not only lying, see Stephen Darwall, ed., *Consequentialism* (Malden, Mass., 2003).

113. For an account of the nuances in the Utilitarian tradition, which argues that Mill in particular was not a rigid consequentialist, see MacIntyre, *Truthfulness, Lies, and Moral Philosophers*. His own position occupies a middle ground between Kant and Mill by arguing that lying is evil because it undermines the integrity of rational relationships. The best rule to follow is therefore "uphold truthfulness in all your actions by being unqualifiedly truthful in all your relationships and by lying to aggressors only in order to protect those truthful relationships against aggressors, and even then only when lying is the least harm that can afford an effective defense against aggression" (357).

114. Simmel, "The Secret and the Secret Society," 316.

115. William James, *The Varieties of Religious Experience* (New York, 1903), 355.

116. Montaigne, "Of Presumption," *Complete Essays*, 491.

117. Montaigne, "Of Liars," ibid., 23.

118. Montaigne, "Of Giving the Lie," ibid., 505.

119. Montaigne, "A Trait of Certain Ambassadors," ibid., 51.

120. The distinction is derived from the thirteenth-century canonist Raymond of Pennafort, *Summa de paenitentia*, and was meant as a way to divide Augustine's eight categories into three. The pernicious lie harms someone without benefiting the liar, the officious lie benefits someone other than the liar, while the jocose lie doesn't harm anyone.

121. The literature on Plato's "noble lie" is extensive. See, for example, Carl Page, "The Truth about Lies in Plato's Republic," *Ancient Philosophy* 11 (1991); D. Dombrowski, "Plato's 'Noble' Lie," *History of Political Thought* 18.4 (Winter 1997); Michèle Broze, "Mensonge et justice chez Platon," *Revue internationale de philosophie* 156–57 (1986). We will return to the question of the noble lie for political purposes in our final section.

122. See Jane S. Zembaty, "Plato's *Republic* and Greek Morality on Lying," *Journal of the History of Philosophy* 26.4 (October 1988).

123. See Jane S. Zembaty, "Aristotle on Lying," *Journal of the History of Philosophy* 31.1 (January 1993).

124. Michel Foucault, *Fearless Speech,* ed. Joseph Pearson (Los Angeles, 2001). According to Marcel Detienne, *The Masters of Truth in Archaic Greece,* trans. Janet Lloyd (New York, 1996), in an even earlier period, the figures of the king, the diviner, and the bard were granted special performative power to tell the truth because of their sharing in divine memory. He situates the transition to a more rational, "secularized" notion of truth in the military assembly, where a dialogic procedure replaced the "magicoreligious" one of the archaic truth-tellers.

125. Ibid., 19.

126. Ibid., 133.

127. Michel Foucault, "Afterword: The Subject and Power," in Hubert L. Dreyfus and Paul Rabinow, *Michel Foucault: Beyond Structuralism and Hermeneutics* (Chicago, 1983), 251.

128. The process by which this new impersonal subject was generated was, to be sure, uneven. Examining the discursive regime supporting the scientific community in seventeenth-century Britain epitomized by the chemist Robert Boyle, Steven Shapin in *A Social History of Truth* shows that it relied heavily on trusting in the truth-telling virtues of certain types of people, in particular Christian gentlemen whose word was taken to be honest and disinterested. Although the ideology of the new science was to question authority and distrust textual in favor of direct sensual testimony, in practice it also respected the civil conversation of those with the cultural capital to engage in the language game of science.

129. There is, to be sure, another, less positive version of the relationship between religion and deception noted by its critics. For example, Max Horkheimer and Theodor W. Adorno comment on the ubiquity of sacrifice as a religious ritual designed to propitiate the gods: "All sacrificial acts, deliberately planned by humans, deceive the god for whom they are performed: by imposing on him the primacy of human purposes, they dissolve away his power, and the fraud against him passes over seamlessly into that perpetrated by unbelieving priests against believing congregations." *Dialectic of Enlightenment,* ed. Gunzelin Schmid Noerr, trans. Edmund Jephcott (Stanford, 2002), 40.

130. St. Augustine, *Treatises on Various Subjects.* For a helpful commentary, see Alan Brinton, "St. Augustine and the Problem of Deception in Religious Persuasion," *Religious Studies* 19 (1983).

131. For example, what could it mean when it is said of Jesus, who presumably was omniscient, that unlike his father, he "knew not the day nor the hour" of the Last Judgment (Matthew 24:36)? For a general discussion of the various positions taken by the church fathers, see Boniface Ramsey, "Two Traditions of Lying and Deception in the Ancient Church," *Thomist* 49.4 (October 1985). He claims that the more permissive one continued in the Eastern Church after Augustine, but his more stringent alternative won out in the West. He also notes that the Islamic tradition, best represented by the twelfth-century author

Ghazālī, was closer to the Eastern Church in its relative tolerance of some lies in certain circumstances, such as in war, in order to reconcile two opponents, between spouses, and when it prevents someone from knowing about something unpleasant about to happen to him.

132. Wisd. 1:11.

133. Augustine, "On Lying," 67–71.

134. Augustine, "Against Lying," 164.

135. Ibid., 166.

136. Ibid., 172.

137. Smyth, *The Habit of Lying,* 21.

138. See Irène Rosier, "Les developments médiévaux de la théorie augustinienne du mensonge," *Hermès* 15 (1995). She shows the growth of an understanding of the intersubjective dimension of the problem, in which the private and communal intentions of the liar could be separated.

139. Albert R. Jonsen and Stephen Toulmin, *The Abuse of Casuisty: A History of Moral Reasoning* (Berkeley, 1988), chap. 10. They show that casuistry had its virtues, although it could be abused for unsavory purposes. See also J. Dobszynski, *Catholic Teaching about the Morality of Falsehood* (Washington, D.C., 1948); Perez Zagorin, *Ways of Lying: Dissimulation, Persecution, and Conformity in Early Modern Europe* (Cambridge, Mass., 1990); and Toon van Houdt et al., eds., *On the Edge of Truth and Honesty: Principles and Strategies of Fraud and Deceit in the Early Modern Period* (Leiden, 2002).

140. It would be historically inaccurate to characterize Jesuit opinion as always permissive. For example, the Emblem Book of the seventeenth-century Bavarian Jesuit Hieremias Drexel, *Orbis Phaëton,* provided an exhaustive critique of the adverse effects of a wide variety of fraudulent ways of speaking and behaving, including "political tongue" (*lingua politica*). See the discussion in Toon van Houdt, "Word Histories, and Beyond: Towards a Conceptualization of Fraud and Deceit in Early Modern Times," in *On the Edge of Truth and Honesty,* ed. van Houdt et al.

141. Probabilism, as developed by Dominicans like Medina and Jesuits like Suárez in Salamanca, did not mean following the most probable opinion when there was a dispute, but rather following the authority of a writ composed by a doctor of the church and of the evidence. For its relationship, not very clear, to the origins of mathematical probability theory, see Ian Hacking, *The Emergence of Probability* (Cambridge, 1975), chap. 3. For a survey of debates over means and ends in politics with several original texts, see Ulrich Kohlmann, ed., *Politik und Moral: Die Zweck-Mittel Debatte in der neueren Philosophie und Politik* (Lünbeger, 2001). Kohlmann's introduction treats the role of the Jesuit-Jansenist debate.

142. See Carlo Ginzburg, *Il Nicodemismo: Simulazione e dissimulazione nell'Europa del '500* (Turin, 1970); and Zagorin, *Ways of Lying,* chap. 4. Nicodemus is discussed in the New Testament, John 3:1–2. Ultimately, Calvin repudiated the term, claiming that it did an injustice to Nicodemus, who abandoned his secrecy to claim Christ's body in public. See Bok, *Lying,* 296.

143. Cited without reference in Bok, *Lying*, 32.

144. Michael T. Gilmore, *Surface and Depth: The Quest for Legibility in American Culture* (New York, 2003).

145. See Judith N. Shklar, *Ordinary Vices* (Cambridge, Mass., 1984), 50–53 for an insightful discussion.

146. See F. Amory, "Whited Sepulchres: The Semantic History of Hypocrisy in the High Middle Ages," *Recherches de théologie ancienne et médiévale* 53 (1986).

147. G. Goedecke, *L'hypocrisie, le vice du siècle: Eine Darstellung des Problems der Heuchlerei in der französischen Literatur des 17. Jahrhunderts* (Berlin, 1968).

148. For discussions, see Jacques Bos, "The Hidden Self of the Hypocrite," in *On the Edge of Truth and Honesty*, ed. van Houdt et al.; and J. W. Smeed, *The Theophrastan "Character": The History of a Literary Genre* (Oxford, 1985).

149. Francis Bacon, "Of Cunning," in *Essays, Civil and Moral* (New York, 1909–14), vol. 3, part 1. Perez Zagorin writes that for Bacon the best position for a statesman "is to enjoy a reputation for openness, to preserve secrecy by habit, to employ dissimulation when needed, and to possess the power of simulation if there is no other remedy." *Francis Bacon* (Princeton, 1998), 145.

150. For an account of Hobbes's defense of necessary mendacity, see Kinch Hoekstra, "The End of Philosophy (The Case of Hobbes)," *Proceedings of the Aristotelian Society* 106.1 (January 2006). One has to be careful to avoid conflating all of these variants of mendacity. As Shapin notes,

> Many early modern moralists discriminated between types of falsehood: *secrecy* was a habit or policy of closeness that might or might not be benign depending upon circumstance; *dissimulation* was an intentional withholding of truth when truth-telling might be deemed appropriate, leading others to believe what was not true; *simulation* was a positive intentional act or utterance that led to the same effect. . . . Secrecy might be laudable, dissimulation circumstantially recommended, and simulation occasionally excused. But the falsehood that went under the name of *lie* found scarcely any defenders in ethical writing *per se* and very few in even the most practical English guides to conduct. (*A Social History of Truth*, 103, 106)

151. See Johannes Trapman, "Erasmus on Lying and Simulation," in *On the Edge of Truth and Honesty*, ed. van Houdt et al.

152. Leo Strauss, *Persecution and the Art of Writing* (Glencoe, 1952).

153. Zagorin, *Ways of Lying*, 330.

154. Lester Gilbert Crocker, "The Problem of Truth and Falsehood in the Age of Enlightenment," *Journal of the History of Ideas* 14 (1953): 575–603.

155. Hugh Grotius, *On the Law of War and Peace*, trans. F. W. Kelsey and others (Indianapolis, 1925), book 3, chap. 1; Samuel Pufendorf, *Of the Law of Nature and Nations*, trans. Basil Kennett (London, 1710), vol. 2.

156. Voltaire to Thierot, October, 28, 1736, *Voltaire's Correspondence*, vol. 5.

Voltaire was referring in particular to disclosing his authorship of *L'enfant prodigue*, which he wanted to protect from the prying eyes of the censors.

157. Reinhart Koselleck, *Critique and Crisis: Enlightenment and the Pathogenesis of Modern Society* (Cambridge, Mass., 1988), 117–18.

158. Frederick of Prussia, *The Refutation of Machiavelli's "Prince" or Anti-Machiavell*, trans. Paul Sonnino (Athens, Ohio, 1981), 113–16.

159. Helvétius, *De l'homme*, section 9, chap. 5; Mercier, *Du théâtre* (Amsterdam, 1773).

160. Antoine de Rivarol, *De l'homme intellectual et moral* (1801), in *Oeuvres choisies* (Paris, 1880).

161. François Vincent Toussaint, *Les moeurs* (Paris, 1748).

162. James Boswell, *The Life of Samuel Johnson*, ed. Bergen Evans (New York, 1952), 504.

163. Trilling, *Sincerity and Authenticity*, 58–67; Marshall Berman, *The Politics of Authenticity: Radical Individualism and the Emergence of Modern Society* (New York, 1972); Alessandro Ferrara, *Modernity and Authenticity: A Study of the Social and Ethical Thought of Jean-Jacques Rousseau* (Albany, 1993).

164. It is first cited in his *Letter to M. d'Alembert*, in *Politics and the Arts, Letter to M. d'Alembart on the Theatre*, trans. Allan Bloom (Ithaca, 1960), 131.

165. Jean Starobinski, *Jean-Jacques Rousseau, la transparence et l'obstacle* (Paris, 1957).

166. Ruth Grant argues that integrity is a more accurate way to describe his ideal than authenticity, a term not employed in his texts. See her *Hypocrisy and Integrity*, 58.

167. Ibid., 102.

168. Derrida, "History of the Lie," 32.

169. Rousseau, *The Reveries of the Solitary Walker*, 29; further citations are in the text.

170. Victor Gourevitch, "Rousseau on Lying: A Provisional Reading of the Fourth *Rêverie*," *Berkshire Review* 15 (1980): 94.

171. Ibid., 100.

172. Grant argues in *Hypocrisy and Integrity* that in such questions as the necessity of a civil religion, which the sovereign could insist be followed at the risk of banishment for unsociability, Rousseau acknowledged in *The Social Contract* that rulers would have to manipulate and lie to the ruled (125).

173. In addition to the original texts, a number of the most important commentaries are collected in *Kant und das Recht der Lüge*, ed. Georg Geismann and Hariolf Oberer (Würzberg, 1986). For another commentary not included in this collection, see Robert J. Benton, "Political Expediency and Lying: Kant vs. Benjamin Constant," *Journal of History of Ideas* 43.1 (January–March 1982). See also Stephen Holmes, *Benjamin Constant and the Making of Modern Liberalism* (New Haven, 1984), chap. 4; and Igor Primoratz, "Lying and the 'Methods of Ethics,'" *International Studies in Philosophy*, 16.3 (1984): 35–57. I call Kant and Constant protoliberals because the political label "liberal" was an invention of a slightly later generation.

174. Kant, *Lectures on Ethics*, ed. Peter Heath and J. B. Schneewind (Cambridge, 1997). Sissela Bok cautions against accepting them as reliable, partly because they suggest a more flexible view of matters than Kant was later to espouse. See *Lying*, 296–97.

175. Kant, "On a Supposed Right to Lie Because of Philanthropic Concerns," in *Grounding for the Metaphysics of Morals*, trans. James Ellington (Indianapolis, 1993), 65.

176. This distinction was, as Norbert Elias has shown, a staple of the German response to the hegemony of the French Enlightenment. See his *The Civilizing Process: The History of Manners*, trans. E. Jephcott (New York, 1978).

177. Kant, "Idea for a Universal History with Cosmopolitan Intent" (1784), in *The Philosophy of Kant*, ed. Carl J. Friedrich (New York, 1993), 139.

178. Carla Hesse, "Kant, Foucault and *Three Women*," in *Foucault and the Writing of History*, ed. Jan Goldstein (Cambridge, 1994). She builds on the work of François Azouvi and Dominque Bourel, *De Königsberg à Paris: La reception de Kant en France (1788–1804)* (Paris, 1991).

179. Hesse, "Kant, Foucault," 89.

180. Benjamin Constant, "Des reactions politique," in *Écrits et discourse politiques*, ed. O. Pozzo di Borgo (Paris, 1964); "On a Suposed Right to Lie because of Philanthropic Concerns."

181. Benton, "Political Expediency and Lying," 137. He claims that Kant was basically identified with the Jacobins and the excesses of the Terror, which the later work of Azouvi and Bourel calls into question.

182. Holmes, *Benjamin Constant and the Making of Modern Liberalism*, 108.

183. Kant seems to have taken the reference to be to himself, but it may have been to the theologian and philosopher Johann David Michaelis, who had also defended the absolute prohibition on lying. Constant did tell the German translator of the piece that he had meant Kant, although Kant had not explicitly said what was attributed to him in anything he had published (and then seems to have forgotten this absence in his own reply!). See the introduction to Kant, *Das Recht der Lüge*, 10–11.

184. It is sometimes argued that Constant's evocation of this example was given added weight by an episode that involved his lover Mme de Staël, who had lied to a spy looking for a fugitive, Mathieu de Montmorency, who was hiding in her house.

185. Because he admitted the importance of principles, Constant can be classed as a "rule utilitarian" rather than an "act utilitarian," who judges only individual actions by their consequences rather than seeing them as exemplars of principles. See Primoratz, "Lying and the 'Methods of Ethics,'" for a discussion of the differences.

186. Later, when he wrote his novel *Adolphe* (1816), Constant would join her in stressing the value of compassion and even enthusiasm, if it had not descended into fanaticism. For a discussion, see K. Steven Vincent, "Charac-

ter, *Sensibilité,* Sociability and Politics in Benjamin Constant's *Adolphe,*" *Historical Reflections/Reflexions Historiques* 28.3 (2002).

187. According to Pierre Manent, "In the end, Constant's political position is that of *opposition,* his intellectual attitude *criticism,* his weapon *irony.* When all its contradictions and tensions are considered, his liberalism is that of a parliamentary orator belonging to the opposition." *An Intellectual History of Liberalism,* trans. Rebecca Balinski (Princeton, 1994), 91. The recent revival of interest in French liberalism has granted Constant a new audience. Compare, for example, the dismissal of him in Sheldon Wolin's *Politics and Vision: Continuity and Innovation in Western Political Thought* (Boston, 1960) as a figure whose work epitomizes "the declining significance of the political" (281) with the praise for him in F. R. Ankersmit, *Aesthetic Politics: Political Philosophy beyond Fact and Value* (Stanford, 1994): "More than anyone else he has contributed to the subtle and well-balanced political instrument we now know by the name of constitutional parliamentary democracy" (139). These judgments reflect differing attitudes toward "the political," which we will examine in the next chapter, and which have different implications for the question of lying in politics, which we will probe in the final chapter.

188. Holmes, *Benjamin Constant the Making of Modern Liberalism,* 118. But he concedes that Constant did not always uphold the virtues of mendacity; "Throughout his life he sustained a divided attitude toward sincerity and hypocrisy. What he consistently valued about hypocrisy, however, was less its educative power than its capacity to protect the individual from political surveillance and control" (125).

189. Ankersmit, *Aesthetic Politics,* 277.

190. Kant proudly reveals his ruse in the preface to his *The Contest of the Faculties.* The episode is discussed in Ernst Cassirer, *Kant's Life and Thought,* trans. James Haden (New Haven, 1981), 393–97. It should be acknowledged, however, to cite Peter Johnson, that "Kant does not say that the moral embargo on lying requires that truth always be volunteered; indeed, there is a considerable moral leeway between discretion and deceit, which Kant acknowledges. Such a margin is politically significant" (*Frames of Deceit,* 60).

191. Kant, *Lectures on Ethics,* 204–5.

192. Kant was not beyond drawing on religious arguments as well, noting that the first evil came into the world not when Cain killed Abel but when Eve, seduced by the serpent, lied to Adam. It was not for nothing, he noted, that Satan was often called the father of all lies.

193. Smyth, *The Habit of Lying,* 18. Much earlier, Thomas de Quincey had called him a virtual accomplice to murder. See his *On Murder Considered as One of the Fine Arts,* in *Collected Writings,* ed. David Masson, vol. 13 (Edinburgh, 1890), 13.

194. Hans Saner, *Kant's Political Thought: Its Origins and Development,* trans. E. B. Ashton (Chicago, 1973), 173.

195. Kant, "Idea for a Universal History with Cosmopolitan Intent," 121.

196. Kant, *The Metaphysics of Morals,* in *Immanuel Kant, Practical Philoso-*

phy, ed. and trans. Mary. J. Gregor (Cambridge, 1996), 552. For a later critique of lying as damaging to the character of the liar, whose personal integrity is jeopardized by saying what he does not believe, and to the deceived, who is disrespected and prevented from exercising his freedom by being given a false view of the world, see Kupfer, "The Moral Presumption against Lying."

197. Kant, *Lectures on Ethics,* 205.

198. As noted earlier, the opposite implication concerning autonomy is drawn by those who note that when the child learns to fib, it gains freedom from the tyranny of the facts. But Kant would respond that this is a spurious freedom, which refers only to the phenomenal realm.

199. MacIntyre, *Truthfulness, Lies and Moral Philosophers,* develops this distinction and notes that whereas Kant generally stresses the former, he also relies on the latter in certain of his arguments.

200. For a discussion of this issue, see Robert N. Van Wyk, "When Is Lying Morally Permissible?: Casuistical Reflections on the Game Analogy, Self-Defense, Social Contract Ethics, and Ideals," *Journal of Value Inquiry* 24.2 (1990).

201. Kant, *Lectures on Ethics,* 203.

202. Derrida, "History of the Lie," 45.

203. Smyth, *The Habit of Lying,* 26.

204. Herbert J. Paton, "An Alleged Right to Lie: A Problem in Kantian Ethics," in *Kant und das Recht der Lüge,* ed. Geismann and Oberer, 54. Paton's larger argument is that if one takes into account his early work on this issue in the 1780s, Kant did not really hold the absolutist position. For a refutation, which restores the traditional understanding, see Norman Gillespie, "Exceptions to the Categorical Imperative" in the same volume.

205. Bok, *Lying,* 41.

206. Ibid., 41–42.

207. Mme de Staël, *De l'Allemagne* (Paris, 1877), 508.

208. Jules Vuillemin, "On Lying: Kant and Benjamin Constant," in *Kant und das Recht der Lüge,* ed. Geismann and Oberer, 115.

209. For a critique of this distinction, see ibid., 106.

210. As Igor Primoratz concludes, "It may well be the case that our moral experience—when it comes to lying at any rate—is so complex, so intricate, that no hard and fast lines can be drawn and no 'method of ethics,' no definite procedure for making the right choices, articulated and applied across the board" ("Lying and the 'Methods of Ethics,'" 54).

211. The issue of cultural difference is a vexed one, since one culture often stigmatizes another as being less truthful. But that there are different standards of veracity in different cultural and historical contexts is not entirely implausible. See the discussion in Barnes, *A Pack of Lies,* chap. 5.

212. Derrida, "History of the Lie," 44.

213. Saner, *Kant's Political Thought,* 346.

214. Max Weber, "Politics as Vocation," in *From Max Weber: Essays in Sociology,* ed. H. H. Gerth and C. Wright Mills (New York, 1958), 120.

215. Saner, *Kant's Political Thought*, 346.

216. See, for example, Arendt, *Lectures on Kant's Political Philosophy*; Kimberly Hutchings, *Kant, Critique and Politics* (London, 1996); and Wolfgang Kersting, "Politics, Freedom and Order: Kant's Political Philosophy," in *The Cambridge Companion to Kant*, ed. Paul Guyer (Cambridge, 1993).

2 ON THE POLITICAL

1. Carl Schmitt, *The Concept of the Political*, trans. George Schwab (Chicago, 1996). This translation is based on the final version.

2. For a critical overview of Schmitt's postwar impact, see Jan-Werner Müller, *A Dangerous Mind: Carl Schmitt in Post-War European Thought* (New Haven, 2003).

3. Weber also had a fairly pedestrian definition of politics as "striving to share power or striving to influence the distribution of power, either among states or among groups within a state." See "Politics as a Vocation," in *From Max Weber: Essays in Sociology*, ed. H. H. Gerth and C. Wright Mills (New York, 1958), 78. But he did share with Machiavelli before him and Schmitt after the antimoralist recognition that "everything that is striven for through political action operating with violent means and following an ethic of responsibility endangers the 'salvation of the soul.' If, however, one chases after the ultimate good in a war of beliefs, following a pure ethic of absolute ends, then the goals may be damaged and discredited for generations, because responsibility for *consequences* is lacking" (126).

It might be noted that the concept of "the political" has been located in a book by one of Weber's contemporaries, Georg Jellinek (*Allgemeine Staatslehre*, 1900), but it was not until Schmitt's treatise that it was put on the conceptual map. See Kari Palonen, *Re-Thinking Politics: Essays from a Quarter Century*, ed. Kia Lindroos (Jyväsklä, Finland, 2007), 171.

4. Reinhart Koselleck, *The Practice of Conceptual History: Timing History, Spacing Concepts*, trans. Todd Samuel Presner et al. (Stanford, 2002).

5. In a later edition of the book, Schmitt tacitly dropped this claim, possibly under the influence of Leo Strauss or Hans Morgenthau, and argued instead that political relations permeate those other spheres as well. See Heinrich Meier, *Carl Schmitt and Leo Strauss: The Hidden Dialogue*, trans. J. Harvey Lomax (Chicago, 1995), for an interpretation stressing Strauss's role and the 1933 edition; see William L. Scheuerman, *Carl Schmitt: The End of Law* (Lanham, Md., 1999), chap. 9, for an alternative emphasis on Morgenthau and the 1932 edition.

6. As might be expected, it enjoyed an earlier popularity in Germany and France than in Britain, where more empirical inclinations ruled. Thus, for example, Bernard Crick entitled his 1962 book simply *In Defense of Politics* (London, 1962). There were, to be sure, isolated instances of British use of the phrase "the concept of the political," for example in Alan Montefiore's introduction to *Neutrality and Impartiality: The University and Political Commitment* (Cambridge, 1975). Schmitt, it might be noted, is absent from Monte-

fiore's discussion, in which the political is blandly identified with "the area of public policy . . . which may affect any (though not necessarily every) non-assignable member of the relevant community" (42).

7. Paul Ricoeur, "Le paradox politique," *Esprit* 26.1 (1957). For another early use, see Julian Freund, *L'essence du politique* (Paris, 1965). For examples of the later widespread adoption of the distinction, see Régis Debray, *Critique de la raison politique* (Paris, 1981); and Denis Kamboucher et al., *Le retrait du politique* (Paris, 1983). In a recent essay, "Ernesto Laclau and the Logic of "the Political," *Philosophy and Social Criticism* 32.1 (2006), Andrew Norris lists nine major theorists who use the term, in addition to Schmitt: Hannah Arendt, Leo Strauss, Claude Lefort, Philippe Lacoue-Labarthe, Jean-Luc Nancy, Chantal Mouffe, Ernesto Laclau, Slavoj Žižek, and Sheldon Wolin. For another discussion, see Oliver Marchart, *Post-foundational Political Thought: Political Difference in Nancy, Lefort, Badiou and Laclau* (Edinburgh, 2007), who examines its role in the French "Heideggerian Left."

8. For an account of the French case, see F. W. J. Hemmings, *Culture and Society in France, 1848–1898* (New York, 1971). The German intellectual retreat from politics is discussed in Fritz Stern, "The Political Consequences of the Unpolitical German," in *The Failure of Illiberalism: Essays on the Political Culture of Modern Germany* (New York, 1972). More recent historians have found a less impoverished political life in the Second Reich. See Margaret Lavinia Anderson, *Practicing Democracy: Elections and Political Culture in Imperial Germany* (Princeton, 2000).

9. See, for example, Tim Mason, "The Primacy of the Political: Politics and Economics in National Socialist Germany," in *Nazism, Fascism and the Working Class: Essays by Tim Mason,* ed. Jane Caplan (Cambridge, 1995). It is, of course, possible to argue that totalitarianism really meant the negation of "genuine" politics, according to certain definitions of the term. For some commentators, it meant "metapolitics" instead; see, for example, Peter Viereck, *Metapolitics: From Wagner and the German Romantics to Hitler,* 2nd ed. (Piscatawy, N.J., 2003). In another, more recent book also called *Metapolitics* (trans. Jason Barker [London, 2005]), the French philosopher Alain Badiou notes that "it has often been remarked that what characterized Soviet society was the death of politics rather than politics being 'placed in command'" (69). For an earlier example of the same argument, which focuses on Lenin's utopian book *The State and Revolution,* with its forecast of the withering away of the state under communism, see A. J. Polan, *Lenin and the End of Politics* (Berkeley, 1984).

10. The first to introduce the Bonapartist analysis for fascism was August Thalheimer in the late 1920s. The "state capitalist" analysis was developed with varying explanations by Friedrich Pollock, Rudolf Hilferding, and Richard Löwenthal. For a general overview of the issue, see William David Jones, *The Lost Debate: German Socialist Intellectuals and Totalitarianism* (Urbana, 1999).

11. Antonio Gramsci, "The Revolution against 'Capital,'" in *Selections from*

Prison Writings 1910–1920, ed. Quinton Hoare, trans. John Mathews (New York, 1977).

12. For a discussion, see Hans Sluga, "Stanley Cavell and the Pursuits of Happiness," in *The Claim to Community: Essays on Stanley Cavell and Political Philosophy* (Stanford, 2006). Sluga contrasts the model of inclusivity beginning with the Sophist Protagoras to that associated with Plato and Aristotle, which defined a more circumscribed political domain.

13. See, for example, Paul Thomas, *Alien Politics: Marxist State Theory Retrieved* (New York, 1994).

14. Chantal Mouffe, *The Return of the Political* (London, 1993) and *On the Political* (London, 2005).

15. Agnes Heller, "The Concept of the Political Revisited," in *Political Theory Today,* ed. David Held (Stanford, 1991), 330.

16. The series is edited by Keith Ansell Pearson and Simon Critchley for Routledge.

17. Husserl's reduction is specifically identified as a source of the search for "the political" by Palonen, *Re-Thinking Politics,* 16.

18. Mouffe, *On The Political,* 5–6. Heidegger also claimed that ontology can be historical rather than transcendental—this was the meaning of his notion of *Geschichtlichkeit* or historicity—but many critics have noted that he rarely engaged with historical developments on more than the most cosmic level. The importance of the unbridgeable conceptual difference between the two levels as a marker of left Heideggerian "post-foundational" political theory, neither essentialist nor nominalist, is elaborated by Marchart, *Post-foundational Political Thought,* chap. 2.

19. Pierre Rosenvallon, *Democracy Past and Future,* ed. Samuel Moyn (New York, 2006), 36.

20. Carl Schmitt, *Political Theology,* trans. George Schwab (Cambridge, Mass., 1985).

21. The metaphor is developed by Hannah Fenichel Pitkin, *The Attack of the Blob: Hannah Arendt's Concept of the Social* (Chicago, 1998).

22. Not all theorists of "the political" consider it a separate domain, preferring to stress its function as an activity, for example, Schmitt in *The Concept of the Political,* 26. In his 1919 lecture "Politics as a Vocation," Max Weber also famously identified it with an activity, the striving to share or influence power and lead political associations. For a useful discussion of his concept of politics and references to further reading, see the entry in Richard Swedberg, *The Max Weber Dictionary: Key Words and Central Concepts* (Stanford, 2005).

23. Jacques Rancière, *On the Shores of Politics,* trans. Liz Heron (London, 2007), 1.

24. Palonen, *Re-Thinking Politics,* 99. He explores in depth the implications of the spatial concept of politics, which he contrasts with ones based on a discipline model, stemming from Aristotle, and an activities model, which he claims is more frequent today. The latter is inherently temporal rather than spatial.

25. The crucial distinction between "place" and "space" is discussed with great acuity in Edward S. Casey, *The Fate of Place: A Philosophical History* (Berkeley, 1998).

26. Marcel Detienne, "The Gods of Politics in Early Greek Cities," in *Political Theologies: Public Religions in a Post-Secular World,* ed. Hent deVries and Lawrence E. Sullivan (New York, 2006), 97. He notes that the word "agora" could stand not only for the space but also for the men who deliberated there and their speech. The same would be true of modern equivalents like the Congress.

27. For more on the metaphoric dangers of seafaring, political or otherwise, see Hans Blumenberg, *Shipwreck with Spectator: Paradigm of a Metaphor for Existence,* trans. Steven Rendall (Cambridge, Mass., 1997).

28. Hannah Arendt, *The Promise of Politics,* ed. Jerome Kohn (New York, 2005), 167.

29. Hannah Arendt, *The Human Condition* (Garden City, N.Y., 1959), 178.

30. Hannah Arendt, *The Origins of Totalitarianism* (Cleveland, 1964), 466. Totalitarianism, she suggests, is even worse than the desert of tyranny because the latter "still provides some room for the fear-guided movements and suspicion-ridden actions of its inhabitants," while the former presses men together, destroying any space at all and with it the possibility of motion. For more on the metaphor of politics as an "oasis" in the desert where the blinding "sandstorms" of totalitarianism blow, see *The Promise of Politics,* epilogue.

31. Margaret Kohn, *Radical Space: Building the House of the People* (Ithaca, 2003).

32. Although the modern state system is normally understood to begin with the treaties that ended the Thirty Years' War, the historian Jeremy Black cautions against giving them too much weight: "First, effective autonomy had long existed within the [Holy Roman] Empire, second the process of Imperial disunity and the effective sovereignty of individual princes had been greatly advanced as a result of the Reformation, and, third, the changes should be seen as an adaptation of a weak federal system, rather than as a turning point." *European International Relations, 1648–1815* (New York, 2002), 74.

33. Andrea Wilson Nightingale, *Spectacles of Truth in Classical Greek Philosophy: "Theoria" in Its Cultural Context* (Stanford, 2004), 70.

34. Arendt, "Introduction *into* Politics," in *The Promise of Politics,* 129, 183.

35. Where, it might be asked, are salient political traditions like anarchism and Marxism in this schema? In both cases, there is a tendency to fold the political into the larger totality of social relations, denying it its own inherent domain. Marx derided the goal of mere "political emancipation" in his quarrel with Left Hegelians like Bruno Bauer, and most anarchists were hostile to the state, parliamentarism, and other traditional political institutions. Although there were some twentieth-century Marxists such as Louis Althusser and his followers, most notably Nicos Poulantzas, who did allow the "relative autonomy" of the political, they claimed that the economy remained determinant "in the last instance."

As for the question of mendacity in politics, Marx himself seems to have upheld a conventional view of its dangers. In 1872 an anonymous attack was launched in the Berlin *Concordia: Zeitschrift für die Arbeiterfrage* against Marx for having allegedly falsified a quotation from an 1863 parliamentary speech by Gladstone in his own Inaugural Address to the First International in 1864. The polemic was written, so it was later disclosed, by the eminent liberal political economist Lujo Brentano. Marx vigorously defended himself in a response published later that year in *Der Volksstaat*, launching a bitter debate that would drag on for two decades, involving Marx's daughter Eleanor, an obscure Cambridge don named Sedly Taylor, and even Gladstone himself, who backed Brentano's version. Finally, Friedrich Engels summed it all up in 1891 in a long pamphlet with all the relevant materials reprinted called "In the Case of Brentano vs. Marx." The entire dossier is available at http://marxists .anu.edu.au/archive/marx/works/download/Marx_vs_Brentano.pdf.

36. Schmitt's target was the legal positivism of neo-Kantian *Rechtstaat* theorists like Hans Kelsen. His contempt for the priority of legality over legitimacy has been linked to his anti-Semitism, since he claimed that belief in the sovereignty of the law was typical of the Jewish mentality. See the discussion in Helmut Lethen, *Cool Conduct: The Culture of Distance in Weimar Germany,* trans. Don Reneau (Berkeley, 2002), 180.

37. The distinction between mere power (*potestas*) and acknowledged authority (*auctoritas*) is, of course, an ancient one. For one discussion, see Hannah Arendt, "What Is Authority?" in *Between Past and Future: Six Exercises in Political Thought* (Cleveland, 1965). For another, see Richard Sennett, *Authority* (New York, 1980). The classic account of three basic types of legitimate authority—traditional, rational-legal, and charismatic—can be found in Max Weber, *The Theory of Social and Economic Organization,* ed. Talcott Parsons, trans. A. M. Henderson and Talcott Parsons (New York, 1947).

38. The reversal of Clausewitz's famous phrase was explicitly advocated by the Weimar right-wing publicist Ernst von Salomon after World War I. See Robert G. L. Waite, *Vanguard of Nazism: The Free Corps Movement in Postwar Germany, 1918–1923* (New York, 1952), 269.

39. Precisely what Schmitt meant by "existential" was never fully clear. As Herbert Marcuse pointed out in "The Struggle against Liberalism in the Totalitarian View of the State," "In political existentialism there is not even an attempt to define the 'existential' conceptually. . . . The existential appears essentially as a contrast to the 'normative,' i.e. as something that cannot be placed under any norm lying outside itself. . . . There is no fundamental or general criterion in existentialism for determining which facts and conditions are to be considered existential." *Negations: Essays in Critical Theory,* trans. Jeremy J. Shapiro (Boston, 1968), 31. Schmitt was, we now know from his diary, deeply influenced by Kierkegaard in 1914. See the discussion in Hans Sluga, *The Care of the Common: The Concept of the Political in an Age of Uncertainty* (forthcoming), chap. 5.

40. Schmitt, *The Concept of the Political,* 52.

41. Schmitt, "Politik" (1936), reprinted in *Staat, Großraum, Nomos: Arbeiten aus den Jahren 1916–1969*, ed. Günter Maschke (Berlin, 1995), 133.

42. Ernst-Wolfgang Böckenförde, "The Concept of the Political: A Key to Understanding Carl Schmitt's Constitutional Theory," in *Law as Politics: Carl Schmitt's Critique of Liberalism*, ed. David Dyzenhaus (Durham, 1998), 39.

43. Carl Schmitt, *The Crisis of Parliamentary Democracy*, trans. Ellen Kennedy (Cambridge, Mass., 1985), 9. This very dubious proposition is belied by the experience of democracies like Canada, Belgium, Swizerland, and India.

44. Schmitt, *The Concept of the Political*, 28. It should be noted that Schmitt spends far more time talking about enemies than friends in his discussion of "the political."

45. For a discussion of Schmitt's critique of the liberal fetish of technology, see John P. McCormick, *Carl Schmitt's Critique of Liberalism: Against Politics as Technology* (New York, 1997).

46. Schmitt, "Politik," 134.

47. Ernesto Laclau and Chantal Mouffe, *Hegemony and Socialist Strategy: Towards a Radical Democratic Politics*, trans. Winston Moore and Paul Cammack (London, 1985), chap. 3.

48. Schmitt, "Politik," 137. Written in 1936, when Schmitt was struggling to retain his position as Nazi crown jurist, the article ends by praising Hitler for being political in the sense of knowing when to use war for other ends, not for its own sake.

49. The word is derived from the Latin "status," which means a condition or a matter of standing. It emerged in the early modern period as something more than just the prince's personal estate to become an entity with its own separate apparatus of governance. For an account, see Quentin Skinner, "The State," in *Political Innovation and Conceptual Change*, ed. T. Ball, J. Farr, and R. L. Hansen (Cambridge, 1989).

50. One theorist who preferred diplomacy to war as the model of "the political" was the Weimar philosopher Helmuth Plessner. See the discussion in Jan-Werner Müller, "The Soul in the Age of Society and Technology: Helmuth Plessner's Defensive Liberalism," in *Confronting Mass Democracy and Industrial Technology: Political and Social Theory from Nietzsche to Habermas*, ed. John P. McCormick (Durham, 2002).

51. There were, to be sure, always those who defended intervening in the internal affairs of other nations on moral or ideological grounds, such as the Abbé Raynal and Thomas Paine in the late eighteenth century. See Reinhard Koselleck, *Critique and Crisis: Enlightenment and the Pathogenesis of Modern Society* (Cambridge, Mass., 1988), 174–86. Koselleck's debt to Carl Schmitt is discussed in William E. Scheuerman, "Unresolved Paradoxes: Conservative Thought in Adenauer's Germany," in *Confronting Mass Democracy*, ed. McCormick, 234–40.

52. The claim that some states are naturally expansive can be found not only in the Nazi quest for *Lebensraum* but also in the imperative to dominate

continents that fueled American and Russian expansion during much of their histories.

53. The classic positive account is Friedrich Meinecke, *Cosmopolitanism and the National State*, trans. Robert B. Kimber (Princeton, 1970). For a critical rejoinder, see Georg G. Iggers, *The German Conception of History: The National Conception of Historical Thought from Herder to the Present* (Middletown, 1968).

54. Friedrich Meinecke, *Machiavellism: The Doctrine of "Raison d'État" and Its Place in Modern History*, trans. Douglas Scott (New York, 1965), 350.

55. For discussions, see Z. A. Pelczynski, ed., *Hegel's Political Philosophy: Problems and Perspectives* (Cambridge, 1971); Shlomo Avineri, *Hegel's Theory of the Modern State* (Cambridge, 1972); and George Armstrong Kelly, *Hegel's Retreat from Eleusis: Studies in Political Thought* (Princeton, 1978).

56. For discussions of Hegel's attitude toward the ancient city-state, see Kelly, *Hegel's Retreat from Eleusis;* and Judith Shklar, "Hegel's Phenomenology: An Elegy for Hellas," in *Hegel's Political Philosophy*.

57. Hegel, *Philosophy of Right and Law*, in *The Philosophy of Hegel*, ed. Carl J. Friedrich (New York, 1954), 280.

58. Ibid., 296.

59. Warren Breckman, *Marx, the Young Hegelians, and the Origins of Radical Social Theory: Dethroning the Self* (Cambridge, 1999), 78.

60. Hegel, *Philosophy of Right and Law*, 322.

61. For a critical discussion of the importance of the "ethical state" ideal in Britain from a Marxist point of view, see David Lloyd and Paul Thomas, *Culture and the State* (New York, 1998).

62. Mouffe, *On the Political*, 20. There is a certain slippage in her terminology, however, as earlier, on p. 9, she writes, "By 'the political' I mean the dimension of antagonism which I take to be constitutive of human societies, while by 'politics' I mean the set of practices and institutions through which an order is created, organizing human coexistence in the context of conflictuality provided by the political."

63. Ibid., 52. One might, of course, ask the question, why is there a shared set of rules if there was no deliberative consensus producing their formation?

64. There were, to be sure, more pluralist strains of liberalism that stressed the importance of intermediate bodies as antidotes to the excessive power of the centralizing state or the threat of atomizing individualism. In French liberalism, they were particularly strong. For a recent account of what she calls "aristocratic liberalism," see Annelien de Dijn, *French Political Thought from Montesquieu to Tocqueville: Liberty in a Levelled Society?* (Cambridge, 2008). It was also possible to infuse liberalism with certain republican values, as Andrew Jainchill has shown in *Reimagining Politics after the Terror: The Republican Origins of French Liberalism* (Ithaca, 2008). French liberalism, however, was relatively weak compared to its British counterpart, which was far more individualist in character.

65. Leo Strauss, "Notes on Carl Schmitt's *Concept of the Political,*" appended to Schmitt, *The Concept of the Political,* 90–93 For a discussion of Strauss's relation to Schmitt, see Meier, *Carl Schmitt and Leo Strauss.* For a critique of his reading, see Robert Howse, "From Legitimacy to Dictatorship—and Back Again: Leo Strauss's Critique of the Anti-Liberalism of Carl Schmitt," in *Law as Politics,* ed. Dyzenhaus; and William E. Scheuerman, *Carl Schmitt: The End of Law* (Lanham, Md., 1999), 226–37.

66. John Rawls, *Political Liberalism* (New York, 2005), 374 (italics in original).

67. Nancy Fraser, "Rethinking the Public Sphere: A Contribution to the Critique of Actual Existing Democracy," in *Habermas and the Public Sphere,* ed. Craig Calhoun (Cambridge, Mass., 1992), 121.

68. For a discussion of Locke and trust, see J. W. Gough, *John Locke's Political Philosophy: Eight Studies* (Oxford, 1950), chap. 7.

69. See Shapin, *A Social History of Truth,* 95, for a discussion of Defoe on truth and trade.

70. Peter Johnson, *Frames of Deceit: A Study of the Loss and Recovery of Public and Private Trust* (Cambridge, 1993), 54.

71. Crick, *In Defense of Politics,* 123.

72. Wolin, *Politics and Vision,* 343–51.

73. Any sustained attempt to deal with his political legacy would have to probe the differences among these texts. For a helpful analysis, see Trevor J. Saunders, "Plato's Later Political Thought," in *The Cambridge Companion to Plato,* ed. Richard Kraut (Cambridge, 1992).

74. Plato's hostility to Sophism has not prevented him from being called "an incomparable sophist" himself by Cornelius Castoriadis, who continues, "One cannot count the number of intentional sophisms and paralogisms that are there in the dialogues. The *Republic* itself is one huge articulated sophism, a multi-leveled and multi-staged sophism." *On Plato's "Statesman,"* trans. David Ames Curtis (Stanford, 1999), 3. In fact, because of his presentation of his thoughts in dialogic form, it can be argued that Plato may have been less monologic than his detractors have claimed.

75. For a discussion of this metaphor and the role of metaphor in general in Plato's seemingly antirhetorical prose, see Frank Ankersmit, *Aesthetic Politics: Political Philosophy beyond Fact and Value* (Stanford, 1996), 257–60.

76. Wolin, *Politics and Vision,* 42.

77. Hans Sluga, *Heidegger's Crisis: Philosophy and Politics in Nazi Germany* (Cambridge, Mass., 1993), 175. Perhaps the most virulent critique of Plato as a totalitarian came in Karl Popper's *The Open Society and Its Enemies,* 2 vols. (London, 1945). He reversed the previous veneration of Plato's political philosophy by humanists like Benjamin Jowett, A. E. Taylor, and Ernst Barker. See the discussion of Plato's positive reputation among the Victorians, even liberals like J. S. Mill, in Richard Jenkyns, *The Victorians and Ancient Greece* (Cambridge, 1980), chap. 10. For the larger context of the reversal of Plato's reputation, which mentions other critics before Popper, see Malachi Haim

Hacohen, *Karl Popper: The Formative Years, 1902–1945* (Cambridge, 2000), chap. 9.

78. See Arendt, "Socrates," in *The Promise of Politics*. She sees Socrates as a mediating figure between the Sophists' reliance on the plurality of uncertain opinion and Plato's belief in the uniformity of the single truth. The difficulty of distinguishing between Plato and Socrates is, of course, enormous because virtually all we know of the latter comes from the words in the dialogues presented by the former, his student. Does Plato identify with Socrates's position or simply include it in the dialectical exchange of opinions he is trying to overcome? Does he identify with it in certain of the dialogues, but not in others? For one attempt to untangle the differences, see Terry Penner, "Socrates and the Early Dialogues," in *The Cambridge Companion to Plato*, ed. Kraut.

79. See, for example, Alan Gilbert, "Do Philosophers Council Tyrants?" *Constellations* 16.1 (March 2009).

80. Leo Strauss, *What Is Political Philosophy? And Other Studies* (Chicago, 1988), 36.

81. Ibid., 85–86.

82. Benjamin Constant, *The Spirit of Conquest and Usurpation and their Relation to European Civilization* (1814), in *Political Writings*, trans. and ed. Biancamaria Fontana (Cambridge, 1988), 102.

83. See Philip Pettit, *Republicanism: A Theory of Freedom and Government* (Oxford, 1997); and Daniel Weinstock and Christian Nadeau, eds., *Republicanism: History, Theory and Practice* (London, 2004). The history of republicanism is, to be sure, very complicated, with many different variations over time and in national contexts. For a comparison of two of them, see Dick Howard, "Intersecting Trajectories of Republicanism in France and the United States," in *The Specter of Democracy* (New York, 2002).

84. Arendt, *Between Past and Future*, 108. Arendt's disdain for rulership extended as well to all types of what the Germans called *Herrschaft*, which Max Weber had seen in the modern era as more rational-legal than traditional or charismatic. For a comparison of her position with his on this issue, see Kari Palonen, "Imagining Max Weber's Reply to Hannah Arendt: Remarks on the Arendtian Critique of Representative Democracy," *Constellations* 15.1 (March 2008).

85. Claude Lefort, *Writing: The Political Test*, ed. David Ames Curtis (Durham, 2000), 133.

86. For a discussion of its impact on America, see J. G. A. Pocock, "Civic Humanism and Its Role in Anglo-American Thought," in *Politics, Language and Time: Essays on Political Thought and History* (New York, 1973). For a contrast with the proto-liberal individualism of Hobbes, see Quentin Skinner, *Liberty before Liberalism* (Cambridge, 1998). John Rawls has argued that there is an important distinction between classical republicanism, which argues only for the active participation of citizens needed to maintain a constitutional regime, and civic humanism, which more ambitiously claims that man's essential nature is only realized with such participation. Whereas the former

is compatible with liberalism, the latter, he argues, is not. See Rawls, *Political Liberalism*, 205–6.

87. In Arendt's case, the balance between the agonistic and accommodational impulses seems to have shifted over time in the direction of the latter. See the discussion in Peter Fuss, "Hannah Arendt's Conception of Political Community," in *Hannah Arendt: The Recovery of the Public World*, ed. Melvyn A. Hill (New York, 1979).

88. David Hume, *Essays: Moral, Political and Literary*, ed. Eugene F. Miller (Indianapolis, 1987), 25.

89. For a good introduction to the idea of governmentality, see Mitchell Dean, *Governmentality: Power and Rule in Modern Society* (London, 1999).

90. For the mature version of his argument, see *Between Facts and Norms: Contributions to a Discourse Theory of Law and Democracy*, trans. William Rehg (Cambridge, Mass., 1998).

91. See Jürgen Habermas, "The Horrors of Autonomy: Carl Schmitt in English," in *The New Conservativism: Cultural Criticism and the Historian's Debate*, ed. and trans. Shierry Weber Nicholsen (Cambridge, Mass., 1989), 128–29; and Habermas, "Carl Schmitt in the Political Intellectual History of the Federal Republic," in *A Berlin Republic: Writings on Germany*, trans. Steven Rendell (Lincoln, Neb., 1997).

92. Rawls, *Political Liberalism*, 420.

93. Seyla Benhabib, *Situating the Self: Gender, Community and Postmodernism in Contemporary Ethics* (New York, 1992), 105.

94. For example, in *Between Facts and Norms* Habermas writes that "politics cannot coincide as a whole with the practice of those who talk to one another in order to act in a politically autonomous manner. The exercise of political autonomy implies the discursive formation of a common will, not the implementation of the laws issuing therefrom. The concept of the political in its full sense *also* includes the use of administrative power within the political system, as well as the competition for access to that system" (150). Law, he argues, is the medium through which discursive will formation leads to administrative power.

95. Jürgen Habermas, "What Is Universal Pragmatics?," in *Communication and the Evolution of Society*, trans. Thomas McCarthy (Boston, 1979), 3.

96. Walter Benjamin, "The Work of Art in the Age of Mechanical Reproduction," in *Illuminations*, ed. Hannah Arendt, trans. Harry Zohn (New York, 1968), 244.

97. Carl Schorske, *Fin-de-Siècle Vienna: Politics and Culture* (New York, 1980), chap. 3.

98. Murray Edelman, *From Art to Politics: How Artistic Creations Shape Political Conceptions* (Chicago, 1995), 91.

99. For a general analysis of the links between anarchism and Symbolism, see Richard D. Sonn, *Anarchism and Cultural Politics in Fin-de-Siècle France* (Lincoln, Neb., 1989).

100. For a consideration of the debate over Schmitt's alleged aestheticiza-

tion of politics, see Neil Levi, "Carl Schmitt and the Question of the Aesthetic," *New German Critique* 101 (Summer 2007).

101. For an earlier attempt to sort it out, see my essay "The 'Aesthetic Ideology' as Ideology; or What Does it Mean to Aestheticize Politics," in *Force Fields: Between Intellectual History and Cultural Critique* (New York, 1993).

102. Judith Squires, "In Different Voices: Deliberative Democracy and Deliberative Politics," in *The Politics of Postmodernity*, ed. James Good and Irving Velody (Cambridge, 1998), 126.

103. For one account of its fortunes, see Nicholas Mirzoeff, *Bodyscape: Art, Modernity and the Ideal Figure* (New York, 1995), chap. 2.

104. For a survey of the tradition in Germany, see Josef Chytry, *The Aesthetic State: A Quest in Modern German Thought* (Berkeley, 1989).

105. See, for example, Philippe Lacoue-Labarthe and Jean-Luc Nancy, *The Literary Absolute: The Theory of Literature in German Romanticism,* trans. Philip Barnard and Cheryl Lester (Albany, 1988); Terry Eagleton, *The Ideology of the Aesthetic* (Cambridge, Mass., 1990); Paul de Man, *Aesthetic Ideology,* ed. Andrzej Warminski (Minneapolis, 1996).

106. Arendt, *The Human Condition,* chap. 4.

107. Arendt's debt to the Aristotelian notion of *praxis* is often acknowledged. For a dissenting evaluation, which emphasizes the influence of Heidegger instead and says Aristotle's version of action was too teleological for Arendt, see Dana R. Villa, *Arendt and Heidegger: The Fate of the Political* (Princeton, 1996), chap. 1.

108. Arendt did acknowledge the importance of the initial act of lawgiving that creates the space for a political performance, an act of foundation that often involves the very violence that politics, rightly understood, keeps at bay. See in particular her discussion in *On Revolution* (New York, 1965), where she expresses admiration for the American Constitution.

109. The classic account of the tropological underpinnings of historical narrative can be found in Hayden White, *Metahistory: The Historical Imagination in Nineteenth-Century Europe* (Baltimore, 1973).

110. Walter Bagehot, *The English Constitution* (London, 1963), 248. Bagehot, to be sure, meant this to be a positive description of a polity wisely ruled by those who deserved to rule over the mass of "ignorant men and women." But more democratic observers have been less enthusiastic.

111. Arendt, *The Human Condition,* 167.

112. Arendt, *The Promise of Politics,* 14.

113. Ibid., 16.

114. Ibid., 277.

115. Sheldon Wolin, "Hannah Arendt: Democracy and the Political," in *Hannah Arendt: Critical Essays,* ed. Lewis P. Hinchman and Sandra K. Hinchman (Albany, 1994), 303–4.

116. Arendt, *The Human Condition,* 210.

117. Jacques Rancière, *The Politics of Aesthetics: The Distribution of the Sensible,* trans. Gabriel Rockhill (London, 2004), 13.

118. Ibid., 14.

119. Arendt, *Lectures on Kant's Political Philosophy*, ed. Ronald Beiner (Chicago, 1982).

120. Palonen, *Re-Thinking Politics*, 33.

121. For a suggestive reading of the complexities of this Marxist formula from *The Eighteenth Brumaire of Louis Bonaparte*, see Jeffrey Mehlman, *Revolution and Repetition: Marx/Hugo/Balzac* (Berkeley, 1977).

122. Michael Steinberg, *The Meaning of the Salzburg Festival: Austria as Theater and Ideology, 1890–1938* (Ithaca, 1990), 38–39.

123. Lefort is a former Marxist, a founder of the group Socialism or Barbarism with Cornelius Castoriadis, and a student of Maurice Merleau-Ponty. Rosenvallon is a colleague of Lefort's at the École des Hautes Études en Sciences Sociales in Paris and much influenced by him. See Samuel Moyn, introduction to Pierre Rosenvallon, *Democracy Past and Future*, ed. Moyn (New York, 2006), 8. Rancière was also a Marxist, but more closely associated with Louis Althusser. In his afterword to Rancière's *The Politics of Aesthetics*, Slavoj Žižek argues that Lefort's version of democracy is more formal than Rancière's, which he claims still believes that "within the multitude of real political agents, there is a privileged One, the 'supernumerary' which occupies the place of the 'symptomal torsion' of the whole and thus allows us access to the truth" (74). This argument aligns Rancière more closely to Alain Badiou and other Leninist post-Althusserians like Žižek himself than I think is warranted.

124. Claude Lefort, *Le travail de l'oeuvre Machiavel* (Paris, 1972). For an extensive commentary, see Bernard Flynn, *The Philosophy of Claude Lefort: Interpreting the Political* (Evanston, 2005), part 1.

125. Lefort, *Writing*, 132–33.

126. Ankersmit, *Aesthetic Politics*, 18. Because of this stress on brokenness, it might well seem that "allegorical" rather than "symbolic," in the sense that Walter Benjamin famously imputed to these terms, would be a more appropriate way to define the aesthetic version of politics we are discussing. But we will remain with the vocabulary of its exponents.

127. Claude Lefort, *The Political Forms of Modern Society: Bureaucracy, Democracy, Totalitarianism*, ed. John B. Thompson (Cambridge, 1986), 297.

128. Ankersmit, *Aesthetic Politics*, 127.

129. According to Ankersmit, "Political debate in democracy is positively antidialectic: it does not attempt to retain the best out of two opposing opinions, but to put displeasing opinions in quarantine, so to speak. It is here that political debate is quite unlike the kind of debate that one may find in the sciences. . . . In political debate, by contrast, the argument of one's opponent has to be encapsulated, rendered innocuous, shown as not deserving serious consideration. Such a strategy entails that one should avoid the cognitive heart of the position of one's opponent as much as possible" (ibid., 106–7). Rancière agrees: "Democracy is closely linked to tragedy—to unsettled grievance. . . . The subject that gives voice and substance to the grievance is not qualified to declare it satisfied. Nor is there any justification for setting up an opposition,

as Habermas does, between the discursive formation of a will to democracy and liberal compromise between interests. Democracy is neither compromise between interests nor the formation of a common will. Its kind of dialogue is that of a divided community" (*On the Shores of Politics*, 102–3).

130. See Rosenvallon's critique of Foucault in *Democracy Past and Future*, 75.

131. Ernst H. Kantorowicz, *The King's Two Bodies: A Study of Medieval Political Thought* (Princeton, 1957).

132. For a comparison of Schmitt's political theology with Kantorowicz's argument, see Lior Barshack, "Constituent Power as Body: Outline of a Constitutional Theology," *University of Toronto Law Journal* 56 (2006). Of the defenders of "aesthetic politics" discussed here, it is only Ankersmit who embraces a more immanentist version of the argument, although not in Schmitt's sense. He writes that "Lefort's (theologically inspired) search for a symbolic political meaning outside of or transcending the political machinery itself is replaced here by a consistent immanence. Though neither Lefort nor the aesthetic political philosopher [i.e., Ankersmit] wishes to attribute legitimate political power to either the ruler or the ruled (or to both, for that matter), Lefort situates its origin in a sphere beyond both the ruler and the ruled, whereas the aesthetic political philosopher discovers this origin between them" (*Aesthetic Politics*, 105).

133. In the 1930s, so David Bates has argued, Schmitt also moved closer to a Catholic corporatist position, leaving behind decisionism for institutional thinking. See Bates, "Political Theology and the Nazi State: Carl Schmitt's Concept of the Institution," *Modern Intellectual History* 3.3 (November 2006).

134. Charles Taylor, *A Secular Age* (Cambridge, Mass., 2007), 712. See also Jim Egan, *Authorizing Experience: Refigurations of the Body Politic in Seventeenth-Century New England Writing* (Princeton, 1999).

135. Jürgen Habermas, *The Structural Transformation of the Public Sphere: An Inquiry into a Category of Bourgeois Society*, trans. Thomas Burger (Cambridge, Mass., 1991), 99.

136. Lefort, *The Political Forms of Modern Society*, 302.

137. Ibid.

138. Ibid., 303.

139. It might be noted that at the very moment when "the people" was transformed into the source of popular sovereignty during the French Revolution, it was crossed with another meaning, which restricted it to the common people opposed to the ruling elites and willing to use violence to overturn the old order. As William H. Sewell Jr. has claimed with regard to the term,

> On the one hand, *le peuple* could mean the entire French population. It was the people in this highly generalized and somewhat mystical sense that was designated as sovereign in the political theory adopted by the National Assembly. On the other hand, *le peuple* could mean the ordinary people, commoners as opposed to nobles and clergy, or the poor as op-

posed to the cultured and wealthy. It was, of course, the people in this latter sense who were thought to be capable of acts of crowd violence. The semantic slippage between the two meanings of "the people" made possible an equation of the people who rose up and took the Bastille (sense two) and the sovereign form of government that suited it best (sense one).

Logics of History: Social Theory and Social Transformation (Chicago, 2005), 246–47. As the history of populism shows, this semantic uncertainty has never been fully shed.

140. Rosenvallon, *Democracy Past and Future,* 37.

141. Derrida's comments on politics and democracy are to be found in many places in his work. For a useful summary, see the entry "Democracy" in Niall Lucy, *A Derrida Dictionary* (Oxford, 2004).

142. Ankersmit, *Aesthetic Politics,* chap. 2.

143. Lefort, *The Political Forms of Modern Society,* 303.

144. Rosenvallon, *Democracy Past and Future,* 50.

145. Lefort, *Complications: Communism and the Dilemmas of Democracy,* trans. Julian Bourg (New York, 2007), 140. How beholden Lefort actually was to Lacan is discussed in a long footnote in Bourg's introduction (195).

146. Rosenvallon, *Democracy Past and Future,* 42.

147. Gustave Flaubert, *Sentimental Education,* trans. Robert Baldick (London, 1964), 181.

148. Rancière, *On the Shores of Politics,* 93.

149. Ibid., 94.

150. Flynn, *The Philosophy of Claude Lefort,* 121.

151. Lacoue-Labarthe and Nancy, *The Literary Absolute.*

152. Carl Schmitt, *Political Romanticism,* trans. Guy Oakes (Cambridge, Mass., 1986).

153. Ankersmit, *Aesthetic Politics,* 129.

154. More than just a political slogan, this argument also informed scholarly attempts to break down the barrier between "high" politics and "low" domestic life. See, for example, the complaint of the distinguished feminist historian Joan Wallach Scott that "by studying power as it is exercised by and in relation to formal governmental authorities, historians necessarily eliminate whole realms of experience from consideration. This would not happen if a broader notion of 'politics' were employed, one that took all unequal relationships as somehow 'political' because involving unequal distributions of power, and asked how they were established, refused, or maintained." *Gender and the Politics of History* (New York, 1988), 26.

155. Michael McKeon, *The Secret History of Domesticity* (Baltimore, 2005), 7.

156. Ibid.

157. Schmitt, "Politik," 135.

158. Benhabib, *Situating the Self,* 94.

159. Mouffe, *On the Political,* 18.

160. The secularization thesis, to be sure, has not gone uncontested. The most trenchant critique was launched by Hans Blumenberg in *The Legitimacy of the Modern Age*, trans. Robert M. Wallace (Cambridge, Mass., 1983), chap. 8. See also Taylor, *A Secular Age*.

161. Pierre Manent, "Europe and the Theologico-Political Problem," in *An Intellectual History of Liberalism*, trans. Rebecca Balinski (Princeton, 1994).

162. Leo Strauss, "Preface to *Hobbes Politisches Wissenschaft*" (1965), in *Jewish Philosophy and the Crisis of Modernity: Essays and Lectures in Modern Jewish Thought*, ed. Kenneth Hart Green (Albany, 1997), 453.

163. Derrida, "Faith and Knowledge."

164. Lefort, "The Permanence of the Theological-Political," in *Political Theologies: Public Religions in a Post-Secular World*, ed. Hent de Vries and Lawrence E. Sullivan (New York, 2006). This collection contains many examples of the imbrication of the political and the theological in our allegedly postsecular age, as does Creston Davis, John Milbank, and Slavoj Žižek, eds., *Theology and the Political: The New Debate* (Durham, 2005). See also the issue of *New German Critique* 35.3 (Fall 2008) devoted to "political theology."

165. Habermas, "On the Relation between the Secular Liberal State and Religion," in *The Frankfurt School on Religion: Key Writings by the Major Thinkers*, ed. Eduardo Mendieta (New York, 2005), 346. This collection brings together many texts from other Frankfurt School theorists demonstrating the complicated dialectic of religion and politics in at least this tradition of Marxist thought.

166. Shapin, *A Social History of Truth*, 72.

167. In his 1921 *Dictatorship*, Schmitt distinguished between "commissarial" dictatorships, which sought to restore an earlier legal order, and "sovereign" ones, which instituted a new order. In subsequent works, like *Political Theology*, he emphasized the importance of the latter.

168. Arendt, *The Human Condition*, 173.

169. For a useful comparison of the two on this and other issues, see William E. Scheuerman, "Revolutions and Constitutions: Hannah Arendt's Challenge to Carl Schmitt," in *Law as Politics*, ed. Dyzenhaus.

170. James Bohman, "The Moral Costs of Political Pluralism: The Dilemmas of Difference and Equality in Arendt's 'Reflections on Little Rock,'" in *Hannah Arendt Twenty Years Later*, ed. Larry May and Jerome Kahn (Cambridge, Mass., 1997), 63.

171. For an insightful discussion of this issue, see Hanna Fenichel Pitkin, *Wittgenstein and Justice* (Berkeley, 1972), 280–86. Her remarks are aimed at Max Weber's attempt to disentangle normative from descriptive notions of legitimacy, but can just as easily be applied to Schmitt. For other considerations of this issue, see Franz L. Neumann and Otto Kirchheimer, *The Rule of Law under Siege*, ed. William E. Scheuerman (Berkeley, 1996).

172. Cornelius Castoriadis, *Philosophy, Politics, Autonomy: Essays in Political Philosophy*, ed. David Ames Curtis (New York, 1991), 158.

173. Michael Halberstam, *Totalitarianism and the Modern Conception of*

Politics (New Haven, 1999), 117. Of course, the conclusion that totalitarianism politicizes all aspects of life begs the question of whether it is more metapolitical than genuinely political in the first place. Halberstam, for example, follows Arendt in seeing it as the denial of politics, properly understood.

174. Eric Alterman, *When Presidents Lie: A History of Official Deception and Its Consequences* (New York, 2004), 13. Joseph McCarthy, it will be recalled, made wild accusations against alleged Communist influence in government. Alterman claims that the willingness to believe him was an unintended consequence of lies President Roosevelt had told about the Yalta agreement with Stalin a few years earlier (76).

175. The full sentence reads: "I, . . . , do solemnly swear that I will support and defend the Constitution of the United States against all enemies, foreign and domestic; that I will bear true faith and allegiance to the same; that I take this obligation freely without any mental reservation or purpose of evasion; and that I will well and faithfully discharge the duties of the office on which I am about to enter, so help me God."

176. Michael D. Gordon, "The Invention of a Common Law Crime: Perjury and the Elizabethan Courts," *American Journal of Legal History* 24.2 (April 1980).

177. In October 2007 the Washington Supreme Court struck down a law that attempted to ban political lying. See Adam Liptak, "Law on Lies by Politicians Is Found Unconstitutional," *New York Times,* October 7, 2007, 24. The article does mention that some similar laws in other states have survived challenges to their constitutionality.

3 ON LYING IN POLITICS

1. Jonathan Swift, *The Prose Works of Jonathan Swift, D.D.,* vol. 9, ed. Temple Scott (London, 1902), 78.

2. Ibid., 79.

3. Reprinted in George A. Aitkin, *The Life and Works of John Arbuthnot* (New York, 1968). The Greek means "political pseudology."

4. Ibid., 298, 295.

5. Ibid., 299. Grudgeons were a kind of coarse meal.

6. Ibid., 302.

7. Oscar Wilde, "The Decay of Lying," in *Aesthetes and Decadents of the 1890's,* ed. Karl Beckson (Chicago, 1981), 169–70.

8. On the issue of cunning in general, with an insightful discussion of its implications for politics, see Don Herzog, *Cunning* (Princeton, 2006). After Machiavelli, identifying it with politics has become, Herzog argues, "a bit of fatuous complacency" (48).

9. The phrase was popularized by Jean-Paul Sartre in his play *Les mains sales* of 1948. For subsequent discussions of the issue, see Michael Walzer, "The Problem of Dirty Hands," *Philosophy and Public Affairs* 2.2 (Winter 1973); Thomas Nagel, "Ruthless in Public Life," in *Moral Questions* (Cambridge,

1979); and Martin Hollis, "Dirty Hands," *British Journal of Political Studies* 12.4 (October 1982).

10. Agnes Heller, "The Concept of the Political Revisited," in *Political Theory Today,* ed. David Held (Stanford, 1991), 338.

11. Gandhi writes: "For me truth is the sovereign principle, which includes numerous other principles. This truth is not only truthfulness in word, but truthfulness in thought also, and not only the relative truth of our conception, but the Absolute Truth, the Eternal Principle that is God. . . . I worship God as Truth only." *The Mind of Mahatma Gandhi,* ed. R. K. Prabhu and U. R. Rao (Ahmedabad, 1967), 42–43. Gandhi's autobiography was entitled *My Experiments with Truth,* and Erik H. Erikson's psychoanalytic biography of him was called *Gandhi's Truth.* What precisely he meant by truth would require a far more extensive discussion than is possible here.

Havel's pledge is made in "The Power of the Powerless," in *Open Letters* (New York, 1991), 132.

12. James C. Scott, *Domination and the Arts of Resistance* (New Haven, 1990).

13. Perez Zagorin, *Ways of Lying: Dissimulation, Persecution, and Conformity in Early Modern Europe* (Cambridge, Mass., 1990).

14. See Dwight M. Donaldson, *The Shi'ite Religion* (London, 1933), 195.

15. Perhaps the most famous crypto-Jew in Iberia was the Portuguese priest Antônio Vieria, the author of *Clavis Prophetarium,* who lived for a while in Brazil. See Anita Novinsky, "O judaismo dissimulado do padre Antônio Vieria," *Sigila* 8 (Autumn–Winter 2001).

16. Jurek Becker, *Jacob the Liar,* trans. Leila Venniwitz (New York, 1990).

17. Louis Begley, *Wartime Lies* (New York, 1991).

18. Franz Neumann, *The Democratic and the Authoritarian State: Essays in Political and Legal Theory,* ed. Herbert Marcuse (New York, 1957), 18. Neumann adds in a footnote that the novels of Stendhal are filled with examples.

19. As Bernard Williams notes, "In our world, in which there is much private life and many particular contracts, it is easier to keep a secret without telling lies, and there is a marked difference between the two. If someone wants to know too much, the first resort, as the casuists said, is a refusal to answer, and a proper pride drawn from the motivations of honor and shame can be a great help in this regard, but under pressure, and particularly if other interests need to be protected, silence may have to turn into evasion and evasion into deceit." *Truth and Truthfulness: An Essay in Genealogy* (Princeton, 2002), 117. For more on the issue of secrecy and its relation to lying, see Sisella Bok, *Secrets: On the Ethics of Concealment and Revelation* (New York, 1989).

20. The phrase seems to go back to the eighteenth century, but it became prominent when the American Friends Service Committee published a pamphlet called *To Speak Truth to Power* in the mid-1950s. http://www.quaker.org/sttp.html.

21. For recent histories of the development of the concept, see William David Jones, *The Lost Debate: German Socialist Intellectuals and Totalitarian-*

ism (Urbana, 1999); David Roberts, *The Totalitarian Experiment in Twentieth-Century Europe: Understanding the Poverty of Great Politics* (London, 2006); and Enzo Traverso, *Le totalitarisme: Le XXe siècle en debat* (Paris, 2001).

22. Ciliga's book was translated as *The Russian Enigma* by Fernand G. Renier and Anne Cliff (London, 1940).

23. Alexandre Koyré, "The Political Function of the Modern Lie," *Contemporary Jewish Record* 8.3 (June 1945): 291.

24. Leszek Kolakowski, "Totalitarianism and the Virtue of the Lie," in *"1984" Revisited: Totalitarianism in Our Century,* ed. Irving Howe (New York, 1983), 127.

25. Cornelius Castoriadis, "The Destinies of Totalitarianism," *Salmagundi* 60 (Spring–Summer 1983): 110.

26. Thierry Meyssan, *9/11: The Big Lie* (London, 2002).

27. In *The Origins of Totalitarianism* (Cleveland, 1958), Arendt could still talk about "totalitarian politics" (464), but by the time she outlined her normative notion of "the political" in *The Human Condition* (Garden City, N.Y., 1958), it was clear that totalitarianism was seen as the death of genuine political action. For Lefort's position, see *The Political Forms of Modern Society: Bureaucracy, Democracy, Totalitarianism* (Cambridge, 1986).

28. Peter Viereck, *Metapolitics: From Wagner and the German Romantics to Hitler* (Edison, N.J., 2004).

29. Carl Schmitt, *The Concept of the Political,* trans. George Schwab (Chicago, 1996), 32.

30. Robert Howse, "From Legitimacy to Dictatorship—and Back Again: Leo Strauss's Critique of the Anti-Liberalism of Carl Schmitt," in *Law as Politics: Carl Schmitt's Critique of Liberalism,* ed. David Dyzenhaus (Durham, 1998), 65.

31. Schmitt, *The Concept of the Political,* 54. As early as Leo Strauss's critique of this book, the cryptonormativism of Schmitt's position has been noted. Despite his surface hostility to morality, he passes a moral judgment against pacifism and humanitarianism as undermining the high seriousness of the life-and-death struggle of politics rightly understood. See Strauss, "Notes on Carl Schmitt's *The Concept of the Political,*" appended to the 1996 edition of the book.

32. Heinrich Meier, *Carl Schmitt and Leo Strauss: The Hidden Dialogue,* trans. J. Harvey Lomax (Chicago, 1995), 19.

33. Schmitt, *The Concept of the Political,* 77.

34. Sun Tzu, *The Art of War,* part 1, 18 and 19.

35. Xenophon, *Memorabilia,* 4.2.15–17. The other justified cases he cites are a father lying to make his son take medicine and a friend lying to prevent a suicide.

36. Amos Perlmutter and John Gooch, introduction to the special issue "Military Deception and Strategic Surprise," *Journal of Strategic Studies* 5.1 (March 1982): 1.

37. Koyré, "The Political Implications of the Modern Lie," 293.

38. Sissela Bok, *Lying: Moral Choice in Public and Private Life,* 2nd ed. (New York, 1999), 141, but she argues that it is important not to extend the concept of "enemy" too widely to justify lying. Perhaps only those in a declared war are fair game.

39. Recent research has demonstrated that there was, in fact, a deliberate German campaign of terror against Belgian civilians. See Jeff Lipkes, *Rehearsals: The German Army in Belgium, August 1914* (Ithaca, 2008).

40. Arthur Ponsonby, *Falsehood in War-Time: Propaganda of the First World War* (London, 1928).

41. John J. Mearsheimer, "Lying in International Politics," address to the American Political Science Association, August 22, 2004, http://www.learned hand.com/mearsheimer_lying.htm, 1.

42. Ibid., 11.

43. Alfred Bäumler, *Das Irrationalitätsproblem in der Ästhetik und Logik des 18. Jahrhundert bis zur Kritik der Urteilskraft* (Tübingen, 1967), 19–22.

44. Wotton wrote it in the autograph album of a merchant Christopher Fleckmore in Italy in 1604.

45. My thanks to my colleague Donald Friedman for drawing this etymology to my attention.

46. Ruth W. Grant, *Hypocrisy and Integrity: Machiavelli, Rousseau, and the Ethics of Politics* (Chicago, 1997), 41.

47. A useful place to begin is the anthology *Western Liberalism: A History in Documents from Locke to Croce,* ed. E. K. Bramsted and K. J. Melhuish (London, 1978).

48. Grant, *Hypocrisy and Integrity,* 177.

49. Michael Walzer, *Thick and Thin: Moral Argument at Home and Abroad* (Notre Dame, 1994), 10.

50. Bernard Williams, *Truth and Truthfulness: An Essay in Genealogy* (Princeton, 2002), 93–94. For a more sustained discussion of the issue of trust, see Peter Johnson, *Frames of Deceit: A Study of the Loss and Recovery of Public and Private Trust* (Cambridge, 1993).

51. For a dissenting view of liberalism that deemphasizes its faith in reason and puts in its place anxiety about scarcity and the importance of desire, see Sheldon Wolin, *Politics and Vision: Continuity and Innovation in Western Political Thought* (Boston, 1960), chap. 9.

52. Kinch Hoekstra, "The End of Philosophy (The Case of Hobbes)," *Proceedings of the Aristotelian Society* 106.1 (January 2006). One can, of course, question the inclusion of Hobbes as a proto-liberal, although he is often seen as a crucial predecessor in a number of ways, such as belief in the ontological priority of the individual and the importance of contracts.

53. See C. K. Ogden, *Bentham's Theory of Fictions* (London, 1932); and Ross Harrison, *Bentham* (Boston, 1983), chaps. 2–4, for a discussion of Bentham on fictions.

54. For a discussion of the implications and limits of this metaphor, see Williams, *Truth and Truthfulness,* 213–19.

55. John Stuart Mill, *On Liberty and Other Writings*, ed. Stefan Collini (Cambridge, 1989), 25.

56. For a discussion of his imperfect emancipation from the first assumption, see Alan Ryan, *J. S. Mill* (London, 1974), 42–43. On the second inclination, see J. H. Burns, "J. S. Mill and Democracy, 1828–1861," in *Mill: A Collection of Critical Essays*, ed. J. B. Schneewind (Garden City, N.Y., 1968), 284.

57. Mill, *On Liberty and Other Writings*, 13–14.

58. J. S. Mill, *Thoughts on Parliamentary Reform* (1859), in *Collected Works of John Stuart Mill*, vol. 19, ed. John M. Robson (Toronto, 1977). Most subsequent opinion, liberal or not, has gone against Mill on this issue. For a recent consideration, see Annabelle Lever, "Mill and the Secret Ballot: Beyond Coercion and Corruption," *Utilitas* 19.3 (2007).

59. For an account of their arguments, see David Runciman, *Political Hypocrisy: The Mask of Power, from Hobbes to Orwell and Beyond* (Princeton, 2008), chap. 5.

60. In its long history, liberalism did at times, of course, turn into more narrowly based interest politics, representing bourgeois class interests (its official parties evolving from what the Germans call a *Weltanschauungspartei* to an *Interessenpartei*). For an argument that from the beginning liberalism was headed in this direction despite its proclaimed belief in reason, see Wolin, *Politics and Vision*, 331–42.

61. Runciman, *Political Hypocrisy*, 154.

62. Andrew Klavan, "The Big White Lie," *City Journal* (Spring 2007), http://www.city-journal.org/html/issue_17_2.html.

63. Grant, *Hypocrisy and Integrity*, 178–79.

64. For a critical discussion of Mandeville's complicated contribution to the liberal tradition and the issue of hypocrisy in politics, see Runciman, *Political Hypocrisy*, chap. 2. See also Danielle Allen, "Burning *The Fable of the Bees*: The Incendiary Authority of Nature," in *The Moral Authority of Nature*, ed. Lorraine Daston and Fernando Vidal (Chicago, 2003), for an account of his demystification of arguments that draw on allegedly natural norms.

65. Bernard de Mandeville, *The Fable of the Bees: Or Private Vices, Public Benefits* (London, 1934), 30.

66. Ibid., 41.

67. The comparison between Mandeville and Leibniz is made by Alain Renaut, *The Era of the Individual: A Contribution to a History of Subjectivity*, trans. M. B. DeBevoise and Franklin Philip (Princeton, 1997), 80–82.

68. See the discussion in Michèle Broze, "Mensonge et justice chez Platon," *Revue internationale de philosophie*, 156–57 (1986).

69. For a general account of his hostility, see Iris Murdoch, *The Fire and the Sun: Why Plato Banished the Artists* (Oxford, 1977).

70. Plato, *Ion, Hippias Minor, Laches, Protagoras*, trans. R. E. Allen (New Haven, 1996). For an insightful discussion of the ambiguities of this dialogue, see Jean-Michel Rabaté, *The Ethics of the Lie*, trans. Susanne Verderber (New York, 2007), 176–83.

71. Ibid., 45.

72. Plato, *The Republic*, in *The Collected Dialogues of Plato*, ed. Edith Hamilton and Huntington Cairns (Princeton, 1973). The Greek comes from *Platonis Opera*, ed. J. Burnet (Oxford, 1978), vol. 4. The first target of the noble lie is the guardians themselves, who are misled by the philosopher or founder of the state, but if that fails, it can be told to the masses as well.

73. D. Dombrowski, "Plato's 'Noble' Lie," *History of Political Thought* 18.4 (Winter 1997): 575.

74. For this claim, see Catherine Zuckert and Michael Zuckert, *The Truth about Leo Strauss: Political Philosophy and American Democracy* (Chicago, 2006), 131.

75. Plato, *The Republic*, 459c–460d.

76. Ibid., 389b–d.

77. Claude Lefort, *Writing: The Political Test*, trans. David Ames Curtis (Durham, 2000), 133.

78. "I am sorry to see him, after such noble superiorities, permitting the lie to governors. Plato plays Providence a little with the baser sort, as people allow themselves with their dogs and cats." "Plato," in *The Essays of Ralph Waldo Emerson* (New York, 1944), 417.

79. Edmund Burke, *Reflections on the Revolution in France*, ed. J. G. A. Pocock (Indianapolis, 1987), 67. Oddly, John Vignaux Symth neglects to mention this passage with its brilliant metaphors of drapery and nudity in *The Habit of Lying: Sacrificial Studies in Literature, Philosophy, and Fashion Theory* (Durham, 2002), which explores many other examples of the link between fashion and deception.

80. Hegel, *Philosophy of Right and Law*, in *The Philosophy of Hegel*, ed. Carl J. Friedrich (New York, 1954), 319.

81. Friedrich Nietzsche, *Untimely Meditations*, trans. R. J. Hollingdale (Cambridge, 1997), 118.

82. R. H. Crossman, *Plato Today* (Oxford, 1939); Karl Popper, *The Open Society and Its Enemies: The Spell of Plato* (London, 1962).

83. Bok, *Lying*, 169.

84. Loyal Rue, *By the Grace of Guile: The Role of Deception in Natural History and Human Affairs* (Oxford, 1994), chap. 5.

85. See, for example, Earl Shorris, "Ignoble Liars: Leo Strauss, George Bush, and the Philosophy of Mass Deception," *Harper's*, June 2004; and Nicholas Xenox, "Leo Strauss and the Rhetoric of the War on Terror," *Logos*, Spring 2004. For an earlier account of Strauss's influence, which sees it as entirely baleful, see Shadia B. Drury, *Leo Strauss and the American Right* (New York, 1997). For an attempted rebuttal, see Zuckert and Zuckert, *The Truth about Leo Strauss.*

86. Shadia B. Drury, *The Political Ideas of Leo Strauss* (New York, 1988), 188.

87. For a recent version of the third of these positions, see Daniel Tanguay,

Leo Strauss: An Intellectual Biography, trans. Christopher Nadon (New Haven, 2003).

88. Leo Strauss, "Letter to Karl Löwith," May, 19, 1933, in *Constellations* 16.1 (March, 2009), introduced by Alan Gilbert, 82.

89. Leo Strauss, *Persecution and the Art of Writing* (Glencoe, 1952). His first inkling of this idea came in the late 1930s, after his recent escape from Nazi oppression. See his *Gesammelte Schriften,* ed. Heinrich Meier (Stuttgart, 2001), 3:548–83.

90. Steven B. Smith, *Reading Leo Strauss: Politics, Philosophy, Judaism* (Chicago, 2006), 163–64.

91. Leo Strauss, *On Tyranny* (Ithaca, 1968), 211. For a general account of his attitude toward truth, see Jürgen Gebhardt, "Leo Strauss: The Quest for Truth in Times of Perplexity," in *Hannah Arendt and Leo Strauss: German Émigrés and American Political Thought after World War II,* ed. Peter Graf Kielmansegg, Horst Mewes, and Elisabeth Glaser-Schmidt (Cambridge, 1995).

92. Leo Strauss, *What Is Political Philosophy?,* 145.

93. His defenders, however, have done it for him. See, for example, Zuckert and Zuckert, who in *The Truth about Leo Strauss* claim that "in the recent discussions of Strauss, in the accusation that he justifies, even advocates the use of 'lies' and manipulation, the most significant fact about the esotericism thesis has been lost to view: it is first and foremost a method for historically understanding writers in the past who incontestably lived in nonliberal societies, and not a prescription for writers living today" (121).

94. In a letter to Eric Voegelin on December 17, 1949, Strauss confided that "the sophist is a man to whom the truth does not matter—but in this sense all men except for the *gnēsios philosophountes* are sophists, especially the *polis* as *polis* (and not only the decadent ones)." *Faith and Political Philosophy: The Correspondence between Leo Strauss and Eric Voegelin, 1934–1964,* trans. and ed. Peter Emberley and Barry Cooper (University Park, Pa., 1993), 63.

95. Strauss, *On Tyranny,* 196. See Tanguay, *Leo Strauss,* for a discussion of his adherence to a more skeptical version of Platonism, which argued for "an unceasing quest for truth rather than the expression of a completed science" (201).

96. Michael S. Roth, "Natural Right and the End of History: Leo Strauss and Alexandre Kojève," *Revue de métaphysique et de morale* 3 (1991): 417.

97. Smith, in *Reading Strauss,* argues that he was a liberal democrat rather than an authoritarian conservative. He ignores the letter cited above from Strauss to Löwith. For a thoughtful response to Smith's argument, see Benjamin Lazier, "Natural Right and Liberalism: Leo Strauss in Our Time," *Modern Intellectual History* 6.1 (April 2009).

98. Meier, *Carl Schmitt and Leo Strauss,* 87. The same point is made in Zuckert and Zuckert, *The Truth about Leo Strauss,* 192.

99. Lefort, *Writing,* 172.

100. The issue of what constitutes wisdom and who gets to decide what is wise is not really resolved by Strauss. Indeed, as Alan Gilbert has noted, "As a

Platonist, Strauss never acquired a respect for the rule of law. The easy slippage here between 'wisdom' and the rule of one without laws is, unfortunately, obvious, even in Plato's formulation." "Do Philosophers Council Tyrants?" *Constellations* 16.1 (March 2009): 109.

101. Strauss, *Thoughts on Machiavelli* (Chicago, 1978), 264–65. Strauss's complicated relation to Machiavelli has been the subject of considerable discussion, for as he admitted to Eric Voegelin in a letter of April 29, 1953, "I can't help loving him—in spite of his errors" (*Faith and Political Philosophy,* 98). The most sustained treatment of his response to Machiavelli can be found in Kim A. Sorensen, *Discourses on Strauss: Revelation and Reason in Leo Strauss and His Critical Study of Machiavelli* (Notre Dame, 2006).

102. Leo Strauss, *The City and Man* (Chicago, 1964), 102.

103. Ibid., 103.

104. Leo Strauss, "The Spirit of Sparta or the Taste of Xenophon," *Social Research* 6.4 (November 1939): 535.

105. For a discussion of the distinction, see Tanguay, *Leo Strauss,* 102–9.

106. Strauss, "Restatement on Xenophon's *Hiero,*" in *Faith and Political Philosophy,* 56.

107. Smith, *Reading Leo Strauss,* 137.

108. Tanguay, however, acknowledges it several times in *Leo Strauss* (e.g., 68, 73, 97) without condemning it.

109. See, for example, the Zuckerts' claim in *The Truth about Leo Strauss* that "the lie (if it really is that) is justified not because elites are superior to the masses and have a right to do whatever it takes for them to rule or maintain themselves; insofar as philosophic reticence or accommodation is justified, it is justified by the public good, that is, by the fact that some opinions held by the public do great good and, disturbing them, even if and when they are not strictly true, may do harm" (127). In short, wise men need not worry about demystifying false beliefs if in their judgment about the good, those beliefs are functional for the welfare of the benighted masses. Of course, the question that is begged here is the right of some to judge what is really in everyone's best interest.

110. Strauss to Karl Löwith, August 20, 1946, "Correspondence Concerning Modernity," *Independent Journal of Philosophy* 4 (1983): 111.

111. Hannah Arendt, *The Promise of Politics,* ed. Jerome Kohn (New York, 2005), 11.

112. Ibid., 25.

113. The phrase, she noted, was originally Edmund Burke's. Ibid., 127.

114. Hannah Arendt, "Truth in Politics," in *The Portable Hannah Arendt,* ed. Peter Baehr (New York, 2000), 574–75.

115. Hannah Arendt, *Eichmann in Jerusalem: A Report on the Banality of Evil* (New York, 1963).

116. Hannah Arendt, "Lying in Politics," in *Crises of the Republic* (New York, 1972).

117. Arendt, *The Human Condition,* 253. In calling the zeal for truthfulness

"unprecedented," she was clearly unaware of the tradition of the *parrhesiastes* later discussed by Foucault.

118. Ibid., 369. This is a very odd claim to make for someone who had written her 1929 dissertation on Augustine (*Love and Saint Augustine*, ed. Joanna Vecchiarelli Scott and Judith Chelius Stark [Chicago, 1996]), but it shows Arendt's general distrust of the deontological prohibition of lying under all circumstances.

119. Arendt, *On Revolution* (New York, 1965), 95.

120. For a discussion of her ambivalence concerning masks and full unmasking, see Leora Bilsky, "Citizenship as Mask: Between the Imposter and the Refugee," *Constellations* 15.1 (March 2008).

121. Arendt, "Truth in Politics," 545; further citations are in the text.

122. Hannah Arendt, *Rahel Varnhagen: The Life of a Jewish Woman*, trans. Richard Winston and Clara Winston (New York, 1974), 11–12.

123. Arendt, "Lying in Politics," 4; further citations are in the text.

124. Hanna Fenichel Pitkin goes so far as to write of Arendt's "obvious disdain for deception and rhetoric" and argue that "when rhetoric and deception come to be regarded and used as the only possible modes of speech, public communication becomes meaningless and politics impossible. Deprived of a stable sense of reality, of truth, of the past, of themselves, man becomes incapable of political action, incapable of the kind of public speech that it presupposes." *Wittgenstein and Justice* (Berkeley, 1972), 331–32. In "History of the Lie: Prolegomena" (in *Without Alibi*, ed. and trans. Peggy Kamuf [Stanford, 2002]), Jacques Derrida claims that "by excluding the indefinite survival of mystification, Arendt makes of history, as history of the lie, the epidermic and epiphenomenal accident of a parousia of truth" and writes of her "certainty of a final victory and a certain survival of the truth (and not merely veracity)" (69). For a consideration of his critique of her position, see Martin Jay, "Pseudology: Derrida on Arendt on Lying in Politics," in *Derrida and the Time of the Political*, ed. Pheng Cheah and Suzanne Guerlac (Durham, 2008).

125. Rabaté, *The Ethics of the Lie*, 19.

126. For an insightful discussion of this distinction in Arendt, see Vincenzo Sorrentino, *Il potere invisibile: Ile segreto e la menzogna in politica* (Molfetta, 1998), 115. For another treatment of the ways in which certain lies function to change the future in a positive way, see Benedict Carey, "I'm Not Lying, I'm Telling a Future Truth. Really," *New York Times*, May 6, 2008, D5. He argues that exaggerations in self-presentation are often indications of a plan for improving the self.

127. Harry Frankfurt, *On Bullshit* (Princeton, 2005), 33–34. For a discussion, see Mark Evans, "The Republic of Bullshit: On the Dumbing-up of Democracy," in *Bullshit and Democracy*, ed. Gary L. Hardcastle and George A. Reisch (Chicago, 2006).

128. In *The Structural Transformation of the Public Sphere: An Inquiry into a Category of Bourgeois Society*, trans. Thomas Burger and Frederick Lawrence (Cambridge, Mass., 1992), Habermas notes that Locke overcame the antithesis

between mere opinion and critical reason, which was powerful in the French Enlightenment (90).

129. Amanda Anderson, *The Way We Argue Now: A Study in the Cultures of Theory* (Princeton, 2006), chap. 7.

130. Habermas, *The Structural Transformation of the Public Sphere*, 56.

131. Ibid., 50.

132. Ankersmit does not introduce the Lacanian distinction between imaginary, symbolic, and real, but it is evident in some of the work of Lefort, who sees a link between totalitarianism and the imaginary. See the discussion in Bernard Flynn, *The Philosophy of Claude Lefort: Interpreting the Political* (Evanston, 2005), 118–19, 223–24.

133. Rosenvallon, *Democracy Past and Future*, 54.

134. See the discussion in Runciman, *Political Hypocrisy*, chap. 4.

135. Habermas, *The Structural Transformation of the Public Sphere*, 99.

136. For an insightful account of this process, see Marc Shell, *Children of the Earth: Literature, Politics and Nationhood* (New York, 1993). For a more focused study of the specific case of mythicized nationalism in Germany, see George S. Williamson, *The Longing for Myth in Germany: Religion and Aesthetic Culture from Romanticism to Nietzsche* (Chicago, 2004).

137. Ruth W. Grant, *Hypocrisy and Integrity: Machiavelli and the Ethic of Politics* (Chicago, 1997), 13.

138. Ibid., 14.

139. Ibid., 175.

140. Judith N. Shklar, *Ordinary Vices* (Cambridge, Mass., 1984), 48, 77.

141. It is, of course, no less the case that reality cannot lag too far behind the fiction without the situation deteriorating into a sham. As the case of the "democratic republics" of Communist Eastern Europe demonstrated, there has to be a popular belief in the approximation of the claim to the truth to avoid wholesale cynicism.

142. Runciman, *Political Hypocrisy*, 43.

143. See Catherine Gallagher, *Nobody's Story: The Vanishing Acts of Women Writers in the Marketplace, 1670–1820* (Oxford, 1994).

144. Wilde, "The Decay of Lying." A different version of the argument can be found in Vladimir Nabokov's *Lectures on Literature* (London, 1983), 5, where he argued in a very un-Wildean manner that artists imitate the deceptions to be found in nature.

145. Hannah Arendt, *Lectures on Kant's Political Philosophy*, ed. Ronald Beiner (Chicago, 1982).

146. W. H. Auden, "In Memory of W. B. Yeats," in *Selected Poetry of W. H. Auden* (New York, 1971), 53.

147. An example is the Weimar Republic, understood by many as "the republic of impostors." For an account, see Peter Sloterdijk's *Critique of Cynical Reason*, trans. Michael Eldred, foreword by Andreas Huyssen (Minneapolis, 1987), where he claims that "deception had become an industry and . . . the *expectation of being deceived* (in the double sense: as readiness to let oneself be

deceived and as mistrust that someone would try to pull the wool over their eyes) had become a universal state of consciousness" (484).

148. William Godwin, *Enquiry into Political Justice and Its Influence on Morals and Happiness,* 2 vols. (London, 1842), vol. 1, book 4, chap. 6, p. 161.

149. In *The Discourses,* ed. Bernard Crick (Harmondsworth, 1979), 393–94, Machiavelli examined the case of Piero Soderini (1452–1522), the chief magistrate or head of state in Florence. Virtuous and trusting, Soderini responded to the factionalism he saw around him with patience and amiability. But in rejecting guile and cunning, he ended up betraying the trust of those who had asked him to maintain civil peace. However "wise and good" he may have been as a man, he was weak, Machiavelli concluded, in dealing with the exigencies of political responsibility.

150. Even so powerful a scourge of political mendacity as George Orwell could caution against self-righteousness in 1940 on the eve of the most Manichaean war in modern history: "For Heaven's sake, let us not suppose that we go into this war with clean hands. It is only while we cling to the consciousness that our hands are not clean that we retain the right to defend ourselves." *A Patriot After All, 1940–41,* ed. Peter Davison (London, 1998), 124.

151. Just to take one justly celebrated example, the Japanese consul-general in wartime Lithuania, Chiune Sugihara, saved thousands of Jews by granting them exit visas against the orders of his government. Here an honest man ended up lying not to his adversaries, but to his own government!

152. This precise wording is taken from the Michigan bar oath, but a canvass of other states shows similar language is found in many. For a history of the practice of lawyer's oaths, see Leonard S. Goodman, "The Historic Role of the Oath of Admission," *American Journal of Legal History* 11.4 (October 1967).

153. Stanley Fish, "No Bias, No Merit: The Case against Blind Submission," in *Doing What Comes Naturally: Change, Rhetoric, and the Practice of Theory in Literary and Legal Studies* (Durham, 1989). For a discussion, see "Fish on Blind Submission," by Geoffrey Galt Harpham, Jeffrey Skoblow, James Holstun, Sieglinde Lug, Grace Tiffany, Roger Seamon, Lawrence W. Hyman, and Stanley Fish, *PMLA* 104.2 (March 1989).

154. Take, for example, the case of a figure who is destined to be mentioned prominently in any future study of lying in politics: Vice President Dick Cheney's chief of staff I. Louis "Scooter" Libby Jr. In March 2007 he was convicted of one count of obstruction of justice, two counts of perjury, and one count of making false statements to federal investigators. Although ultimately granted a presidential commutation (short of an outright pardon), Libby became a metonym for all the lies told by the Bush administration in connection with the war it unleashed on Iraq. Libby, a neoconservative who studied political science with Paul Wolfowitz at Yale, has sometimes been seen as an indirect disciple of Leo Strauss and his alleged defense of the "noble lie." (See, e.g., John Walsh, "Lies of the Neocons: From Leo Strauss to Scooter Libby and Beyond," http://cplmcl.newsvine.com/_news/2008/06/19/1591418-lies-of-the-

neocons-from-leo-strauss-to-scooter-libby-and-beyond.) But his real trans-gression, in fact, was disclosing the truth or helping to disseminate it about Valerie Plame, the wife of Ambassador Joseph Wilson and a critic of Bush's rationale for invading Iraq, thus breaking the veil of secrecy that surrounded her work as a CIA agent. It is perhaps no small irony that the book written by Wilson was called *The Politics of Truth: Inside the Lies That Led to War and Betrayed My Wife's CIA Identity* (New York, 2004), or that another politician named Joe Wilson, the conservative congressman from South Carolina, could think of no greater insult to hurl at President Barack Obama from the floor of the House of Representatives than: "You lie!"

INDEX

Montesquieu, Charles de Secondat, Baron, 101
Moore, G. E., 20
moralism, as basic attitude toward lying, 16–18, 66
morality: and lying, 46–75. *See also* consequentialism; deontology; utilitarianism
Morley, John, *On Compromise*, 35, 145
Morrison, Toni, 146
Morris, William, 175
Mouffe, Chantal, 79, 89, 92, 93, 96, 120, 122, 205n7, 210n62
Mucius Scaevola, Quintus, Pontifex, 189
Münsterberg, Hugo, 10

nature: and lying, 19–26, 40, 189nn7–8, 193n75, 228n144; as norm, 19–21, 23, 29, 126
Navarrus, *Handbook for Confessors and Penitents* (*Enchridion, sive Manuale Confessariorum et Paenitentium*), 55
Nazism, 1–3, 13, 17, 76, 98, 106, 122, 136, 139, 140, 152–54, 209n52. *See also* fascism; totalitarianism
Nazi-Soviet Pact, 142
Neumann, Franz, 134, 220n18
Nietzsche, Friedrich, 3, 22, 23, 40, 47, 79, 151, 190n20, 195n105; on "extramoral" view of lying, 22, 23, 47; *The Gay Science*, 23; "Uses and Disadvantages of History for Life," 151
Nightingale, Andrea Wilson, 83
Nixon, Richard, 15
Norris, Andrew, 188n82, 205n7
Nyberg, David, 31, 188n82

Origen, 53
Orwell, George, 11–14, 135, 186n52, 186n54, 190n28, 229n150; *Animal Farm*, 190n28; *Homage to Catalonia*, 186n54; *Nineteen Eighty-Four*, 11, 135; "Politics and the English Language," 11; reputation of, 12, 186n52, 186n54

Palonen, Kari, 111
parrhesia, 51, 52, 62, 152, 227n117
Partisan Review, 12
Pascal, Blaise, 32, 50, 56; *Pensées*, 32; *Provincial Letters*, 56
Paton, Herbert J., 71, 203n204
Peace of Westphalia (1648), 83, 89, 127
Petronius, 19, 189; *Lying and Nature*, 19
Pettit, Philip, 100
phronesis, 31
Piaget, Jean, 22
Pietism, 35, 65
Pitkin, Hanna Fenichel, 12, 218n171, 227n124
Plato, 3, 7, 43, 50, 63, 68, 82, 97–99, 102, 103, 108–11, 147–51, 153–58, 160, 173, 182n8, 206n12, 211n74, 211n75, 211n77, 212n78, 224n78; *Gorgias*, 97, 147; *Hippias Minor*, 147, 148; hostility to opinion, 3, 98, 99, 109, 212n78; *The Laws*, 97, 108, 147, 153; popularity under Nazism, 3, 98; *The Republic*, 3, 43, 97, 99, 147–50, 155, 158, 211n74; and Sophists, 3, 43; *The Statesman*, 97, 147. *See also* lying, forms of: noble lie; political, the, forms of: governance by wise elite; Strauss
Plessner, Helmut, 29, 192n63, 209n50
Pocock, John, 6
poiesis, 108, 125
polis, 3, 37, 52, 81, 85, 87, 97, 99–101, 104, 110, 115, 121, 122, 147, 170
political, the: and academic culture, 177, 179; boundaries of, 75–86, 88, 107, 119–29, 141, 175–79, 206n22, 206n24, 217n154, 218n164; and free press, 177, 178; and French political theory, 77, 79, 205n7; historicity of, 76, 77, 79, 85, 121, 175; and indepen-

political, the (*continued*)
dent judiciary, 177, 178; and language, 104, 105, 117, 118; and law,
125, 126, 213n94, 214n108; as ontological category, 79, 80, 84, 120, 127,
136, 206n18; and organic wholeness, 107, 112, 119, 168; and religion,
123–25, 218nn164–65; and ritual,
106; and the symbolic, 6, 106, 112–
19, 124, 136, 169, 170, 172, 215n126,
216n132, 228n132; and theatricality,
108–12, 168, 173, 183n32; twentieth-
century interest in, 77–79
political, the, forms of: as the aesthetic, 86, 105–19, 137, 168–74; as
antagonism, 85–89, 92–96, 102,
109, 114, 137–39, 154, 157, 210n62; as
agonism, 85, 86, 89–93, 96, 102,
104, 109, 110, 137, 140–42, 154, 157,
170; as contractualism among individuals, 86, 93–97, 112, 137, 142–47
(*see also* liberalism); as governance
by the wise, 86, 97–100, 137, 142,
145, 147–57 (*see also* republicanism); as republican virtue, 86, 100–
105, 112, 137, 142, 157–67 (*see also*
republicanism)
Politicos (Spain), 5
Politiques (France), 5, 130
Pol Pot, 127
Ponsonby, Lord Arthur, *Falsehood in
War-Time,* 139
Popper, Karl, 151, 211n77; *The Open
Society and Its Enemies,* 211n77
Pragmatism, 10, 49
praxis, 108, 125, 214n107
Priscillian, 54
Protagoras, 3, 78, 206n12
Psalms, 19, 189
"public sphere," 16, 34, 82, 103, 104,
112, 166, 179. *See also* Habermas
Pufendorf, Samuel, 58, 64
Puritanism, 7, 9, 13, 35, 56, 57, 160, 176.
See also lying: and early modern
Christianity

raison d'état, 4, 89, 90, 141, 182n14
Rampton, Sheldon, *Weapons of Mass
Deception,* 15
Rancière, Jacques, 81, 82, 110–12, 118,
169, 215n123, 215n129; *The Politics
of Aesthetics,* 110, 215n123
Ranke, Leopold von, 85
rational choice theory, 177
Rawls, John, 95, 96, 104, 212n86
Raymond of Pennafort, *Summa de
paenitentia,* 196n120
Reagan, Ronald, 15, 142, 188n81
realism, as basic attitude toward lying
in politics, 17, 18
Realpolitik, 140
Reformation, 7, 133, 207n32. *See also*
lying: and early modern Christianity
Renaissance, 32, 101, 103
republicanism, 6, 65, 86, 97, 100–105,
112, 116, 137, 142, 157–67, 210n64,
212n83, 212n86
Ricks, Christopher, 42, 194n87
Ricoeur, Paul, 22, 77
Rivarol, Antoine de, 59
Robespierre, Maximilien, 33, 65, 159,
165. *See also* French Revolution
Rochefoucauld, François de la, 171
Romanticism, 34, 60, 67, 107, 119. *See
also* authenticity
Rome (Ancient), 85, 97, 100, 102, 105,
122, 147
Roosevelt, Franklin, 142, 188n81,
219n174
Rosenvallon, Pierre, 79, 112, 116, 117,
120, 169, 215n123, 216n130
Roth, Michael, 154
Rousseau, Jean Jacques, 33, 34, 48,
60–65, 67, 70, 100, 102, 104, 115,
170, 171, 192n48, 200n172; and
amour-propre, 62; *Confessions,* 60,
62; *The Reveries of the Solitary
Walker,* 33, 60; and salon culture,
33, 60, 65; *The Social Contract,* 64,
200n172. *See also* lying, forms of:
hypocrisy, politeness; salons

Spinoza, Baruch, 117, 123; *Theologico-Political Treatise*, 123
Squires, Judith, 107
Staël, Germaine de, 67, 72, 201n184
Stalin, Josef, 136, 142, 219n174
Stalinism, 113
Starobinski, Jean, 60
Stauber, John C., *Weapons of Mass Deception*, 15
Steinberg, Michael, 112
Steiner, George, *After Babel*, 46
Stephanopolous, George, *All Too Human*, x
Stoicism (Ancient), 54, 117
Stone, I. F., 16, 177
Strauss, Leo, 4–6, 14, 21, 58, 93, 99, 101, 123, 147, 151–57, 182n17, 204n5, 205n7, 211n65, 221n31, 224n85, 225n89, 225nn93–95, 225n97, 226nn100–101; and American neoconservatism, 151, 224n85, 230n154; *The City and Man*, 155; "How Fārābī Read Plato's *Laws*," 153; and Machiavelli, 4–6, 101, 154, 155, 182n17, 226n101; *On Tyranny*, 4, 156; and Plato, 99, 101, 153–55, 225n95, 226n100; and Schmitt, 93, 94, 123, 154, 155, 211n65, 221n31; "The Spirit of Sparta or the Taste of Xenophon," 4; and the theologico-political problem, 123; *Thoughts on Machiavelli*, 155; "What is Political Philosophy?" 99. *See also* lying, forms of: esoteric writing, noble lies; political, the, forms of: governance by the wise
Sun Tzu, *Art of War*, 138
Swift, Jonathan, 33, 130, 131, 150; "An Essay upon the Art of Political Lying," 130
Sydney, Algernon, 100, 101
Sydney, Sir Philip, *The Defense of Poesie*, 172

Tailhade, Laurent, 106
Talleyrand, Charles Maurice de, 38

Tasso, Torquato, *Jerusalem Divided*, 26
Taylor, Charles, 115
Taylor, Harriet, 145
technocracy, 10, 96, 99, 185n46
Ten Commandments, 47, 53, 159
Thayer, Abbot, 21
theater, 7, 9, 51, 108–12, 183n32, 195n95. *See also* political, the: and theatricality
Theophrastus, *Characters*, 57
Thierot, Nicolas-Claude, 58
Thirty Years' War, 83, 207n32
Thomas Aquinas, Saint, 55
Thucydides, 118
Tocqueville, Alexis de, 116
totalitarianism, 1, 12, 13, 77, 81, 82, 98, 113, 117, 119, 122, 126–28, 135, 136, 151, 162–64, 169, 170, 205n9, 207n30, 211n77, 219n173, 221n27, 228n132. *See also* fascism; lying, forms of: big lie; Nazism; Soviet Union
Toussaint, François-Vincent, 59
Trilling, Lionel, 12, 13, 186n54; *Sincerity and Authenticity*, 13
trust, 16, 22, 25–28, 31, 36, 38, 39, 42, 48, 50, 71, 95, 96, 105, 138, 139, 144, 149, 171, 191n29, 197n128, 222n50, 229n149
"truth serum," 38
Twain, Mark, 9, 15, 19, 46, 131, 150; 185n44; "On the Decay of the Art of Lying," 19, 46

United States of America: Constitution of, 8, 125, 128, 214n108; as culture of transparency, 6–8; Declaration of Independence of, 161; emphasis on plain speaking in, 8, 9, 13, 14, 35–36; Puritan influence on, 7, 9, 13, 56
utilitarianism (ethics), 26, 49, 59, 61, 75, 96, 112, 144, 145, 148, 174, 196n113, 201n185. *See also* consequentialism

OTHER BOOKS BY MARTIN JAY

The Dialectical Imagination: A History of the Frankfurt School and the Institute of Social Research, 1923–1950 (1973, 1996)

Marxism and Totality: The Adventures of a Concept from Lukács to Habermas (1984)

Adorno (1984)

Permanent Exiles: Essays on the Intellectual Migration from Germany to America (1985)

Fin-de-Siècle Socialism and Other Essays (1989)

Force Fields: Between Intellectual History and Cultural Critique (1993)

Downcast Eyes: The Denigration of Vision in Twentieth-Century French Thought (1993)

Cultural Semantics: Keywords of Our Time (1998)

Refractions of Violence (2003)

La crisis de la experiencia en la era postsubjetiva, ed. Eduard Sabrovsky (2003)

Songs of Experience: Modern American and European Variations on a Universal Theme (2005)